Immigration Nation

Over the past forty years, countries in the Global North have increasingly restricted their migration policies to reduce the arrival of migrants. As part of this, development aid has become a central tool in the migration control strategy pursued by European countries and the US, with donors, IOs, and NGOs becoming prominent actors. In this book, Lorena Gazzotti shows that migration control is not only exercised through fences and deportation. Building on extensive research in Morocco, Gazzotti shows that aid marks the rise of a substantially different mode of migration containment, one where power works beyond fast violence, and its disciplinary potential is augmented precisely by its elusiveness. Where existing studies on border externalisation have essentialised donors, IOs, and NGOs, with countries of 'origin' and 'transit' as compliant subcontractors, and border control as a neat form of intervention, this nuanced study unsettles such assumptions, to show that bordering happens in everyday, mundane fashions, far away from the spectacle of border violence. This title is also available as Open Access on Cambridge Core.

DR LORENA GAZZOTTI is the Alice Tong Sze Research fellow at Lucy Cavendish College and CRASSH, University of Cambridge, where her work explores the intersection between security, containment, and precarity in North Africa and the UK. She has published in the *Sociological Review*, the *Journal of North African Studies*, *The Guardian*, and *Times Higher Education*.

T0382265

Immigration Nation

Aid, Control, and Border Politics in Morocco

LORENA GAZZOTTI
University of Cambridge

CAMBRIDGE
UNIVERSITY PRESS

Shaftesbury Road, Cambridge CB2 8EA, United Kingdom

One Liberty Plaza, 20th Floor, New York, NY 10006, USA

477 Williamstown Road, Port Melbourne, VIC 3207, Australia

314–321, 3rd Floor, Plot 3, Splendor Forum, Jasola District Centre, New Delhi – 110025, India

103 Penang Road, #05–06/07, Visioncrest Commercial, Singapore 238467

Cambridge University Press is part of Cambridge University Press & Assessment, a department of the University of Cambridge.

We share the University's mission to contribute to society through the pursuit of education, learning and research at the highest international levels of excellence.

www.cambridge.org
Information on this title: www.cambridge.org/9781009514002

DOI: 10.1017/9781009024129

First published 2021
First paperback edition 2024

A catalogue record for this publication is available from the British Library

Library of Congress Cataloging-in-Publication data
Names: Gazzotti, Lorena, 1991– author.
Title: Immigration nation : aid, control, and border politics in Morocco / Lorena Gazzotti.
Description: New York : Cambridge University Press, 2021. | Includes bibliographical references and index.
Identifiers: LCCN 2021015098 (print) | LCCN 2021015099 (ebook) | ISBN 9781316519707 (hardback) | ISBN 9781009024129 (ebook)
Subjects: LCSH: Morocco – Emigration and immigration. | BISAC: POLITICAL SCIENCE / World / General
Classification: LCC JV8978 .G39 2021 (print) | LCC JV8978 (ebook) | DDC 325.64–dc23
LC record available at https://lccn.loc.gov/2021015098
LC ebook record available at https://lccn.loc.gov/2021015099

ISBN   978-1-316-51970-7   Hardback
ISBN   978-1-009-51400-2   Paperback

Contents

Figures

Maps

Tables

Abbreviations

AECID   Agencia Española de Cooperación Internacional para el Desarrollo (Spanish Agency for International Development Cooperation)

AFIC   Africa-Frontex Intelligence Community

AFVIC   Association des amis et des familles des victimes de l'immigration clandestine

AMDH   Association Marocaine des Droits de l'Homme (Moroccan Association for Human Rights)

ANAM   Agence Nationale de l'Assurance Maladie (National Agency for Medical Insurance)

AVRR   Assistance to Voluntary Return and Reintegration

CHU   Centre Hospitalier Universitaire

CMSM   Conseil des Migrants sub-Sahariens au Maroc (Council of sub-Saharan Migrants in Morocco)

CMW UN   Convention for the Protection of Migrant Workers and their Families

CNDH   Conseil National des Droits de l'Homme (National Council for Human Rights)

CTB   Coopération Technique Belge (Belgian Technical Cooperation)

DfID   Department for International Development (UK)

EC   European Commission

EIDHR   European Instrument for Democracy and Human Rights

ENI   European Neighbourhood Instrument

ENP   European Neighbourhood Policy

EU   European Union

EUTF EU   Emergency Trust Fund for Africa

FIIAPP   Fundación Internacional y para Iberoamérica de Administración y Políticas Públicas (International

	and Ibero-American Foundation for Administration and Public Policies)
FRONTEX	European Border and Coast Guard Agency
GADEM	Groupe Antiraciste d'Accompagnement des Etrangers et Migrants (Anti-racist Group for the Accompanying of Foreigners and Migrants)
GAM	Global Approach to Migration
GAMM	Global Approach to Migration and Mobility
GFMD	Global Forum on Migration and Development
GIZ	Deutsche Gesellschaft für Internationale Zusammenarbeit (German Organisation for International Cooperation)
ICMPD	International Centre for Migration Policy Development
INDH	Initiative Nationale de Développement Humain (National Initiative for Human Development)
INGO	International Non-Governmental Organisation
IO	International Organisation
IOM	International Organisation for Migration
MAEC	Ministère des Affaires Etrangères et de la Cooperation Internationale (Ministry of Foreign Affairs and International Cooperation)
MCMREAM	Ministère Chargé des Marocains Résidents à l'Etranger et des Affaires de la Migration (Ministry in Charge of Moroccans Residing Abroad and of Migration Affairs)
MDMCREAM	Ministère Délégué Chargé des Marocains Résidents à l'Etranger et des Affaires de la Migration (Delegated Ministry in Charge of Moroccans Residing Abroad and of Migration Affairs)
MEDA	MEsures D'Accompagnement
MSF	Médecins Sans Frontières
NGO	Non-Governmental Organisation
ODA	Official Development Assistance
OECD	Organisation for Economic Co-operation and Development
OMDH	Organisation Marocaine des Droits Humains (Moroccan Organisation for Human Rights)

PNPM	Plateforme Nationale de Protection Migrants (National Platform for Migrants' Protection)
RAMED	Régime d'Assistance Médicale
SIVE	Sistema Integrado de Vigilancia del Exterior (Integrated System of External Vigilance)
SNIA	Stratégie Nationale d'Immigration et d'Asile (National Strategy for Immigration and Asylum)
SPRING	Support for Partnership, Reforms and Inclusive Growth
SSF	Single Support Framework
TPMA	Thematic Programme for Migration and Asylum
UN	United Nations
UNAIDS	Joint United Nations Programme on HIV/AIDS
UNFPA	United Nations Population Fund
UNHCR	United Nations High Commissioner for Refugees
UNICEF	United Nations International Children's Emergency Fund
USAID	United States Agency for International Development

This title is part of the Cambridge University Press *Flip it Open* Open Access Books program and has been "flipped" from a traditional book to an Open Access book through the program.

Flip it Open sells books through regular channels, treating them at the outset in the same way as any other book; they are part of our library collections for Cambridge Core, and sell as hardbacks and ebooks. The one crucial difference is that we make an upfront commitment that when each of these books meets a set revenue threshold we make them available to everyone Open Access via Cambridge Core.

This paperback edition has been released as part of our Open Access commitment and we would like to use this as an opportunity to thank the libraries and other buyers who have helped us flip this and the other titles in the program to Open Access.

To see the full list of libraries that we know have contributed to *Flip it Open*, as well as the other titles in the program please visit www.cambridge.org/fio-acknowledgements

Acknowledgements

In her book *Complaint!*, feminist scholar Sara Ahmed argues that "Power works by making it hard to challenge how power works". In expansive border regimes, power thickens and contracts, it encircles some, it is oblivious of others. Understanding its workings would have been impossible without the generous availability of my interviewees, who kindly offered their time to answer my questions and, more than once, to put me in touch with additional respondents. I will be always grateful for this support.

This book has seen the light thanks to the mentoring and friendship of many great women. Alexandra Winkels had the onerous task of supervising the thesis this book builds on. She did it so graciously – which was not easy, given how overexcited and overconfused a PhD student I was! Mercedes Jiménez has shown an incredible enthusiasm for this project all along. Her generous mentoring, her knowledge of the Strait, and her commitment to social justice are a constant source of inspiration. Maria Hagan has been an unbeatable fieldwork partner during my last field visit. We shared interviews, reflections, laughs, and a twelve-hour bus ride from Agadir to Rabat via Marrakech that we both kind of regret. Leslie Gross-Wyrtzen, Niyousha Bastani, Katharina Natter, Melissa Mouthaan, Melissa Gatter, Cynthia Magallanes Gonzales, Anissa Maâ, Ruth Lawlor, Georgia Cole, Noura Wahby, and Pascaline Chappart also provided feedback on various draft chapters that brought the manuscript to the next level. Sigrid Lupieri volunteered to proofread more of my Southern European English than anyone should ever be obliged to. Francesca Tabloni, Fatima Fernandéz, and Vanessa Tullo have also opened the door of their houses in Casablanca and Rabat to me whenever I needed it, and I cannot express my gratitude enough.

This book is also the product of the support of many great men. Graham Denyer Willis has been everything a mentor should be – constantly encouraging me to do better, think bigger, and think with others. Mehdi Alioua, Nouri Rupert, and Hicham Jamid offered feedback and encouraging support on my early thoughts while this project was still at the fieldwork stage. Michael Collyer was such a good examiner, providing incisive comments while also showing genuine interest in learning from my findings. Gerasimos Tsourapas, Felix Anderl, Matt Mahmoudi, Hassan Ould Oumar, Jo Brandim Howson, and Ted Tregear also provided feedback and reading suggestions on my chapters at different stages.

I wrote a book about elusive power while precariously working in a sector – UK Higher Education – where domination works through camouflage – badly paid teaching jobs are branded as incredible 'opportunities' and taking on additional unpaid work is qualified as a sign of good 'departmental citizenship'. At Cambridge, though, I have found a community of trade union organisers that taught me some terrific lessons about resistance in the face of elusive power. Thanks to Stephanie Mawson, Ted Tregear, Ruth Lawlor, Sandra Cortijo, Rasha Rezk, Torkel Loman, Sue Hakenbeck, Michael Abberton, Lydia Richards, and everyone else at the Cambridge branch of the University and College Union for showing me how to resist and teaching me about the importance of building workers' power from the bottom up.

The research for this book counted on the financial support of the Cambridge Trust, the MariaMarina Foundation, Lucy Cavendish College, the Department of Politics and International Studies at the University of Cambridge, the Centre Jacques Berque pour les Etudes en Sciences Sociales, and the Society for Libyan Studies. I am also thankful to three anonymous reviewers for very helpful feedback on the manuscript, to Maria Marsh and Atifa Jiwa at Cambridge University Press for accompanying me though the editorial process, to Angela Valente for her superhuman patience in the copy-editing stage, and to Philip Stickler for creating the maps that figure in this book.

I finished writing this book in the midst of a global pandemic. It's not easy to support someone at a distance. I am so grateful my family tried and managed to do this in such challenging times. Raffaele Danna, Enrico Daviddi, Ben Jackson, Selina Zhung, Alex Waghorn, Matt Mahmoudi, David Kaloper-Mersinjak, Saksham Sharma, Paola Velasco, Josh Platzky Miller, Lorena Qendro, Guillaume Baverez, Hugo Poplimont, and Romain Alves de Souza provided the necessary mix of grilled meat, humour, and advice on road bikes that any dystopian survival kit requires.

Note on the Text

Chapter 4 is an expanded version of a chapter that will be published in the edited collection 'Money Matters in Migration', by Cambridge University Press in 2021. Chapter 7 is a revised and expanded version of my article 'Deaths, Borders, and the Exception: Humanitarianism at the Spanish–Moroccan Border', published in the *American Behavioral Scientist* in 2020.

Introduction

Power works by making it hard to challenge how power works.

Sara Ahmed, forthcoming

On the morning of 9 September 2016, a large crowd gathered at the convention centre of Hay Riad, one of the wealthiest neighbourhoods of the Moroccan capital Rabat. All those who mattered in the migration world were there: Moroccan high-ranking civil servants, European diplomats, representatives from international, Moroccan, and migrant non-governmental organisations (NGOs), and of course, officers of the International Organisation for Migration (IOM) and the United Nations High Commissioner for Refugees (UNHCR). The occasion was a conference marking the third anniversary of Morocco's new migration policy. Launched by King Mohammed VI in 2013, the policy reform aspired to put human rights and integration at the centre of Morocco's border management strategy. In November 2013, Moroccan authorities announced a campaign to regularise undocumented foreigners. In December 2014, the government adopted a National Strategy for Immigration and Asylum (SNIA, in the French acronym), which aimed at providing Morocco with the legal and institutional infrastructure to integrate migrants, refugees, and asylum seekers (Benjelloun 2017b).

Officially, the new migration policy marked a turning point in the history of migration politics in Morocco, and in the Western Mediterranean more broadly. The announcement made by Mohammed VI in 2013 followed a decade of dire treatment of black migrant people in the country. Violence at the border had caused public outcry from the part of local and international civil society organisations and raised concerns within the National Council for Human Rights (CNDH, in the French acronym). The new migration policy promised to mark a break with this dark past, paving the way for a 'humane' approach to migration regulation (Gross-Wyrtzen

1

2020b). The announcement of such a reform had been publicly welcomed by the international community. The SNIA, in fact, perfectly
suited the border control interests of the European Union (EU) and its
member states, which had long tried to obtain a more significant
cooperation among 'transit' countries in the control of the Western
Mediterranean migratory route connecting Western and Central Africa
to Western Europe. Already in 2015, the EU had manifested its support
by granting Morocco a €10 million aid budget aimed at facilitating the
implementation of the new migration policy (EU Delegation in Rabat
2016). Other donors had followed suit (see Chapter 1). At the time of
the conference, the United Nations (UN) system in Morocco was
lobbying donors to fund a $13 million joint initiative in the field of
migration and asylum (Kingdom of Morocco and United Nations in
Morocco 2016; Nations Unies Maroc 2016). By 2016, aid-funded
projects sponsoring the integration of 'sub-Saharan migrants' were
proliferating around the country, as the entire aid industry embarked
on the mission of supporting Morocco in becoming a model of integration in North Africa (Tyszler 2019).

The morning of the event, I arrived at the convention centre with two
other participants and headed to the registration desk. The atmosphere
was very cheerful, and security extremely relaxed. When the ceremony
started, various high-ranking Moroccan civil servants from the (then)
Ministry in charge of Moroccans Residing Abroad and of Migration
Affairs (MCMREAM),[1] Ministry of Foreign Affairs, and Ministry of
Interior came forward to illustrate Morocco's achievements in the
previous three years, its commitment to being an international pioneer
in the implementation of a 'humane' approach to the regulation of
migration, and the challenges that persisted along the way. "We should

---

[1] On 10 October 2013, the Ministry of Moroccans Residing Abroad was expanded
through the creation of a Department for Migration Affairs. The Ministry's name
was therefore changed into Ministry in Charge of Moroccans Residing Abroad
and of Migration Affairs (MCMREAM, in the French acronym) (Benjelloun
2017b). The Ministry subsequently lost its autonomy and became the Delegated
Ministry in Charge of Moroccans Residing Abroad and of Migration Affairs
(MDMCREAM, in the French acronym), under the Ministry of Foreign Affairs
and Cooperation (MAEC, in the French acronym). After a new institutional
reshuffle, the MDMCREAM has been now transformed into a Delegated
Ministry in Charge of Moroccans Residing abroad, under the Ministry of Foreign
Affairs, African Cooperation, and Moroccans Residing Abroad. See: https://ma
rocainsdumonde.gov.ma/attributions-mcmre/

not forget that Morocco is a developing country, a poor country", one of the speakers mentioned, to emphasise the magnitude of the effort that Morocco was engaging in. Invited to talk on the stage, both the head of the IOM mission, Ana Fonseca, and the then representative of the UNHCR, Jean-Paul Cavalieri, profusely congratulated Moroccan authorities for their pioneering commitment in reforming the country's migration policy, encouraging them to persist.

The optimistic atmosphere at the convention centre in Hay Riad reflected the hopes of the international community vis-à-vis the transition that Morocco had embarked upon. But this cheerful image had its blind spots. On several occasions during the ceremony, sceptical participants raised their eyebrows at the sugar-coated image of the country's integration policies depicted by the speakers. It was no secret that, despite the publicised commitment to engage in the 'humane' treatment of foreigners, the implementation of several substantial integration and legislative measures promised by the Moroccan state was languishing. The treatment of migrants at the border was still dire, with the police regularly raiding migrant camps close to the Spanish enclaves of Ceuta and Melilla, and displacing dwellers to the interior cities of the country. Critical civil society organisations had interpreted the contradictory behaviour of Moroccan authorities as the symptom of an "undecided" migration policy – humanitarian on paper, militarised in practice (FIDH and GADEM 2015). Representatives of IOs, however, maintained a more cautious discourse. In interviews published on 16 September 2016 by the Moroccan newspaper *TelQuel*, both Ana Fonseca, at the IOM, and Jean-Paul Cavalieri, at the UNHCR, declined to comment on a question about violence against migrants. Ana Fonseca specified that she was unable to comment because she had "no information on forced displacements and violence at the border." She then added that "every country has its own way to treat irregular migration but it is important to respect human rights" (*TelQuel* 2016, translation by author).

The sugar-coated picture portrayed by the ceremony definitely faded on 4 October 2016, when the National Platform for Migrants' Protection (PNPM, in the French acronym) published a press release denouncing the fact that Moroccan authorities had unleashed a new wave of violence against migrants attempting to cross the border with the Spanish enclave of Ceuta. According to the PNPM, on 10 September 2016 around 100 migrant people, including 20 minors, had been arrested, several had been injured, and many displaced to the South of the country. Despite not being an isolated episode, this arrest campaign was particularly sinister and paradoxical, because it had taken place the day after the ceremony for the Third Anniversary of Morocco's new, 'humane' migration policy. "This event [...] casts a dark shadow on the outcome of the new Moroccan migration policy" the PNPM stated. "The National Platform for Migrants' Rights [...] denounces this securitarian violence, that tramples human dignity in the name of the protection of the borders of the European Union" (PNPM 2016, translation by author).

Bordering the World through Aid

Over the past forty years, countries in the Global North have increasingly restricted their migration policies to reduce the arrival of migrants, mainly from less well-off countries in the South. The appetite of Northern states to deter, capture, and remove undesired foreigners from their territory has determined a proliferation of migration control instruments. These now include tools ranging from restrictive migration laws to border fences and immigration removal centres (FitzGerald 2019). The sophistication of containment has coincided with the expansion of the border beyond its geographically fixed location. Countries in the North have thus tried to externalise[2] and outsource their borders to states in the South by invoking principles of shared responsibility over the control of migration flows (Pastore 2019). They have thus engaged in multilateral and bilateral negotiations to push countries of so-called origin and transit to police the mobility of their own citizens, and of non-nationals suspected to head towards wealthier destinations (El Qadim 2015; Khrouz 2016b). The expansion of the border has also coincided with the outsourcing of migration control measures to non-state actors, including corporations, NGOs, IOs, and even private citizens (Lahav and Guiraudon 2000). In migration control, as in anti-terrorism policies (Abbas 2019; Heath-Kelly and Strausz 2019), the co-optation of non-traditional security actors has allowed surveillance to infiltrate sectors such as

---

[2] Externalisation is commonly understood as "a series of extraterritorial activities in sending and in transit countries at the request of the (more powerful) receiving states (e.g., the United States or the European Union) for the purpose of controlling the movement of potential migrants" (Menjivar 2014: 357).

healthcare, education, and development cooperation, expanding the reach of the border not only away from the physical edges of the state but also away from the national security apparatus (see Cassidy 2018; Strasser and Tibet 2020). Development aid[3] has thus become a central tool in the migration control strategy pursued by European countries, Australia (Watkins 2017b), and the United States (Williams 2019). Donors, IOs, and NGOs have also become prominent actors in the regulation of international mobility due to their capacity to operate transnationally and implement development and humanitarian projects on the 'management' and 'prevention' of migration along migration routes (Geiger and Pécoud 2010).

How does migration control work beyond the spectacle of border violence? This book analyses aid as an instrument of migration containment, and the involvement of non-state actors, such as NGOs and IOs, in the expansion of the border in contexts of so-called migrant transit. I do this by examining the rise of 'sub-Saharan migrants' as a category of beneficiaries within the development and humanitarian industry in Morocco, a country that has long been at the centre of joint European and African efforts to secure borders in the Western Mediterranean. I argue that aid marks the rise of a substantially different mode of migration containment, one where power works beyond fast violence, and its disciplinary potential is augmented precisely by its elusiveness. Contrary to more conventional security instruments such as fences or deportation, aid thus does not filter border containment power in a neat or spectacular way, by physically preventing the movement of migrants or by inflicting injury. Rather, aid enables more subtle forms of marginalisation that construct 'sub-Saharan migrants' as a problem to be dealt with and promote forms of exclusionary integration into Moroccan society. Because aid does not work through violence and coercion, the kind of border control it supports is not "immediate in time, explosive and spectacular in space, and as erupting into instant sensational visibility" (Nixon 2011, 2). This elusiveness makes it more difficult to apprehend how development

---

[3]   By aid, I refer to the kind of government funding that the Organisation for Economic Co-operation and Development (OECD) defines as Official Development Assistance (ODA), or "government aid designed to promote the economic development and welfare of developing countries," and disbursed under the form of "grants, 'soft' loans (where the grant element is at least 25% of the total) and the provision of technical assistance" (OECD n.d.).

and humanitarian projects expand the border regime: no one can clearly retrace the contours of control or identify its perpetrators. Aid workers enact strategies which allow them *not to see* the work that they do as containment, or to justify their co-optation into the security apparatus. Domination always seems to solidify but not quite, as it could easily camouflage as something else – the case could always be made that identifying such practices as domination relies on misplaced intentionality or misinterpretation of the context. Since control looks a lot like care, or it is enacted through complex architectures of implementation, it can elude resistance and slip through. The border becomes evanescent: nobody can say where it is, how it operates, and who is actually enforcing it.

To say that aid expands the reach of the border, however, does not mean that containment works along predictable patterns. An analysis of the implementation of aid-funded projects reveals that our assumptions about the 'powerful' and the 'powerless' in migration control do not always hold. Scholars and civil society organisations have often maintained that states in the Global North can relatively easily induce countries in the South to collaborate on migration control, fundamentally by using aid as a bargaining chip to 'buy' their cooperation (Arci 2018; Concord 2018; Korvensyrjä 2017).[4] A similar argument is made for IOs and NGOs, and, in particular, the IOM, who are thought to have a high margin of manoeuvre in the contexts of 'origin' and 'transit' where they operate (Caillault 2012; Fine 2018; Pécoud 2018). But in this book, I argue that viewing Global Northern actors as infallible is essentialist. Morocco, in fact, constitutes a formidable example of a setting where national and local authorities selectively support the implementation of aid-funded projects depending on how these fit the domestic political agenda. The involvement of a 'transit' country in migration control cooperation does not automatically denote submission and passivity (Maâ 2020b): the state can capitalise on the activity of NGOs and IOs to implement certain parts of its migration policy – for example, by directly and indirectly entrusting donor-funded actors with the provision of social assistance to poor foreigners. But the autonomy of Morocco as a border control actor appears in a clearer

---

[4]   The title of a report published by the French NGO La Cimade in 2017 succinctly summarises this view: "*Coopération UE-Afrique sur les migrations. Chronique d'un chantage*" [EU-Africa Cooperation on migration. Chronicle of a blackmail] (La Cimade 2017).

light through the analysis of state-led obstruction of aid-funded projects. In the borderlands especially, Moroccan authorities closely monitor humanitarian activities, coming to the point of expelling those actors that speak out about border violence (see Norman 2016).

Talking about Morocco as an 'Immigration Nation' as I do in the book title is, of course, ironic. That Morocco has long been at the centre of border securitisation efforts in the Western Mediterranean does not mean that immigration in the country is demographically significant. Much to the contrary, the number of foreigners living in Morocco is actually very low and has considerably decreased after the country gained independence from colonial rule in 1956. In 2014, foreign residents in Morocco officially constituted only 0.25 per cent of the total population of 33 million people (Haut Commissariat au Plan 2017b), with estimates of the number of 'irregular migrants' ranging between 10,000 and 40,000 individuals (European Commission 2016; Médecins du Monde and Caritas 2016). Politically, however, Morocco became conceptualised by the EU and its member states as an 'Immigration Nation' sometime between the late 1990s and the early 2000s, when European state and non-state actors started regarding the collaboration of non-European countries as essential to reduce the arrival of migrants from less well-off countries in the South. The European drive for migration control and Morocco's capacity to use migration as a foreign policy tool produced an unprecedented escalation of political attention towards people qualified as 'sub-Saharan migrants' living in Morocco. Far from being a natural category, the expression 'sub-Saharan' is imbued with colonial and racist prejudice. After the end of colonisation, in fact, this term replaced the expression "Afrique Noire" (Black Africa) to refer to formerly colonised countries – thus subtly coding racial considerations into a geographic category (Tyszler 2019). In practice, 'sub-Saharan migrant' has now become a label utilised by Moroccan and European policymakers, aid workers, journalists, and private citizens to systematically construct black people as actual or 'potential' migrants suspected to be transiting through Morocco to irregularly cross the border to Europe (El Qadim 2015; Khrouz 2016a). The securitisation of the Euro–African border and the policing of people qualified as 'sub-Saharan migrants' materialised through the rise of fences surrounding the Spanish enclaves of Ceuta and Melilla, the approval of restrictive immigration laws both in European countries and in Morocco, and the establishment of aid policies specifically aimed at supporting border control cooperation (Coleman 2009; El Qadim 2015). Morocco thus became one of the first countries where the EU and its member states fuelled the emergence of a migration industry by using development as an instrument of containment – an approach that was later replicated in countries further away from European borders (Gabrielli 2016).

Scholars and journalists tend to use the term 'migration industry' to refer to a very broad group of actors involved both in the control and in the facilitation of migration, in licit as well as in illicit activities (Andersson 2014; Gammeltoft-Hansen and Sørensen 2013). What is common to organisations as different as faith-based charities and smuggling networks, the literature argues, is that they share "an interest in migration or earn their livelihood by organising migration movements" (Castles et al. 2014, 235). In this book, however, I use the expression[5] in a slightly different way, to refer to the actors involved in the implementation of European aid policy on the ground in countries of 'transit'. Aid, rather than profit, defines the boundaries of the industry, determining who belongs to it and who does not, establishing accountability structures and flows of contestation, co-optation, and aspired belonging. The boundaries of the industry are not stable nor irreversible; organisations like the IOM or the UNHCR, or predominantly donor-funded local and INGOs, certainly form part of it. Smaller, critical organisations generally orbit around the industry but can sometimes become aid-recipients (see Chapter 3).

Studying the working of border power through aid can sometimes feel like chasing a ghost. The aid apparatus in Morocco, in fact, does not even explicitly express itself in terms of border control. As the opening ethnographic vignette shows, donors, NGOs, and IOs rather frame their intervention in terms of 'integration'. One of the ways the migration industry supported Morocco's integration strategy was through the funding of projects facilitating the access of migrants to the labour market. As I will explain in Chapter 5, these projects often failed: given the high rates of unemployment and informality characterising the Moroccan labour market, West and Central African people attending training workshops rarely ended up securing stable employment afterwards. One of the organisations that promoted labour

---

[5] In this book, I use 'migration industry', 'aid industry', and 'development and humanitarian industry' as interchangeable terms.

integration projects was the one that contracted Samuel, a Congolese community-based worker whom I interviewed during my fieldwork. After years of financial struggles with small business initiatives and a dearth of job opportunities, Samuel ended up seeking employment within the aid industry itself. As a community-based worker, Samuel was crucial to the activity of his organisation as he was doing most of the outreach work necessary to secure access to precarious migrant communities. His job was extremely demanding: Samuel would receive calls at any hour of the day (including during our interview) from parents needing help enrolling children in school, from women about to give birth and needing to be transported to the hospital, or from people who had been arrested by Moroccan police. Despite the centrality of his role, however, Samuel did not have a job contract for the work he was performing. Rather, he had a 'volunteer contract', which came with a meagre indemnisation of 1500 dirham/month (€137/month).[6] This was less than the Moroccan minimum wage (2,698.83 MAD/ month in 2019/2020) (CNSS 2019) and considerably less than the salary of the organisation's regular employees (see also Abena Banyomo 2019). Sabrine, a European aid worker employed by the same organisation later explained that community-based workers were not employed full-time. According to Sabrine, contracting these people as volunteers was a solution that allowed migrants such as Samuel to continue their professional activities, while at the same time assisting the organisation to maintain a presence in the area. As a matter of fact, however, being a community-based worker had been Samuel's only source of employment: he had been pushed towards the aid industry by the dearth of alternative job opportunities, and he did not have another job on the side.

The case of Samuel exemplifies the forms of non-explicitly coercive control through which the aid industry contains migrant, refugee, and asylum-seeking people. The organisation that Samuel works for is formally committed to the project of transforming Morocco into a country of integration – it bids for labour integration initiatives, sponsors training workshops, and talks the talk of integration. This official commitment, however, was challenged by the deliberate devaluation of Samuel's work. This devaluation is justified by Sabrine with arguments that have been long used to motivate the

---

[6] All currency conversions relate to the conversion rate on 21 July 2020.

underpayment of workers in the global factory – there are no obligations, Samuel is always free to have another job, volunteering is a way for him to be active and involved. The underpayment of community-based workers is certainly less severe a form of control than other forms of hard border security that contain migrants' presence inside and outside of Morocco. But the financial and contractual downplaying of Samuel's contribution clearly produces a form of marginalisation: Samuel remains impoverished, and he is not integrated into society as a decently paid worker, but rather as a compensated 'volunteer'. In this power game, Samuel becomes a subordinate player that the migration industry feels entitled to extract value from (Andersson 2014). 'Integration' thus becomes an empty signifier: the same organisation that ostensibly tries to facilitate the access of migrants to the labour market easily dismisses, and marginalises, migrant labour.

By taking aid as a vantage point to reflect on the transformation and diffusion of migration control, I complicate our understanding of how power works within the border regime. I build on Foucault's analytic of power to develop a framework that explains the coexistence of fast techniques of bordering with emerging instruments of indirect and elusive rule. Foucauldian tools allow us to apprehend the "friability" of the border – the elusiveness, unexpected alliances, and resistances characterising it (Tazzioli 2014, 9). Discussing the ambiguity of power inevitably leads to complicate our understanding of 'benevolence', 'malevolence', and co-optation into borderwork. I bring in Elizabeth Povinelli's notion of the "quasi-event" (Povinelli 2011, 5) to provide an alternative vocabulary to examine the factors driving the expansion of the border regime. I emphasise that the elusiveness of aid makes containment less visible and thus more difficult to resist for the actors orbiting around the aid industry. I compound these different threads of analysis into a discussion about power relations in the governance of the border. This book thus de-essentialises the workings of border power by discarding four myths common in both scholarly and journalistic prose. Donors are not all-powerful: they rarely manage to get partner countries' full cooperation in migration control, let alone to perfectly transpose their border outsourcing aspirations on the ground (El Qadim 2015; Geha and Talhouk 2018). IOs and NGOs are not almighty: their movements are often critically constrained and policed by domestic authorities (Gazzotti 2019), their projects crafted in such a way as to not hurt the sensibilities of local governments, and their very existence is constantly threatened by donors' shifting strategies (Bartels 2017). But we should not see these organisations as abject either: NGOs and IOs, in fact, also operate as autonomous actors that devise strategies to ensure their own institutional survival and the achievement of their own political mission. This might lead them to take choices that align (or not) with those of donors or of local authorities (Bouilly 2010; Cuttitta 2020; Tyszler 2019). Finally, domestic actors hardly match the image of compliant subcontractors. They pose limits to the presence of external actors on their territory by selectively cooperating into or obstructing aid-funded projects, depending on their own political agenda (Wunderlich 2010). The outcome of migration-related aid projects is thus shaped by the autonomous strategies of actors on the receiving end of border externalisation policies, and by contingencies that make migration control elusive, and unexpected at times.

Bordering beyond Coercion

In a famous passage of *The History of Sexuality*, Foucault observed a historical shift in the workings of sovereign power, understood as the right "to decide life and death" (Foucault 1990, 135). Whereas until the seventeenth century the sovereign used to exercise his prerogative in a *deductive* fashion, "by exercising his right to kill, or by refraining from killing," from that moment onwards sovereignty assumed a new form, one that did not only work through death and destruction, but also through *productive* mechanisms. Foucault defines this new regulatory technology as "a power bent on generating forces, making them grow, and ordering them, rather than one dedicated to impeding them, making them submit, or destroying them" (Foucault 1990, 136). In other words, the power "to *take* life or *let* live" gave way to "a power to *foster* life or *disallow* it to the point of death" (Foucault 1990, 138). Violent forms of sovereignty were therefore obfuscated by two types of power: one focusing on the body ("an anatomo-politics of the body") as a site for the deployment of disciplinary tactics of subjugation; and one focusing on the population as a whole ("bio-politics"). Both discipline and biopolitics "characterized a power whose highest function was perhaps no longer to kill, but to invest life through and through" (Foucault 1990, 139).

The most famous and powerful example that Foucault provided of this historical transformation is the transition in the penal treatment of crimes, which opens the first chapter of *Discipline and Punish*. The philosophy and practice surrounding penality shifted from a public spectacle of torture to "punishment of a less immediately physical kind," where the condemned is contained through techniques that are less obvious because they no longer rely on visible bodily injury (Foucault 1979a, 8). The rise of the prison, and of confinement as a generalised technique of punishment, is symptomatic of the repositioning of the body within this new politics of penal power, which no longer tends towards the destruction of the condemned but to its subjugation. Here, punishment relies on a "studied manipulation of the individual," that is socialised into internalising the implicit and explicit rules regulating their social world, so that authority can function without anyone constantly enforcing it (Foucault 1979a, 128–29). Killing and dying thus become actions that do not just happen in ways that are "catastrophic, crisis-laden, and sublime," but most often in forms that are rather "ordinary, chronic, and cruddy" (Povinelli 2011, 3). Nixon has conceptualised the discrete working of subjugation power as "slow violence," or "a violence that occurs gradually and out of sight, a violence of delayed destruction that is dispersed across time and space, an attritional violence that is typically not viewed as violence at all" (Nixon 2011, 2). Other scholars have named this form of chronic dispossession as "abandonment," or a technique of governance premised on the purposefully inconsistent presence of the state in the everyday life of communities labelled as disposable, dismissible, out of sight (Biehl 2005; Gross-Wyrtzen 2020b; Willis 2018).

This, of course, does not mean that spectacular, cruel manifestations of power have disappeared. Indeed, "necropolitics," or the working of power through death, occupies a distinct place in contemporary societies. Slavery, colonial terror, and contemporary practices of warfare and mass murder all provide evidence that the historical shift in the practice of sovereignty has not produced a unique and homogenously applied model of regulation of the body and the population, but rather that "modernity is at the origin of multiple concepts of sovereignty, and thus also of the biopolitical" (Mbembe 2019, 67). Indeed, discipline and biopolitics did not perfectly replace sovereignty in organising the relations of power in society. Elements of both systems coexist, as violence resurges alongside the enactment of techniques of government that foster life (Foucault 2007), and is regularly deployed against those labelled as undeserving (Ahmed 2017).

The shift from sovereign to disciplinary/biopolitical power did not mark the disappearance of coercive methods of rule either. Coercion remains central to the regulation of a population, but is carried out in a subtler, more discrete fashion. Because discipline works to conquer and transform the subject through a series of habits and regulations, subjugation is achieved through the internalisation of such rules. The obedient subject, that acts according to the rules it has internalised, might not feel as if they were being directed by some form of external authority. Rather, they might be under the impression of operating freely, out of their own choice (Taylor 2017). Foucault clarified the role of power subjectivation when he developed his theory of governmentality. In *Security, Territory, Population* Foucault devotes remarkable attention to the notion of 'conduct', which he loosely understands as conducting others ("conduire"), conducting oneself ("se conduire") (or let oneself be conducted), or behaving "as an effect of a form of conduct (*une conduite*)"(Foucault 2007, 193, italics in original). The action of conducting is not necessarily free of the exercise of force. However, governing remains fundamentally different from dominating because power is not exercised directly, but indirectly, through "a 'conduct of conducts' and a management of possibilities" (Foucault, 2007, in Lemke 2016, 18). The integration of aid into the workings of international politics is an example in such power transition, as it signals a change in the way wealthy countries try to exercise hegemony on other parts of the world. Whereas colonial power was characterised by the repressive and violent submission of colonised territories, development operates biopolitically insofar as it is premised on fostering forces rather than violently repressing them (Brigg 2002). Development thus becomes a way for donors to deploy power beyond coercion – by directing people's actions through their freedom, and through a professed commitment to the improvement of the life of both individuals and their communities (Duffield 2007).

The border is a field of power where control materialises in both spectacular and mundane forms. Undeniably, migration containment is intimately characterised by violence (Minca and Vaughan-Williams 2012), to the point that the traditional Foucauldian biopolitical lens struggles to account for the kind of open, primordial forms of abuse that are unleashed against migrants in the borderlands. Building on an analysis of pushbacks and failures to rescue migrant boats in distress in the Mediterranean, Vaughan-Williams concludes that "letting die" does not adequately reflect the active role that European authorities play in exposing migrants to death. EU member states do not only obliviously let them at the mercy of a hostile physical and political environment. By stripping border crossers of the right to be rescued, EU authorities actively transform migrants into people that *can be left to die* because they do not deserve sanctuary (Vaughan-Williams 2015, 65). Coercive techniques of containment, however, coexist with subtler, non-militarised instruments regulating the movement of people. In her work on the US–Mexico border, Jill Williams defines information campaigns aiming at curbing irregular migration as the "softer side" (Williams 2019, 1) of border governance. She contrasts them with "hard power," militarised techniques of bordering because they infiltrate migrants' mobility capacity from a different spatial and targeting strategy. Fences or deportation try to apprehend migrants in public sites through techniques aimed at physically distancing them from the border, constraining and injuring their bodies. Soft-power bordering strategies, instead, operate in intimate, non-conventional security spaces, targeting not so much the bodies of migrants, but rather their emotional selves by appealing to feelings of fear and empathy (Williams 2019, 1). States can immobilise migrants by preventing them from moving, but at the same time preventing them from really settling (Picozza 2017; Tazzioli 2018, 2019). Waiting is probably the clearest example of how border control operates through slow violence. Keeping people waiting (for resettlement, for their visa application to be processed, for the border to open again) is not visibly harmful, but it effectively consumes people both physically and socially – because it undermines their healthcare and accelerates their financial and social marginalisation (Hyndman 2019). In her work on containment in inner Moroccan urban centres, Gross-Wyrtzen argues that the multiple processes of racialised dispossession activated by border control effectively maintain West and Central African migrants in a condition of protracted waiting – unable to accumulate enough resources to cross the border to Europe and unable to return. This form of destitute waiting is less legible than building fences, but equally effective as a containment device (Gross-Wyrtzen 2020b; see also Coddington 2019). Waiting and unsettlement produce a form of governmentality that is as pervasive as it is discontinuous and inconsistent – migrants are either tightly, physically and administratively controlled or they are left to their own devices, made legible or unlegible by a state that alternates strategies of seeing, not seeing (Aradau and Tazzioli 2019, 201), or not wanting "to be seen seeing" (Gross-Wyrtzen 2020b, 894–95).

The coexistence of spectacular and mundane mechanisms of migration control is strategic to the expansion of the border. In a seminal piece, Nicholas De Genova argues that the state perpetuates the containment of undesirable foreigners by staging a "border spectacle" at its territorial frontiers. Such a scene casts the attention of national and international audiences on the spectacular exclusion of migrants at clearly identifiable crossing points. The routinary consumption of such images by the public elevates some of the most mediatised representations to the role of quintessential portrayals of 'illegality'. Producing and reproducing the "Border Spectacle," De Genova says, naturalises illegality as a given condition: the 'clandestines' are demonised as inherently deviant because of their decision to transgress migration laws. In so doing, the state overshadows the reliance of its economy and social system on cheap, deportable labour, and the central role played by migration law in driving – rather than countering – the irregular movement of people. Staging a spectacle of migrant exclusion at crossing points solidifies a form of public consciousness that identifies "the Border" with the territorial edges of the state, and "bordering" with visible, clear-cutting forms of containment, deployed against people profiled as undeserving and expendable (De Genova 2013).

Benevolence, Malevolence, and the "Quasi-Events" of Border Control

Migration studies and critical humanitarian literature have tended to depict the work of non-state actors as either aligning with (Cuttitta 2016; Scheel and Ratfisch 2014; Valluy 2007c) or resisting border control imperatives (Alioua 2009; Stierl 2015). NGOs and IOs align to migration containment objectives by subcontracting specific border control functions, like the prevention of irregular migration (Rodriguez 2019) or the facilitation of return (Chappart 2015; Maâ 2019). They also expand the border by performing practices of care and assistance to migrant and displaced people that integrate elements of control. This second form of border outsourcing is intimately linked to what

Polly Pallister-Wilkins labels as "humanitarian borderwork," the delivery of emergency relief aimed at protecting life in contexts where
containment endangers migrant existence often to the point of death
(Pallister-Wilkins 2016). Indeed, humanitarianism is characterised by
an intimate tension between practices of care – a will to "do good," to
rescue a suffering humanity during instances of crises (Ticktin 2014,
274) – and attitudes of control – the tendency to see humanity also as
a source of threat that requires monitoring and containment for it to be
saved (Feldman and Ticktin 2010). In the specific field of border
control, this tension between care and control materialises in heter-
ogenous ways. Programmes assisting displaced people can integrate
elements of border policing – it is the case, for example, of humanitarian organisations that tightly control the movement of people in and
out of refugee camps (Turner 2018). In other cases, control might be an
unintended consequence of border humanitarian activities. The struggle of humanitarians to help might end up reinforcing the racialised
logics underpinning border control – for example, when organisations
frame migrants as "victims," or when they support vulnerability frameworks that only conceive the "suffering body" as a legitimate recipient
of assistance (Ticktin 2011). At times, the moral philosophy underpinning charity work, and the longer, situated histories of empire that
marked the global establishment of religious missions facilitate the
anchoring of control in humanitarian borderwork. In her work on
migration control in Morocco, Tyszler highlights how Catholic organisations, whose presence in the country is tied to the history of Spanish
and French colonialism, can turn into providers of humanitarian assistance to migrants stranded in various areas of Morocco. The provision
of assistance inspired by Catholic morals, however, can push them to
endorse certain border control norms which align with their ethics, or
to introduce further disciplinary norms aimed at policing migrant
bodies (Tyszler 2020). The involvement of non-state actors in the
border project should not be essentialised as motivated solely by financial gain: some organisations might be pushed by a moral stance – as
a continuation of their missionary duty (Maâ 2020b), or as a way to
enact solidarity principles (even though this can happen in often racialised and non-reflexive ways) (Agustín 2007).

Describing the border security world as fractured between 'benevolent' and 'malevolent' practices, however, does not go far enough in
explaining the expansion and contraction of the border regime (El

Qadim et al. 2020), or of security apparatus more broadly (see also Gazzotti 2018). Indeed, Agier himself discounts the idea of humanitarianism as so intimately linked to military interventions by means of a "manipulating intentionality," even though the two are undeniably tied by a "functional solidarity" (Agier 2011, 5) (Chapter 7). But if intentionality cannot be considered the primary reason leading non-traditional security actors to support migration control, how do we explain the seemingly endless expansion of the containment apparatus? Answering this question implies understanding that the transition from coercive to elusive modes of societal regulation marked the expansion of ruling mechanisms that can hardly be apprehended as *manifestations* of power. Discipline, in fact, "is not a triumphant power, which because of its own excess can pride itself on its own omnipotence; it is a modest, suspicious power, which functions as a calculated, but permanent economy" (Foucault 1979a, 170). Since we are accustomed to conceptualising power as a deductive force, we are less able to recognise domination when it does not occur through fast violence or explicit coercion (Taylor 2017). Like in other fields of 'soft security' (Busher et al. 2017; O'Neill 2015), we struggle to see containment in aid-funded migration projects not only because power does not expressly work in a negative fashion, but also because it is not enacted by the usual suspects that we generally associate with border control, like the members of the security apparatus.

The proliferation of migration control methods and their diffusion away from the state have determined the enlistment of the most disparate non-security actors into border containment. These now include aid workers employed by NGOs and IOs, donors' employees, but also religious figures (Watkins 2020), youth workers (Rodriguez 2015), and mothers of irregular border crossers who died at sea (Bouilly 2010). Contrary to what we expect of security forces, we tend to automatically perceive non-traditional security professionals as non-threatening. When the control is delegated to individuals that we perceive as carers, "we believe that these individuals are helping us, caring for us, educating us or healing us – as, to some extent, they may be – and thus we submit to them voluntarily and do not see this submission as an effect of power" (Taylor 2017, 54). When non-traditional security agents are drawn into border control, the most unlikely social spaces – youth centres, schools, or cinemas – become the frontline of a containment policy that has become all the more elusive; it is implemented by actors that are not *really* security agents, and through methods that are not *really* security instruments.

Due to their ordinary appearance, Povinelli labels quieter, mundane forms of suffering as "quasi-events": in comparison with faster forms of power and violence, they are "never anything huge" (Povinelli 2011, 144), but are rather chronic forms of misery and domination that exist "between this state of neither great crisis nor final redemption" (Povinelli 2011, 4). The ordinariness of quasi-events adds to their lethality because they tend to go unnoticed – "it is hard to say when they occurred let alone what caused them" (Povinelli 2011, 144). Although the presence of power is also marked by the formation of resistance (Foucault 1990, 95), resistance struggles to rise and endure when the contours of domination and suffering are not neat. Whereas fast violence seems "to demand, as if authored from outside human agency, an ethical response" (Povinelli 2011, 14), one struggles to feel the same impulse to "take sides" (Povinelli 2011, 146) if there is not a blatant injustice to feel strongly about, a perpetrator that can clearly be held accountable, or an easily identifiable cause to someone's misery.

The kind of border control that I discuss in this book can be understood as a series of "quasi-events". Aid does not systematically filter border containment power in a way that is neat, eye-catching, or clearly painful. The refusal of IOM and UNHCR representatives to comment on border violence is not an action that directly harms anyone. Samuel does not sustain physical injury for being contracted as a volunteer rather than as a proper employee. But aid-funded projects do not need to physically injure migrant people to be *rooted in* and *conducive to* containment. The lack of honest criticism from a large portion of the UN community in Morocco perpetuates an international image of the state as respectful of (migrants') rights in a moment when the country's human right record is clearly deteriorating (Chapter 7). The distance from the field and embodied privilege enjoyed by the heads of the IOM and UNHCR allow them to make such statements without experiencing their consequences. Being underpaid as a 'volunteer' impoverishes Samuel, thus impairing his social mobility and capacity to live a dignified life. The caring angle and complex geopolitical entanglement that characterise the operations of development and humanitarian actors always lead to mitigating discourses – there is always a *but* or a *however*. Frontline bureaucrats, in general, tend to adopt rationalising strategies to cope with the impossible requests that their functions oblige them to reconcile (Zacka 2017; see also Ahmed 2012). Atypical security bureaucrats particularly tend to enact sense-making strategies in order *not to see* the work that they do as control (Busher et al. 2017). They might rationalise their co-optation into security policies as legitimate by describing their work either as 'business as usual', or by framing it within a greater mission to achieve social justice (Ahmed 2012). For a care actor, receiving aid money disbursed through an anti-terrorism or border control budget line is legitimate *if* the activities funded are the same that were funded before, or *if* the money enables the funding of welfare programmes that would be otherwise impossible to offer (Bastani and Gazzotti in press). By enacting such strategies, frontline border workers further undo the "perceptual" (Povinelli 2011b, 14) dimension of border control: it just takes a sentence, a polite shrug, and containment fades into the background, too subtle to sustain concerns, too present to completely appease them.

Who Governs the Border?

Understanding border power as slippery and non-traditional security bureaucrats as patchy migration control actors, confronts us with a question that has been central in migration and border debates: who governs the border? The discussion about the apparent omnipresence and multidirectionality of power (Foucault 1990) in migration politics is particularly heated because it is enmeshed with questions about external pressures, the afterlives of coloniality, and the agency of so-called 'subaltern' states. Scholars have long tended to see the workings of border control in non-European countries predominantly as the result of the externalisation of European migration containment (Belguendouz 2005; Casas-Cortes et al. 2014; Watkins 2017a). According to this body of scholarship, the EU and its member states would be able to export and 'impose' the implementation of restrictive border control measures in the territories of countries labelled of migrant 'origin' and 'transit', which often includes former European colonies. Compliance with European requests would be obtained through incentives – like the offer of preferential trade agreements, development aid, or dedicated visa quotas for nationals of partner countries – or more coercive forms of conditionality (Coleman 2009; Korvensyrjä 2017). This approach, however, has now been widely recognised as essentialist, because it ignores the agency of countries in the Global South. Partially inspired by post-colonial theory, more recent work has shifted towards a position which acknowledges that countries of 'origin' and 'transit' can oppose fierce resistance to European externalisation attempts, discontinuously engaging in border control cooperation and steering it according to their own political priorities. Resistance to EU pressures is common where the adoption of restrictive border control measures would come at unsustainable financial and political costs – like alienating a country's diaspora or electorate (Mouthaan 2019), undermining the management of domestic security concerns (Zardo and Loschi 2020), hampering other foreign policy aspirations, or placing a disproportionate amount of responsibilities over border control on Southern actors (El Qadim 2015).

Both approaches, however, tend to adopt a one-sided understanding of reality, which does not acknowledge the broader complexity of migration control cooperation (Maâ 2020b). In a recent piece on the new Moroccan migration policy, Leslie Gross-Wyrtzen and I build on Ann Laura Stoler's work on colonial presences to acknowledge that the capacity of action of countries in the Global South *also* coexists with long-lasting, yet unevenly durable, forms of coloniality that have shaped Moroccan history. The securitisation of borders in the Western Mediterranean cannot therefore be read "as either imperialism in a new guise or as a definitive break from the colonial past" (Gross-Wyrtzen and Gazzotti 2020, 5). The externalised border is rather a space in tension where different, unevenly durable forms of colonial domination overlap, influencing the current migration landscape and clashing with contemporary forms of resistance to migration control. It is undeniable that colonial infrastructures and present European pressures heavily condition the field of migration policy in the South. However, it is also true that cooperating with the EU on border control cooperation is not necessarily a marker of submission to neo-colonial imperatives for countries on the receiving end of externalisation policies (Maâ 2020b, 2). Countries of 'origin' and 'transit' can decide to proactively engage in border control cooperation if that increases their international legitimacy (Benjelloun 2017a; Natter 2014; Paoletti 2011), or if that allows them to accumulate other financial or diplomatic resources. Tsourapas labels "refugee rentier states" those states that leverage the presence of displaced communities on their territory as a bargaining chip to gain power and revenues from state and non-state actors (Tsourapas 2019b, 464).

Aid perfectly captures how border control is not only about externalisation nor about Southern agency, but rather a bit of both: it emerges out of a will of Northern countries to externalise their borders, but its implementation is distributed and contested, and its workings are rarely the ones intended by donors. In recent work on migration policymaking in Morocco, Turkey, and Egypt, Kelsey Norman highlights that North African and Middle Eastern countries can allow aid-funded IOs and NGOs to deliver services to migrant and refugee people on their territory as part of a political strategy of "strategic indifference." By outsourcing the implementation of integration measures to non-state, externally-funded actors, states gain international legitimacy for their participation in border control cooperation by investing minimal public resources (Norman 2019; see also Geha and Talhouk 2018). Taking the case of Senegal and Mauritania, Frowd argues instead that cooperation in EU-sponsored projects can constitute a form of state-building for countries of 'transit' and 'origin'. European-funded projects, in fact, can allow these countries to strengthen state outreach, and better assert their sovereign prerogative over their own borders and nationals (Frowd 2018; see also Dini 2017).[7] The cooperation of countries of 'origin' and 'transit' into donor-funded projects does not therefore automatically denote passivity, as aid-recipient countries can proactively direct aid to fulfil their own political strategies.

The reason why much of the existing literature tends to see border control as spectacular, countries of "origin" and "transit" as easily compliant, and donors as all-powerful, is that scholars have mostly privileged the analysis of the aspirational dimension of aid as a border containment instrument, substantially basing research on the analysis of official documents outlining the policy as it exists on paper. This is problematic because the kind of containment filtered by aid-funded projects can be too little "event focused, time bound, and body bound" (Nixon 2011, 3) to actually appear between the lines of project factsheets or even of an evaluation document. But more obviously, the politics of communication that donors, NGOs, IOs, and aid-recipient

---

[7] This argument is also true for other fields of EU intervention, like democracy promotion (Schuetze 2019).

countries adopt to talk about migration control cooperation is either reticent, or crafted in such vague terms that it sounds purposefully critic-proof (Geiger and Pécoud 2010, 6).

To address this problem, my methodological approach builds on a body of scholarship more attentive to the *practice* of containment, that analyses "actually existing" border policy through a focus on its implementation (Bartels 2017; Dini 2017; Frowd 2018; Infantino 2016). Implementation is the dimension where a policy is delivered and executed on the ground (Lipsky 1980). Focusing on migration control as it exists in practice rather than in the ideal allows us to deconstruct the image of the border as a set of grandiose and neat operations, an almost almighty, tenacious entity that flawlessly manages to immobilise people along migration routes (Burridge et al. 2017). The border is much more fragile than it seems: during implementation, in fact, the policy scripts conceived by policymakers have to come to terms with the political tensions, organisational factors, and everyday life dynamics marking the world of the street, which policymakers are not always able to predict at the policy-design stage (Zacka 2017). This is particularly true when policymaking takes place at the transnational level, in contexts that are far removed from the reality that policy instruments seek to govern. Policy outcomes therefore cannot be easily predicted, as power does not work along foreseeable and pre-determined pathways (Foucault 1990). The implementation turn in border studies has foregrounded a view of migration control more attentive to the everyday, situated, and contingent practices characterising the work of security agents. Power does not flow neatly from top to bottom: border policy is made of a myriad mid-level spaces of cooperation, negotiation, domination, and resistance (Ellermann 2009). The inherent multi-layered character of border control transforms mid- and street-level bureaucrats into power brokers, who are able to open bargaining spaces far away from the mainstream sites of the political (El Qadim 2014). Concerns that have very little to do with border control can play a substantial role in the way border bureaucrats apprehend their roles: the imperative to deliver results in a timely way, and to repurpose resources according to political and economic considerations affect the way decisions over visa, asylum, and financial help applications are made (Satzewich 2015; Slack 2019). The study of implementation thus foregrounds a picture of containment where borders are "never simply 'present', nor fully established, nor obviously

accessible" (Parker and Vaughan-Williams 2012, 728): they are mut-
able entities, dynamic in nature, always in becoming (Burridge et al.
2017).

A Note on Methods and Ethics

This book is the product of eleven months of fieldwork conducted
between March 2016 and August 2019, and of years of engagement
with some of the people whose stories are featured in these pages.
Semi-structured interviews constitute the main source of data for my
analysis. I conducted 126 semi-structured interviews with donor representatives, officers of IOs and NGOs, Moroccan civil servants,
people from West and Central Africa who had participated into aid-
funded projects as 'beneficiaries', African and European diplomats,
academics, and development consultants. Interviewees were selected
based on their involvement in or knowledge of the implementation of
aid-funded projects in the field of migration in Morocco from 2000 to
2018. Depending on the person, interviews were conducted in French,
Spanish, English, or Italian. Nine of these interviews were conducted
with Maria Hagan, who joined me on fieldwork in July 2019 to collect
data for her own research project. Around half of the interviews were
recorded. For the others, I rely on notes that I took during and after
the conversation. I integrated interview data with the analysis of
primary documents compiled by development and humanitarian
organisations, as well as newspaper articles, reports, and official
communiqués drafted by human rights organisations and by
Moroccan authorities. During my time in Morocco, I also conducted
participant observation of events organised by NGOs and IOs – mainly
conferences, round-table discussions, and project launches, as well as
training sessions organised in the framework of two different development projects. When I conducted participant observation, I was introduced – or I introduced myself – to all the participants of the workshop
(migrant people, aid workers, and consultants) as a researcher in the field
of migration. During and in between periods of fieldwork, I kept up to
date with real-time developments in the field through various media
platforms.

Geographically, I followed the migration industry around the country. For most of my fieldwork, I was based in Rabat, where donors, IOs,
and many NGOs had their headquarters – which, at times, constituted

the only offices in the country. I conducted regular field trips in other areas of project implementation, such as Oujda, Tangier, Tétouan, Nador, and Casablanca. I also conducted field visits to places that have been drawn into the violent map of internal displacement in the period after the announcement of the new Moroccan migration policy. These include Fes, Meknes, Beni Mellal, Tiznit, and Agadir (see Map 1). Unlike border cities and large coastal centres, these places only sporadically receive the interests of aid-funded NGOs and IOs, although migrants find themselves stranded in these areas. I conducted many other interviews via Skype and WhatsApp to reach development and humanitarian practitioners who were no longer operating in Morocco. To protect my respondents, I have anonymised all interviews and informal conversations, and have altered some details in ways that do not impact the analysis. For ease of reading, the names of respondents, as well as the names of some of the NGOs they worked for, have been pseudonymised. For clarity, pseudonymised NGOs are marked as starred (*) throughout the text.

My identity and my privilege (as a middle-class, white European woman studying at a prestigious UK university) followed me on fieldwork. Though allowing for only a modest living in the United Kingdom, my PhD salary allowed me to live comfortably in Morocco, where I was

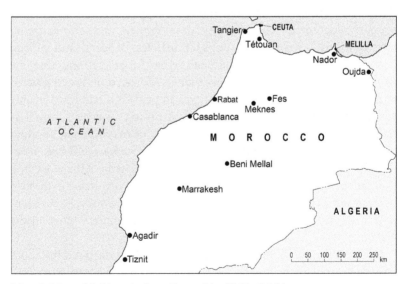

Map 1 Map of fieldwork sites. Created by Philip Stickler.

living and socialising in the same spaces as well-off Moroccans and the 'expatriate' community – which, in Rabat, is largely formed by aid workers (Boudarssa 2017). Informal and serendipitous encounters made me appear more familiar to some of my potential interlocutors, providing me with a chance to establish some trust that any study of (aid) bureaucracy requires in order to go beyond institutional rhetoric (see Pascucci 2018). Although my privileged respondents and I shared the same upper-middle-class networks and urban spaces, most West and Central African people navigating the aid industry as civil society leaders or project beneficiaries that I met during fieldwork did not, because their social and economic background was much more disadvantaged. This of course did not mean that this second category of informants and I never crossed paths: I bumped into many of them at conferences organised by IOs in upscale venues (see Chapter 3), or on the premises of NGOs. These encounters, however, cannot be read in a colour-blind fashion. In aid spaces funded by European donors and populated by white aid workers, my whiteness made people presume I was yet another aid worker. When entering the drop-in centres of certain NGOs, people queuing to speak to the NGO officers would ask me whether I was the new social assistant, whether I had worked for this or that other NGO, or simply "who I was in the project," assuming that all the lighter-skinned people in the room were Moroccans or Europeans employed by that particular charity. I always made sure to draw a neat distinction between myself and the employees of aid organisations when I introduced myself to someone in the field.

As I will explain in Chapter 3, embarking on a research project on border control in Morocco means entering a field that is overcrowded and extra politicised. 'Migration' has become a sort of extractive sector in Morocco, where states, non-state actors, and even researchers extract monetary and social value from the plights of migrant people targeted by border control. Although my research focused on the structures of border power rather than on people subjected to it, I was acutely aware that my work was also inextricably tied to the extractivism characterising the industry (Andersson 2014; Sukarieh and Tannock 2019). When I started my research, I became very quickly aware that many of my potential interviewees experienced research fatigue, because they had already granted interviews to too many researchers, journalists, and development consultants (Omata 2019). This was particularly true for West and Central African migrants and civil society leaders who were navigating the aid industry as beneficiaries, or as unpaid or underpaid workers (see Tyszler 2019). To mitigate existing power imbalances, I questioned the necessity of each interview, made all possible attempts to minimise the discomfort in terms of time commitment and transportation costs, and tried to 'give back' whenever I could.

I embarked on the thesis that this book is based on without any direct experience of working in international development cooperation. This changed when, in 2018, I briefly became part of the migration industry myself. Once the writing of the first draft of my thesis had been almost completed, I was hired for a short research consultancy by the IOM. The legal boundaries defining my consultancy prevent me from using any of the information I accessed during my short professional relation with the IOM for the purpose of my research. This experience, however, allowed me to read some of my research data in a much clearer light, and gave me deeper insights into the world of frontline borderwork.

As Gentile ironically puts it in his reflections on empirical research, "sometimes, the realities of fieldwork are at odds with the quiet setting described in textbooks – one in which interviewees are largely cooperative, authorities permissive and the data trustworthy" (Gentile 2013, 426). Whether male or female, Moroccan or foreigner, researchers do not go unnoticed in Morocco. In the borderlands especially, my movements appeared to raise attention. In Oujda, I received a series of calls from a man who declined to state his identity – he simply said "Moi, je suis quelqu'un" (I am someone) – but who knew where I had been the day before and the names of the people I had spoken to the previous afternoon. In Nador, I had the clear impression I was being followed by a man in his forties dressed in a brown leather jacket and wearing sunglasses, which, as a friend and colleague put it to me once during a conversation, seems to be the uniform of plainclothes Moroccan policemen. NGOs in Oujda and Nador were also less comfortable with meeting me than their counterparts in other parts of the country. My informants there sometimes prevented me from seeing them in their offices, preferring to keep the contact informal, while other times they asked me who they should say I was, in case the police asked. The 'spectre' of police surveillance, sometimes presumed, sometimes real, was something that lingered in the daily lives of most people surrounding me. During my entire fieldwork, interviewees repeatedly asked me whether I had been under surveillance. Some of them asked with curiosity, others to alert me to be careful, and others yet because they had experienced it themselves.

This book does not, of course, deal with all the aid-funded projects that have been implemented in Morocco in relation to 'sub-Saharan migration'. Due to my focus on the expansion of border security away from the state, I concentrated my attention on projects implemented by IOs and NGOs (either local or international). I thus exclude aid-funded initiatives directly implemented by more traditional security providers, such as the state and private companies, whose involvement in border control is more generously analysed in other works (Frowd 2018; Garelli and Tazzioli 2016; Rodier 2012). Although this book is obviously concerned with the spectacular flourishing of the migration business in countries at the receiving end of externalisation policies, my focus here is not so much on the financial productivity that the fight against irregular migration triggers, but rather on the elusive forms of border power that it generates. I direct the reader to Ruben Andersson's *Illegality Inc.* to find out about the absurdities and paradoxes that migration control generates (Andersson 2014). Finally, the research is focused on the aid actors regulating the presence of migrants in Morocco. As the reader will note, civil society actors lying outside the aid circuit and migrants themselves are not the specific focus of my analysis, but they come up here and there in the book as they overlap with, challenge, and question the working of the migration industry. I must specify, however, that the fact that migrants are mentioned only in their interactions and tensions with NGOs and IOs does not mean that I consider them to be powerless or dependent upon development and humanitarian organisations. Migration scholars have widely discussed the acts of contestation through which migrants cope with and organise against the forms of domination enacted by state and non-state actors mandated with migration containment (Moulin and Nyers 2007; Scheel and Ratfisch 2014). My interest here is circumscribed to the circumstances in which these two worlds – the world of the exiled and the world of aid – collide, and to which governing rationalities emerge from this collision.

Outline of the Book

This book explores how aid filters border control on the ground in Morocco. To do so, I follow aid policy as it expands beyond the traditional sites of state security, permeating mundane societal sectors that are not habitually the locus of migration containment. The empirical chapters will explore how aid contributes to the production of 'sub-Saharan migrants' as a population group of concern by following the workings of aid through six societal fields: public discourse, civil society relations, welfare, labour, voluntary return, and humanitarian assistance.

Chapter 1 provides the contextual background for the rest of the monograph. It retraces patterns of immigration into Morocco and discusses how processes of bordering securitised the presence and movement of people profiled as 'sub-Saharan migrants'. I reconstruct the tightening of borders in the Western Mediterranean, highlighting the efforts undertaken by European countries to prevent the irregular movement of people and the border externalisation process which accompanied such a project. I discuss the involvement of Moroccan authorities in the bordering and militarisation of the Western Mediterranean, outlining the main developments that occurred in the domestic migration policy strategy. The end of the chapter provides an overview of the actors involved in the aid industry.

Chapter 2 explores how aid constructs Morocco into an 'Immigration Nation', by fostering a hegemonic imaginary of immigration in the country as a predominantly 'black', 'African', and 'irregular' experience. This performance is subsumed by discourses and practices de-historicising immigration in Morocco and normalising the idea of 'sub-Saharan migrants' as the main group of foreigners living in the country. This escalates the political attention over Western and Central African migration to levels which are not supported by demographic data. I identify two critical junctures that allowed the migration industry to consolidate narratives of 'transit' and 'settlement' migration throughout the country, trivialising projects targeting 'sub-Saharan migrants' along the major stopovers of migrant routes in Morocco.

Chapter 3 examines how aid creates conflicts and entrenches existing racialised inequalities within the civil society sector. I show that funding injections shake Moroccan civil society by producing three kinds of organisational subjectivities. The first group are the newcomers, which decide to accept donors' funding, while enacting sense-making strategies to justify their work as not explicitly in support of border security policies. The second group are the radicals: organisations which consider aid money as an instrument of border externalisation, and therefore decide to reject it or distance themselves from it. The last group of civil society organisations are those remaining on the doorstep. Mainly migrant-led organisations, these actors aspire to be part of the aid industry but are unable to bid for aid-funded projects and are confined to play a subordinate role in the migration market. Funding injections therefore alter relations between civil society organisations by favouring phenomena of co-optation, conflict and subordination. This leads to the emergence of conflict among civil society actors, who do not manage to take a unified stance in favour or against the border regime.

Chapter 4 examines how the entanglement between care and control transforms aid into a tool that filters marginalisation without directly excluding migrants from basic service provision. By looking at projects providing social assistance to migrants living in the big Moroccan urban centres, I argue that aid rather mediates the marginalisation of migrants through their inclusion in a parallel network of care. Developing in the interstices of a tight border and of an indifferent Moroccan state, this care is volatile: it rests on bureaucratised logics of filtering that normalise the abandonment of migrants. This care is also unaccountable: the actors providing assistance enact mechanisms which allow them not to see themselves as responsible for migrants' grievances.

Chapter 5 shows that aid facilitates the creation of a political architecture of control that pushes refugee people into self-disciplining behaviours, in the hope to be seen by aid agencies as conforming to a certain style of refugeehood. Specifically, I look at projects favouring labour integration to show that migrant people can be attracted to or can decide to distance themselves from aid-funded projects for reasons that have nothing to do with the stated purpose of the initiative (in this case, favouring migrants' integration into the labour market). Rather, the structural constraints characterising the life of migrant people in Morocco (lack of legal mobility avenues, lack of access to public services, lack of access to decent work) pushes project beneficiaries to read aid-funded projects as disciplinary tools through which aid agencies can observe their behaviours.

Chapter 6 examines the Assistance to Voluntary Return and Reintegration (AVRR) programme run by the IOM. I argue that the AVRR elusively expand the deportation capacity of countries of 'transit'. I label the function played by aid as elusive because the AVRR is not coercively imposed by the IOM or European states on Moroccan authorities, countries of origin, or migrants. Moroccan authorities consider it a cheaper and more diplomatically acceptable alternative to deportations. Embassies of countries of origin see it as an economically advantageous way to outsource assistance to their citizens abroad in distress. Migrants themselves see it as a last resort opportunity – or so argue IOM officers.

Chapter 7 looks at humanitarian projects assisting migrants in the Moroccan borderlands. I argue that the fast violence pervading the border allows us to see the inclusionary-exclusionary stance of the aid apparatus in a clearer light. It shows that aid sustains the rise of a silent, threatened apparatus of emergency relief. Donor-funded projects providing humanitarian assistance to migrants enter a symbiotic relation with border violence. Although abuses against migrants perpetually trigger humanitarian intervention, NGOs and IOs engage in a form of "minimal biopolitics" (Redfield 2013), that mitigates migrants' death without fully investing in life.

Immigration Nation takes aid as a prism to conceptualise the sophistication of migration control. It shows that donor-funded projects do not participate in the construction of the border regime by physically immobilising migrants along migratory routes. Rather, it enables a form of slow containment, that is as pervasive as it is difficult to apprehend. Highlighting how aid facilitates the expansion of the border regime in Morocco provides useful analytical insights that illuminate the workings of the migration industry in other countries of 'transit' in the broader Middle East and in Africa. Although countries like Turkey and Libya have long been in the spotlight of European policymakers, the Arab uprisings in 2011 and the onset of the "migration crisis" in 2015 have expanded the spatiality of aid-funded interventions aimed at remotely securing the borders of the EU and of its member states. As projects aiming at providing social assistance, labour integration, and voluntary return to migrants and refugees proliferate in countries like Mauritania, Niger, Tunisia, Lebanon, and Jordan, *Immigration Nation* provides a lens to decipher migration control beyond the spectacle of border violence.

1 | Bordering the Western Mediterranean

I visited the Spanish enclave of Melilla for the first time in the summer 2019, while on a stopover before my last research stay in Morocco. There, I spent a few days conducting interviews, looking for books on the history of the city in the local library, and visiting the general archive. During my short stay, I met Rafael, a young Spanish photographer from the *peninsula* (mainland Spain) at the beginning of his career. When I asked Rafael why he had decided to take up a job in Melilla, he told me that being in the North African enclave would give him a chance to take pictures *de los migrantes que saltan la valla*, of the migrants that jump the triple fences dividing Spain from Morocco (see Figure 1). But that summer, Rafael complained, there had been no attempts of irregular border crossing. What Rafael did not seem to know, however, was that the reason why the number of migrants crossing the fence had decreased so dramatically that summer was that Morocco had been conducting an extremely harsh deterrence campaign on the other side of the border. Since August 2018, Moroccan police forces had been arresting and dispersing migrant people living in the North of Morocco, not only in forest camps, but also in Tangier and, at times, also in Casablanca and Rabat (Gazzotti and Hagan 2020). In a report released in the fall 2018, the Moroccan NGO Groupe Antiraciste d'Accompagnement et de Défense des Étrangers et migrants (GADEM, in the French acronym) estimated that at least 6,500 people had been victims of these arrest-and-disperse campaigns between July and September 2018 alone (GADEM 2018a). "When nothing happens here [in Melilla] it's because a lot of things are going on in Morocco" (Díaz 2018) Spanish activist José Palazón declared in an interview to the Spanish press in the summer 2018.

The escalation of arrest-and-disperse campaigns recorded in 2018 constituted the culmination of the long-term securitisation of the Western Mediterranean. Started in the 1970s, this process unfolded

31

Figure 1 The fence dividing Melilla (on the left) from Morocco (on the right), summer 2019. Photographed by the author.

in three stages: the securitisation of European borders; the externalisation of European migration control; and the emergence of autonomous migration control strategies in African countries. The different sections of this chapter will provide a historical overview of the bordering of the Western Mediterranean, and will begin to introduce the main actors inhabiting the migration industry.

The Rise of the Southern European Border

European countries started closing their borders in the aftermath of the 1973 oil shock, and more decisively after the signature of the Schengen Agreement in 1985 (De Haas 2007). The creation of an area of free circulation within signatory states displaced the border of 'Fortress Europe' southward (Geddes 2000, 2008), increasing pressure on Southern Mediterranean countries to monitor their frontiers and prevent the entry of undocumented migrants into the Schengen area (Boswell 2003). After Spain became an EU country, the Spanish–

Figure 2 Crossing the border between Ceuta (Spain) and Fnideq (Morocco), summer 2014. Photographed by the author.

Moroccan border became the *Frontera Sur*, the Southern border of the European Union (Ferrer-Gallardo 2008).

By the early 1990s, European countries had started tightening their migration policies, with the aim to ensure the dissuasion, interception, and removal of irregular border crossers (Boswell 2003). Both Spain and Italy reformed their immigration law between the mid-1980s and the early 1990s (Arab 2009). Legal amendments went hand in hand with infrastructural bordering. Since 1995, Spain has repeatedly reinforced the fences surrounding the Spanish enclaves of Ceuta and Melilla (Ferrer-Gallardo 2008), largely benefitting from the financial support of the EU (Zaragoza-Christiani 2016) (see Figure 2).

Spain and the EU have also tried to seal the Mediterranean and Atlantic maritime routes by equipping their sea borders with techno-logical systems of interception able to track the movements of boats. In 2002, Spanish authorities launched the Integrated System of External Vigilance (SIVE, in the Spanish acronym), which was first activated in the Gibraltar Strait and later off the shores of the Canary Islands to detect boats coming from Morocco, Mauritania, and Senegal (Vives 2017a, 2017b).

European leaders quickly realised that this unilateral strategy of border control would not produce the desired effects in terms of management of irregular crossings. For this reason, they soon started soliciting 'sending' and 'transit' countries to cooperate in migration control (Boswell 2003). This approach has been implemented both at the bilateral level, with individual European countries trying to negotiate migration-related agreements with 'sending' and 'transit' countries (see Paoletti 2011 for the Italian–Libyan case; El Qadim 2015; Zaragoza-Christiani 2016 for the Spanish–Moroccan case), and at the multilateral level. After the signature of the Tampere Agreement in 1999, the EU formally adopted the "external dimension" of its migration and asylum policy, giving way to the Commission to incorporate discussions over migration in the foreign policy of the EU (Lavenex and UçArer 2004).[1]

Morocco has always ranked highly in the external migration governance strategy of the EU. In 1998, the high-level working group on migration and asylum identified Morocco, Iraq, Albania, Somalia, Sri Lanka, and Afghanistan as countries with which it was necessary to develop action plans on the fight against irregular emigration and border control (Belguendouz 2005; El Qadim 2015). In the following years, the European Commission has rather opted for 'dialogues' gathering European and African countries to discuss issues related to migration. It is in this spirit that the Euro–African Ministerial Conference on Migration and Development was organised in 2006 in Rabat. This laid the basis for what would later become the Rabat process (Collyer 2009, 2016), a multilateral dialogue grouping European, North African, Central African, and Western African countries as well as IOs (ICMPD n.d.). As part of these border externalisation efforts, the EU, its member states, and Morocco have cooperated in the joint

---

[1] This approach was further sanctioned in the Hague Programme (Afailal 2016; Collyer 2012; Jiménez Álvarez 2011), which included a section on the "external dimension of migration and asylum" in the part addressing the specific orientations on "strengthening freedom' (Council of the European Union 2005). It is interesting to note that the document lists the provision in matter of migration control right after the first article insisting on the freedom of mobility within EU border for EU citizens, therefore directly opposing the freedom of circulation within EU territory with the need to tighten the external borders (Council of the European Union 2005).

implementation of migration control measures. Morocco has signed a number of bilateral agreements to facilitate the return of Moroccan irregular migrants from different European countries, including Italy, France, Germany, and Spain (Cassarino 2018). In practice, the implementation of these legal instruments has been patchy. As an example, in 1992, Spain and Morocco signed a readmission agreement which would facilitate the repatriation of Moroccan nationals and non-Moroccan migrants that had allegedly 'transited' through Morocco before reaching Spain (El Qadim 2015). Morocco, however, generally refused to honour the readmission of this second group of migrants, and their official return to Morocco has always been conducted as an exceptional measure (Zaragoza-Christiani 2016)[2] – as happened, for example, in August 2018, when Spain summarily deported 113 migrants from the Spanish enclave of Ceuta to Morocco (GADEM 2018b). Since 2003, the EU has tried to negotiate a readmission agreement with Morocco, so far unsuccessfully due to the resistance of Moroccan authorities (El Qadim 2015). The refusal of Morocco to sign the readmission agreement with the EU testifies to the country's capacity to prioritise its geopolitical priorities over European border externalisation pressure, and to formulate a selective involvement in migration control cooperation (Benjelloun 2017a; Natter 2014).

Countries on both banks of the Mediterranean have also cooperated on border surveillance and the interception of irregular border crossing attempts, either through data exchanges on migratory events or through direct collaboration in border patrol. In 2007, the European Border and Coast Guard Agency (FRONTEX) started operating off the Mediterranean coasts of Morocco (Vacchiano 2013). Morocco is part of the Africa-Frontex Intelligence Community (AFIC), a working group created in 2010 by FRONTEX to strengthen information exchange with African partners (FRONTEX 2017). Spanish and Moroccan authorities carry out joint patrols over maritime and land borders (Zaragoza-Christiani 2016), and some members of the Moroccan Royal Gendarmerie are trained in Spain (GADEM et al. 2015). Spanish and Moroccan police have also collaborated in the implementation of unlawful border control practices, such as the summary expulsions of "sub-Saharan" nationals from the Spanish enclaves

---

[2] El Qadim signals that this readmission agreement has been "partially applied," but just after 2004 (El Qadim 2015, 62).

of Ceuta and Melilla. Conducted since the early 2000s, summary push-backs breach international law, and have been condemned by the United Nations High Commissioner for Human Rights (Committee on the Rights of the Child 2018; UN Office of the High Commissioner for Human Rights 2015) and the European Court of Human Rights (European Court of Human Rights 2017). Despite strong opposition from human rights bodies, Spanish authorities have continued return-ing migrants illegally at the borders of Ceuta and Melila. In 2015, the Spanish immigration law was updated in an attempt to 'legalise' these violent border control practices in open contradiction with inter-national law (Caminando Fronteras 2017; Migreurop & GADEM 2015). Despite early declarations made by Pedro Sanchez vis-à-vis the need to 'humanise' border control when he became Spanish Prime Minister in 2018, recent developments suggest that Spanish authorities do not seem intentioned to repeal this amendment and to discontinue pushbacks (Sanchez 2018).

Migration Policymaking in Morocco

Morocco has not been a passive recipient of European border external-isation, but has rather developed its own art of migration governance. Until the late 1990s neither migration, nor the presence of 'sub-Saharan migrants' were matters of public concern in the country (Benjelloun 2017c; Natter 2014). In the early 2000s, this attitude changed. In 2002, the Moroccan Ministry of Interior formulated its own border surveil-lance strategy, aiming at "controlling borders, dismantling human trafficking networks and disrupting irregular departure attempts" (MCMREAM 2016, 78) (see Figure 3). In 2003, the Moroccan parlia-ment approved Law 02–03, which has become widely known for its repressive tone and for the clear stigmatisation of 'sub-Saharan' migra-tion. Replacing former colonial Immigration Acts, the new legislation criminalises irregular entry and exit from the country. It introduced fines and detention sentences for Moroccan and foreign undocumented migrants and for people enabling irregular emigration (Khrouz 2016b). This migration policy shift is part of a broader regional trend. In the span of a few years, Tunisia (2004), Algeria (2008), Libya (2010), and Mauritania (2010) modified their migration acts or introduced law criminalising undocumented migration and smuggling (Perrin 2016). This migration policy turn has led to the construction of a "securitarian

Figure 3 Member of the Moroccan Auxiliary Forces patrolling the coast beside the entry to the port of Tangier, summer 2018. Photographed by the author.

belt" surrounding Europe (Jiménez Álvarez 2011, 105). The introduction of Law 02–03 fulfils three main functions, as it seeks to control the mobility of Moroccan nationals, of Maghrebi nationals seeking to reach Spain through Moroccan shores and of migrants coming from West and Central Africa 'in transit' through Morocco (Jiménez Álvarez 2011). The media treatment that irregular migration received in Morocco (Natter 2014) and the legal distinction that Law 02–03 makes between transit and settlement (Perrin 2008) framed undocumented migration as a phenomenon concerning mainly migrants from West and Central Africa (Natter 2014).

Scholars have foregrounded different hypotheses as to why Morocco decided to adopt such a restrictive migration law in the early 2000s. Early analyses highlighted that European pressure over migration control was pushing Morocco to play "Europe's gendarme" (Belguendouz 2003, 2005). Later works, however, suggest reading Morocco's enlistment into Europe's "war against migrants" (Migreurop 2006) as an expression of Morocco's capacity to develop a "migration diplomacy,"

(Wihtol de Wenden 2010, 13), or a tactical capacity to use migration as a bargaining chip in their unequal diplomatic relations with European actors (El Qadim 2015; Zaragoza-Christiani 2016). Morocco has not always smoothly complied with European pressures on border control cooperation, showing a fierce capacity to transform migration into a "geographical rent" (Bensaâd 2009, 274). As Natter highlights, Morocco's initial repressive engagement in migration control cooperation still allowed the country to challenge the diplomatic isolation to which it had been confined in the 1980s and 1990s. The approval of Law 02–03 should therefore be read not only as a result of European pressure, but also of Morocco's ambition to become a precious partner for the EU (Natter 2014).

The securitisation of migration in North Africa has resulted into the emergence and normalisation of institutional and criminal abuses against migrants, especially at border crossings. In fact, the approval of Law 02–03 inaugurated a decade marked by a securitarian approach to migration governance. Identified as 'potential border crossers', West and Central African migrants started being tracked by the Moroccan police. Security forces widely employed coercive deterrence measures to discourage people from crossing the border with Spain and from settling in Morocco (Escoffier 2006). The 'Ceuta and Melilla events' have become the symbol of this dark escalation of border control. The night between 28 and 29 September 2005, around 500 people tried to cross the fence surrounding the Spanish enclave of Ceuta. Spanish and Moroccan border guards reacted by teargassing and shooting both in the air and on border crossers, as reported by witnesses. At least five migrant people died as a result. Between 5 and 6 October 2005, at least six migrants died in similar circumstances during another attempt to cross the fence in Melilla (Migreurop 2006). Hundreds of people were then raided and forcibly displaced south of Figuig, in the desert at the border between Morocco and Algeria, where they were subsequently found by a team of MSF. Left without water or food, many of the migrants were injured and many of them were women and children (Jiménez 2005; Peraldi 2011), all categories of people which are entitled to legal protection.

Moroccan civil society did not remain silent vis-à-vis the brutal treatment of migrants at the hands of both Spanish and Moroccan security forces. Some of the most important human rights groups advocating for the defence of migrants' rights emerged in the 2000s

(Natter 2014, 2018). Moroccan and migrant-led civil society organisations joined INGOs and transnational human rights movements, like the Migreurop network, to denounce the effects of border, and the human rights violations committed by Moroccan authorities (Alioua 2011a). The presence of a vibrant network of civil society actors has been essential to monitor and denounce the behaviour of Moroccan authorities, characterised by an exclusively security-oriented approach to migration governance (Natter 2018; Norman 2016), with peaks of violence in moments of heightened presence of migrants in the borderlands (CMSM and GADEM 2012; MSF 2013c).

A decade after the approval of Law 02–03, Moroccan migration policy underwent a further, seemingly decisive shift. After a year of heightened border violence and humanitarian critique, on 9 September 2013, the CNDH released a report entitled *Foreigners and Human Rights: For a Radically New Immigration and Asylum Policy*. The CNDH recognised that the implementation of border control by Moroccan police forces had resulted in the open violation of migrants' rights and in the infringement of national and international legislation.

[The CNDH] does not contest in principle the rights of Moroccan authorities to control the entry and stay of foreigners and their duty to fight against trafficking in human beings. However, the CNDH considers that public authorities cannot, in the accomplishment of such missions, avoid constitutional obligations in terms of [respect of] human rights and the right of aliens, the international engagements taken through the ratification of the ensemble of instruments on the protection of human rights.

(CNDH 2013, 3, translation by author)

The report listed a series of recommendations to Moroccan authorities. Policy advice included, among others, the respect of current legislation on migrants', refugees', and asylum seekers' rights, the formulation of a law on asylum, the review of the legislation regulating the fight against human trafficking, the launch of a regularisation campaign, the creation of an integration policy, and a broader consultation with civil society organisations (CNDH 2013). These events were followed by a rapid sequence of reforms. On 10 September 2013, King Mohammed VI announced his High Royal Orientations for the new migration policy during a working session with various members of the government (MAP 2013b).

At least initially, Moroccan authorities radically changed their attitude towards migrants in the country. The state shifted from firmly
denying that Morocco could become a country of settlement and asylum
for 'sub-Saharan' migrants, to a more tolerant approach towards
migrant presence in the country. This transformed integration, rather
than security, into a key strategy of migration governance (Alioua et al.
2017; Cherti and Collyer 2015). In December 2014, the government
elaborated the SNIA (MCMREAM 2016). The policy reform included
three main components. First, a process of legislative reform had been
put in place. The Moroccan authorities announced three new laws on
migration, asylum, and human trafficking. Second, Moroccan authorities formulated an integration policy. Since the launch of the new
migration policy, Morocco has run two regularisation campaigns in
2014 and 2017 respectively. Moroccan authorities had also taken
some timid steps to facilitate the social and economic integration of
immigrants in the country. In October 2013, the Ministry of Education
issued a circular allowing foreign students "from the Sahel and sub-
Saharan countries" (Ministère de l'Education Nationale, Royaume du
Maroc 2013). The authorities also discussed measures to facilitate
migrants' inclusion in the Moroccan labour market and in the main
instruments of social insurance for vulnerable populations (PNPM
2017b). Third, in the initial phase of the policy reform, there was
a decrease in violence against migrants in cities far away from the border.
Moroccan police forces discontinued mass arrests in most cities. This
halted the generalised harassment of black migrants in the country
(Cherti and Collyer 2015). Deportations of migrants to the desert at
the border with Algeria were also discontinued between 2013 and the
summer of 2018, when police repression against migrants reappeared
strongly in the Moroccan borderscape (GADEM 2018a).

Whereas the launch of Law 02–03 allowed Morocco to gain geostra-
tegic leverage, the new migration policy magnified a broader diplomatic
exercise, for it speaks to multiple possible allies and constituencies. On
the one hand, Morocco's more benevolent attitude vis-à-vis African
migrants symbolises its will to strengthen its diplomatic ties with the
rest of Africa (Cherti and Collyer 2015; Natter 2018).[3] On the other

---

[3] As the Moroccan sociologist Mehdi Alioua put it in an interview to the Moroccan
    press, the new migration policy aimed to build a link between migration
    governance and foreign diplomacy, because "if Morocco wants to be in Africa,
    Africa must be in Morocco" (Ait Akdim 2016, translation by author).

hand, the new migration policy was also a reaction of Moroccan authorities to international shaming (Norman 2016). In March 2013, MSF published a very critical and negative report on the situation of West and Central African migrants in Morocco. The INGO denounced the precarious living conditions suffered by migrants in the country, and violent abuses inflicted by Moroccan, Spanish, and Algerian police forces. That same year, MSF closed its mission in Morocco and left the country after sixteen years of operations. As the 2013 report had highlighted, the NGO had acknowledged that the cases treated by its staff were not the result of sporadic crises, but the victims of structural border violence (MSF 2013c) (Chapter 7). Chronologically, the release of the CNDH report overlapped with the evaluation of Morocco's compliance with the International Convention for the Protection of Migrant Workers and their Families (CMW) (Jiménez Álvarez et al. 2020). The UN Committee responsible for the Convention considered six reports: one written by Moroccan authorities, and five critical reports authored by civil society organisations. One of these reports, written by a coalition of human rights groups led by GADEM, minutely detailed how the Moroccan strategy of migration control infringed many of the points stipulated by the Convention, highlighting the systematic ill-treatment of black migrants by the security forces of the Alaouite state (GADEM 2013a, 2013b). These strongly publicised criticisms risked undermining the public image of a modern, stable country on its way to democracy that Morocco had projected internationally (Norman 2016).

The new migration policy allowed Morocco to address some of the reputational damage produced by international shaming. From the very beginning, Morocco has framed the policy reform as part of a wider strategy to uphold its international commitments on human rights respect. The authorities also actively involved civil society organisations into policy formulation and implementation. This move has been fruitful and allowed Morocco to gain further international consensus. European leaders, as well as the local IOM and UNHCR mission staff, tirelessly applaud Morocco for its political engagement in migrant integration. At the same time, civil society co-optation allowed the government to reduce the criticism and credibility of its most radical internal observers (Natter 2020; Norman 2016).

The implementation of the new migration policy, however, does not follow a linear pattern (Natter 2018; Norman 2018). Although the law on human trafficking was adopted by the parliament in 2016 (Legal

Flash 2016), the discussion and approval of the two laws on migration and asylum has been constantly delayed over the past six years and their approval does not seem to be close. None of the measures put in place to facilitate the access of migrants to public services and welfare provision is considered to be fully operational at the moment (GADEM 2018a; PNPM 2017b). Moroccan authorities continue to ill-treat migrants in the areas surrounding the Spanish enclaves of Ceuta and Melilla and, even if less systematically, also in Tangier (Human Rights Watch 2014). As I have mentioned in the opening paragraph, the summer of 2018 witnessed one of the harshest arrest campaigns against migrants. Following a (modest) increase in the number of border crossings in the Western Mediterranean route,[4] European countries demanded Moroccan authorities ramp up border control. Arrest-and-disperse campaigns continued throughout 2019 (Gazzotti and Hagan 2020). These forced displacements do not comply with the legal provisions guaranteed by Moroccan migration law, as they also indiscriminately targeted refugees, asylum seekers, people holding a regular residency permit, pregnant women, and children (GADEM 2018a, 2018b).[5] Various high-ranking Moroccan civil servants tried to justify this new wave of violence by resorting to the rhetoric of fighting "against irregular migration and trafficking networks" to justify arbitrary arrests and internal displacement. In August 2018, The Moroccan Minister of Communications Mustapha El Khalfi declared that "these are not forced returns, but operations aimed at transferring migrants to other cities, conducted in conformity with national laws aimed at fighting illegal migration" (Amnesty International 2018). Particularly, worrying is the attitude of the former President of the CNDH, Driss El Yazami, who had been one of the main figures behind the formulation of the

---

[4] According to data compiled by FRONTEX, 57,034 irregular border crossing attempts were detected on the Western Mediterranean route in 2018, up from 23,063 in the previous year. This increase, however, occurred in the context of an overall decrease of irregular migration in the EU, as 2018 marked the lowest number of irregular arrivals detected at EU external borders in five years (Statewatch 2019). GADEM argues that the increase of police harassment occurred after 602 migrants managed to enter the Spanish enclave of Ceuta on 26 July 2018 (GADEM 2018a).

[5] Emblematic was the fact that one of the earliest victims of the raids was a sixteen-year-old Malian adolescent, Moumoune Traoré, who died 'falling' from the bus onto which he had been forced by Moroccan authorities while he was being displaced from Tangier to the South of Morocco (Maleno Garzon 2018).

new migration policy. During a meeting with African diplomats on 30 August 2018, El Yazami stated that the "transfers" of migrants from the North to the South of Morocco were "in compliance with Moroccan law" (Benargane 2018, translation by author). These attempts to represent forced displacements and massive arrest campaigns as complying with Moroccan law expose the tenuous advancement in terms of respect for human rights achieved by the new migration policy, and its vulnerability to international pressures over border control (Jiménez Álvarez et al. 2020).

An Introduction to the Moroccan Migration Industry

Before delving into the slow workings of aid as a border containment instrument, it is necessary to pause and discuss the various actors that inhabit (and overcrowd) the Moroccan migration industry. The implementation of aid projects on the ground in Morocco, in fact, relies on the intervention of a complex set of actors, including donors, IOs, local and international NGOs, and Moroccan authorities themselves. Each actor intervenes at a different scale of the implementation process, and has therefore a different capacity to directly intervene in the life of migrants. The next paragraphs will provide an overview about who the main actors peopling the migration industry are, how they started operating in the migration sector in Morocco, and how their historical trajectory intersects with European and Moroccan pressures for border control.

Who are the Donors?

The **European Union** has undoubtedly been the most prominent donor in the field of migration in Morocco. In fact, the EU already had a long history of economic and technical cooperation with Morocco, starting in the 1970s as part of a broader Mediterranean politics aiming at establishing a dialogue between the North and the South of the Mediterranean in the post-colonial period. Over the decades, this political and economic cooperation has been formalised with the establishment of the Global Mediterranean Policy (1972), the Euro-Mediterranean Partnership (1995), the European Neighbourhood Policy (ENP) (2004) and the Union for the Mediterranean (2008) (Bialasiewicz et al. 2013; Collyer 2016). Since the Barcelona Declaration in 1995 – and more firmly after the signature of the ENP – security has become increasingly relevant in the articulation of the strategic priorities for the EU-Mediterranean partnership. Development cooperation has become perceived as a way to protect EU citizens from the 'risks' emerging in the South of the Mediterranean, including by political unrest, drug trafficking, terrorism and, of course, irregular migration (Afailal 2016; Jiménez Álvarez 2011). Development cooperation funding constitutes the backbone of the implementation of the EU "external dimension" approach to migration control. Soon after the 1999 Tampere Council, the negotiators of the EU's Directorate-General Justice and Home Affairs realised that implementing an external action directed at third countries in the field of migration would have proven very difficult without any specific thematic instrument available (Coleman 2009). Furthermore, the EU also realised that an approach solely focused on the security aspects of migration control would have been ineffective to secure the collaboration of third countries. In response to this "need for a balanced, global and coherent approach" (European Council 2005, 2), in 2005 the European Council adopted the Global Approach to Migration (GAM) – renamed Global Approach to Migration and Mobility (GAMM) in 2011 – (Collyer 2012; Hampshire 2016). The GAM set on paper the need to frame actions in the field of the prevention of irregular migration within broader cooperation initiatives, tackling also the development of 'sending' and 'transit' countries and legal migration of the latter's nationals within broader migration debates (Collett 2007). The 'balanced' aspect of the 'partnership' between Morocco, the EU, and its member states was publicly reasserted by the Mobility Partnership, which Morocco and the European Union signed in 2013 (den Hertog 2016; Limam and Del Sarto 2015). EU funding on migration and asylum is scattered into a panoply of financial instruments (García Andrade and Martín 2015; den Hertog 2016). In 2001, the EU created B7-667, the first dedicated funding line for migration control cooperation with third countries, which ran from 2001 to 2003 with a budget of €42.5 million. In 2004, the B7-667 was substituted by the AENEAS regulation (Coleman 2009), which ran until 2006 with an overall budget of €250 million. In 2007, the Commission created the Thematic Programme for Migration and Asylum (TPMA), which lasted until 2013 with an overall budget of €384 million (García Andrade and Martìn 2015). Since 2016, projects on migration governance in Morocco began to also be funded through the EU Emergency Trust Fund for Africa (EUTF), the financial instrument created by the EU to spur migration control cooperation with African countries in the wake of the so-called migration crisis (Gabrielli 2016). Although initially Morocco was not among the priority countries addressed by the EUTF (Gazzotti 2018), this has substantially changed after the 'migration crisis' declared by Spanish authorities in the summer 2018. Between December 2018 and December 2019, the European Commission adopted two different programmes worth almost €146 million in total to support Moroccan authorities in the "integrated management of borders and migration in Morocco" (European Commission n.d.d) and in the "support to the actions of Moroccan authorities against the networks facilitating irregular migratory flows" (European Commission n.d.b) (see Conclusion). Beside migration-specific programmes, Morocco has received migration-related funding also within the framework of other financial instruments, like the MEDA programme (El Qadim 2015), the European Instrument for Democracy and Human Rights (EIDHR) and the ENP (EU Delegation in Rabat 2016, 2017b). Migration and border control, in fact, figured prominently as issues of cooperation both in the 2005–10 EU/Morocco Action Plan[6] as well as in the most recent European Neighbourhood Instrument (ENI) Single Support Framework (SSF) 2014–17, through which Morocco received €807.5 million in development assistance (for all sectors of development cooperation) between 2014 and 2017.[7]

Together with the EU, **Switzerland** is one of the longest-standing donors to have operated in the field of migration in Morocco. After starting work in the country in 2004 in the field of disaster management, Switzerland decided to engage in the migration sector in the aftermath of the Ceuta and Melilla events in 2005.[8] Switzerland and Morocco, in fact, already had a bilateral dialogue over the question of return of irregular migrants. Not being an EU member, Switzerland was not bound by the strategic priorities of the EU in terms of migration control cooperation. This has allowed the donor more space of manoeuvre to operate in the field of migrant protection, including allowing funding to organisations advocating for the defence of migrant rights and humanitarian actors operating in the

---

[6] See https://library.euneighbours.eu/content/eu-morocco-enp-action-plan
[7] See https://ec.europa.eu/neighbourhood-enlargement/neighbourhood/countries/morocco_en
[8] Interview, Officer of the Swiss Development Cooperation, Rabat, July 2016.

borderlands.[9] In 2017, the donor announced its intention to stop funding migration-related projects (see Chapter 7).

Germany has just recently, albeit rapidly, gained a prominent role as a donor in the field of migration in Morocco. Migration is part of the "governance" operation sector of the Deutsche Gesellschaft für Internationale Zusammenarbeit (GIZ), which implements most German-funded projects in Morocco. Between the late 2000s and the early 2010s, the agency had gained some experience in the field of diaspora programmes, and began working more intensely in the field of migration in 2015.[10] Den Hertog identifies three main factors which contributed to the politicisation of migration in German–Moroccan development cooperation: the Arab uprisings, following which German authorities established a series of economic instruments targeting the Middle East and North Africa regions; the 2016 events in Köln, which likely spurred pressure on the German government to accelerate the deportation of Moroccan irregular migrants; and the joint chairmanship of the Global Forum on Migration and Development (GFMD). The donor has therefore pursued initiatives in the field of immigration management in Morocco, while positioning itself in the field of return of Moroccan irregular migrants (den Hertog 2017).

Although **Belgium** had already funded projects in the field of migration in the past, the donor has recently assumed a more central role in this sector. The most recent cooperation programme (2016–20) signed by Belgium and Morocco listed migration as a strategic field of operation.[11] The five-year-programme includes supporting the implementation of the Moroccan National Strategy on Migration and Asylum, namely on the labour integration of migrants. The migration axe of the five-year-strategy was officially launched in early 2018 (Enabel 2018). The Belgian Technical Cooperation (Enabel) is also managing a €4.6 million programme funded by the EUTF on migrants' access to justice in Morocco (European Commission 2018a).

As the oldest bilateral partner of Morocco in migration control cooperation, **Spain** had already began associating its development

---

[9] Interview, Officer of the Swiss Development Cooperation, WhatsApp, September 2017.
[10] Interview, two GIZ officers, Rabat, August 2016.
[11] Email, Coopération Technique Belge (CTB) officer, 6 October 2016; see also: www.enabel.be/content/enabel-morocco

and migration policies in the early 2000s, and more ostensibly after the critical juncture between the Ceuta and Melilla events in 2005 and the Cayuco 'crisis' in 2006 (Azkona and Sagastagoitita 2011). This approach was institutionalised by the 2009–12 Plan Director, which mentioned "Migration and Development" as one of the priority sectors of Spanish Development cooperation in Morocco (Ministerio de Asuntos Exteriores y de Cooperaciòn, Gobierno de Espana 2009). During that period, however, Spanish efforts to govern migration through development were mainly focused on controlling Moroccan mobility, especially in relation to the presence of Moroccan 'unaccompanied minors' in Spain (Suárez-Navaz and Jiménez Álvarez 2011). Since 2016, Spain has become more directly implicated in the funding and implementation of cooperation projects related to the governance of 'sub-Saharan' migration in Morocco. Between 2016 and 2017, the Agencia Española de Cooperación Internacional para el Desarrollo (AECID) and the Fundación Internacional y para Iberoamérica de Administración y Políticas Públicas (FIIAPP) were delegated the implementation of a €5.5 million project on the fight against xenophobia and discrimination funded by the EUTF. Furthermore, the AECID also provides technical support to the MDCMREAM in the field of migration management (European Commission n.d.a). The FIIAPP is now in charge of the implementation of the €44 million EU-funded project on the "integrated management of borders and migration in Morocco" mentioned above.

Many other state donors have funded projects in the field of governance of 'sub-Saharan' migration, but their implication has been more discontinuous. Amongst these are:

Monaco
USAID
Finland
The Netherlands
Denmark
Norway
Italy
Morocco
United Kingdom
Spanish Decentralised Cooperation
IOM Development Fund

UNAIDS
UNHCR
UNFPA

Who Implements the Projects?

UN Agencies

UN agencies perform a wide range of tasks in the field of migration in Morocco. These include providing capacity building to Moroccan authorities, and replacing the Moroccan state in the delivery of certain social and legal policies, such as determining who deserves international protection. The IOM and the UNHCR clearly represent the most prominent actors in this field. As I mentioned in the previous section, the IOM began operating in Morocco in 2001 (Caillault 2012), before signing the formal mission agreement with the Moroccan government in 2007. Although the agency has its formal headquarters in Rabat, it has other support structures around the country, namely offices in Tangier and Tétouan,[12] and a focal point in Oujda. As I will explain more in detail in Chapter 2, the UNHCR has been formally present in Morocco since the 1950s, but it was not fully operational until 2004, when the number of asylum requests received by the agency spiked (Valluy 2007c). This other UN agency has its headquarters in Rabat but has never managed to establish a formal presence in other areas of the country. Since the late 2000s, the agency has a formal collaboration with the Moroccan Organisation for Human Rights (OMDH, in the French acronym) in Oujda, which refers potential asylum seekers from the border to UNHCR staff in Rabat[13] (see Chapter 7).

Other UN agencies have a more sporadic presence in the field of migration, generally limited to the sector of intervention of each specific organisation. UNWomen implemented a project on the access to legal services for women and children victims of human trafficking (UNWomen n.d.). The UN Office for Drugs and Crime (UNODC) led an EU-funded programme on the fight against human trafficking and

---

[12] These two offices, to my understanding, exclusively implements the USAID-funded counter-terrorism project – see (Gazzotti 2018).

[13] Interview, UNHCR Officer, Rabat, August 2016; Interview, former officer of the UNHCR Morocco, Skype, October 2017.

smuggling, run in collaboration with the IOM and UNICEF (UNODC 2016).

International Centre for Migration Policy Development (ICMPD)
ICMPD is an IO headquartered in Vienna. It consists of eighteen Member States[14] and provides technical expertise to governments on 'migration management' (Hess 2010). In Morocco – as everywhere else, the ICMPD mainly implements projects related to multilateral dialogues on migration and advises Moroccan authorities in the elaboration of migration policy strategies. Most recently, the ICMPD has been tasked with the coordination of a project on border security (see Conclusion).

International NGOs
INGOs include Italian, Spanish, Belgian, and French organisations, some of which converted their activities to the field of migration to better adapt their organisational structure to the Moroccan political and funding landscape. Like IOs, INGOs operating in this sector occupy a grey area, as they often directly manage the capacity-building activities but outsource most direct interventions to local NGOs.

Faith-Based Organisations
Faith-based, especially Catholic, organisations have been at the forefront of the assistance to migrant people targeted by border control in Morocco, like in other countries in North Africa (Robin 2014; Tyszler 2020), the Middle East (Wagner 2018), and Latin America (Slack 2019). These organisations occupy a middle ground between local and INGOs: despite being distributed on the Moroccan territory and having direct contact with migrant people, they are also connected and/ or organised in broader networks of faith-based organisations.

Local NGOs
Local NGOs – including grassroot organisations and migrant NGOs (see Chapter 3) – are crucial actors in the migration industry, as they conduct most of the work on the ground involving direct interaction with migrants. Most local charities play a subordinated role within the

---

[14] See: www.icmpd.org/about-us/

funding landscape, as they are integrated within the development cooperation apparatus as project beneficiaries, in the framework of capacity-building programmes seeking to promote the capacity of local 'civil society' in the management of migration[15]; as project partners or subcontractors for bigger programmes managed by INGOs or IOs; or, more rarely, as direct beneficiaries of donors' funding.

Moroccan Authorities

Moroccan authorities play a double role in the implementation of development cooperation projects in the field of migration. On the one hand, Moroccan ministries – and, in particular, the former MCMREAM and now the Ministry of Foreign Affairs – constitute the main interlocutors for diplomats seeking to set the development cooperation agenda of the country they represent.[16] On the other hand, Moroccan national and local authorities are also involved in the phase of project implementation, either as direct aid-recipients or, more often, serving as project partners for programmes implemented by IOs and NGOs.

How Is Aid Allocated and Disbursed?

The way development and humanitarian aid is allocated depends on the donor and on the financial instrument taken into consideration. Donors can decide to allocate development aid directly to a certain organisation (Caillault 2012). Alternatively, donors can launch a call for tenders, to which Moroccan state authorities, NGOs, and IOs can apply presenting project proposals of various lengths – rarely for periods exceeding thirty-six months. This funding option is the one generally used by the EU both for migration-specific and for general programmes.

Both IOs and INGOs generally operate through local NGO partners when it comes to direct assistance to migrants, refugees, and asylum seekers. The UNHCR, for example, directly runs all the duties related to the determination of refugee status, but then outsources the provision of healthcare, professional training, social and legal assistance to Moroccan NGOs. Similarly, the IOM outsources all services related to

---

[15] This is the case in particular for NGOs formed by migrants from West and Central Africa – see Chapter 3.
[16] Interview, GIZ officer, August 2016; Interview, CTB Officer, December 2016.

direct assistance to local NGOs – except for the Voluntary Return programme, which is run directly by IOM staff in Rabat, although always in collaboration with other NGOs (see Chapter 6).

Over the years, development actors have created mechanisms to coordinate operations in the field of migration, both at the funding and at the implementation level. In 2007, Italy and Spain co-launched an inter-donor working group on migration in development (Gazzotti 2018), which, however, lasted just for a couple of years.[17] Recently, the MDMCREAM has also launched a donor coordination group, led by the Cooperation Direction of the Ministry (European Commission 2016).[18] The EU sometimes organises meetings with its aid-recipients to coordinate actions and avoid project duplication.[19] The UN system in Morocco has a working group on migration, which has been functioning since at least 2007.[20] In 2009, NGOs have created the PNPM, which gathers organisations working in the entire Moroccan territory. The organisations composing the PNPM have changed over the years, as some INGOs have left the country and others have deliberately decided to withdraw from the platform (Rachidi 2016).[21] Small coordination platforms – Protection Working Groups – have emerged in Oujda, Tangier, and Casablanca, although these differ from the PNPM because they also include the IOM and the UNHCR among their participants (UNHCR Morocco 2020). Despite the existence of formal mechanisms of cooperation, coordination between different donors, UN agencies, and also NGOs is hampered by issues of competition over funding, with consequences that I will highlight in more detail in the next chapters.

Conclusion

Since the late 1990s, Morocco has been on the receiving end of the border externalisation policies implemented by the EU and European countries. The involvement of Morocco into the sealing of the Western

---

[17] Interview, former officer of the Italian Development Cooperation, Skype, January 2017.
[18] Interview, officer of the MDMCREAM, Rabat, September 2017.
[19] Interview, NGO officer, Rabat, September 2017.
[20] The first strategic document of the UN Migration working group dates back to September 2007 (Groupe Thématique Migrations 2007).
[21] Interview, NGO officer, Rabat, September 2016.

Mediterranean should not be solely interpreted as a consequence of European pressure. Over the past twenty-five years, Morocco pursued its own migration diplomacy, which uses migration as a bargaining chip in its foreign policy, either to reassert its political power with European countries or to open diplomatic avenues in Africa. Aid has been a prominent instrument in the European border externalisation strategy. The implementation of aid-funded projects has always relied on a complicated network of donors, implementing agencies, and subcontracting organisations, with different proximities to the centres of decisional power in migration policy and to migrants themselves. The next chapters will explain how this aid-funded migration industry filters border containment power on the ground in Morocco.

2 | How Morocco Became an 'Immigration Nation'

In a recent document related to the EU Trust Fund for Africa, the European Commission stated that "the distribution of the migrant population on Moroccan territory is in evolution. In 2013, the estimated migrant population in Morocco ranged between 20,000 and 40,000 people" (European Commission, n.d.c, 2, translation by author). This sentence, however, contained an evident lapse: "20,000 – 40,000 people" is the figure most currently cited in governmental and non-governmental reports estimating the number of *irregular* migrants present in Morocco (see, for example, Médecins du Monde and Caritas 2016) – often more explicitly qualified as 'irregular sub-Saharan' in both written texts and in oral common use (see, for example, Karibi 2015). In this document, however, the Commission used this figure to refer to the total number of *migrants* residing in the country. In other words, the report equated the condition of foreigners in Morocco with the condition of irregularity, and implicitly, blackness.

'Migrant' and 'migration' have become, by and large, racialised words in Morocco. Despite the diversity of immigrant communities that Morocco has historically hosted, a new narrative is gaining ground which recognises the country as an 'Immigration Nation' only in reference to the allegedly 'new' population of 'black', 'transit', 'irregular' migrants allegedly proceeding from West and Central Africa towards Europe. This description, however, is deceptive. Immigration in Morocco is neither novel, nor exclusively or predominantly involving black people from other parts of Africa. Morocco has hosted immigrant communities well before the signature of the Schengen Agreement, to such an extent that the official number of foreign residents captured by Moroccan records was seven times higher in 1952, at the time of the Protectorate, than in the 2014 census. European migrants have always formed an important foreign presence in Morocco, which outnumbers that of Africans in the official census. Although it is true that censuses do not capture irregular migration, this logic works both ways: if it is difficult to estimate how many irregular West and Central Africans are not counted by official records, the same thing can be said for irregular Europeans and North Americans.

This chapter examines the role that the migration industry plays in the political production of Morocco as an 'Immigration Nation'. I argue that aid agencies stage discourses and practices that normalise an understanding of immigration in Morocco as a predominantly 'black', 'transit', 'irregular' experience. This historically selective image of migration ignores the multifaceted dynamics of incoming mobility in Morocco, and it tallies with the concerns of European donors over a potential 'African invasion' (de Haas 2008). By creating, socialising, and reproducing such a biased representation of immigration in Morocco, aid agencies produce what Foucault calls a "regime of truth," a system of implicit rules and ideologies that produce certain statements and facts as *obviously* true or even common sense (Foucault 1980, 132).

Although thinking of Morocco as a recent country of immigration has become mainstream discourse, this image is not a foregone conclusion obtained through an objective reading of Moroccan migration history. A regime of truth does not simply exist. It needs to be produced, socialised, and learnt, so that it can become hegemonic over alternative forms of knowledge (Berger and Luckmann 1979). The capacity to influence and shape the constitution of a specific regime of truth is uneven, as is the distribution of power within society. Actors with the capacity to concentrate "physical force," "economic," "informational" and, more importantly, "symbolic" power have more leverage in the creation and reproduction of reality (Bourdieu 1994, 13; see also Cronin 1996). In countries on the receiving end of externalisation policies, development and humanitarian organisations have such capacity. They produce leaflets, presentations, and factsheets about immigration in Morocco, thus localising resources that transform migration into a visible theme of intervention. During an interview, Daniele, an Italian development consultant, invited me to think differently about how donors managed to push their political agenda in an aid-recipient context like Morocco. "The EU does not impose," he told me, "but the EU has more weight, and therefore its political vision matters more than the political vision of another country, but it is not a constant will to impose [its political vision], in my opinion."[1]

---

[1] Interview with Daniele, Italian development consultant, Rabat, November 2016.

The rest of the chapter falls into three sections. First, I retrace the history of immigration in Morocco, highlighting both its multidirectionality and its intimate connection with broader histories of empire. In so doing, I propose an alternative "regime of truth" against which to read the intervention of the migration industry. By casting attention on the multifaceted, longer histories of mobility in the country, I de-exceptionalise the significance of 'sub-Saharan transit migration' within the broader migratory landscape characterising Sahelian and Mediterranean Africa. The following two sections unravel the discourses and practices through which Morocco is produced as an 'Immigration Nation'. I contend that donors, NGOs, and IOs entrench ideas about binary categories of migrant 'transit' and 'settlement' onto the ground. They do it not only by promoting specific narratives about migration, but also by spatialising aid projects through migration routes and by adapting project activities to the boundaries of permissibility allowed by Moroccan authorities.

An Overview of Immigration in Morocco

Stating that Morocco is a recent country of immigration elides the role that the Alaouite Kingdom has historically played in the political economy of military, commercial, and touristic exchanges in the Maghreb, and in the Mediterranean more broadly. Foreigners from West and Central Africa were a steady presence in Morocco well before the twenty-first century. Especially after the Arab conquest, the Maghrib and Sahelian Africa were connected by caravan trade. Through the trans-Saharan route, goods, precious materials, and captives were transported from the Bilad al-Sudan to North Africa. As Morocco was well connected in the trans-Saharan slave trade, the presence of enslaved populations in the country was recorded from as early as the ninth century (Ennaji 1999). Although estimating how many black Africans arrived in Morocco as captives through the slave trade is challenging, Wright reports that in the eighteenth and nineteenth centuries the figure ranged between 2,500 and 4,000 slaves per year (Wright 2007). The institution of slavery was never officially abolished as such, its practice continued until the twentieth century, and its memory is still deeply inscribed in the minds and rituals of slave descendants (Becker 2002). However, a series of reforms introduced in the latest stage of the Sherifian Empire (Ennaji 1999) and then during the Protectorate practically led to its slow disappearance (El Hamel 2012). The trans-Saharan slave trade obviously did not exhaust the network of exchanges connecting West and Central Africa to Morocco. Morocco was a destination for religious pilgrims, especially from Senegal, heading to the mausoleum of Ahmed al-Tijani, founder of the Tijaniyya brotherhood in Fes (Berriane et al. 2013; Lanza 2014). From the start of the twentieth century until the late 1980s, Casablanca was a procurement hub for small Senegalese traders who bought merchandise which they would later resell back home (Pian 2005). Since the 1970s, the diplomatic cooperation of Morocco with West and Central African countries has transformed Moroccan universities into a pole of attraction for students and a centre of formation for future African bureaucrats (Berriane 2015; Infantino 2011).

Labelling Morocco as a country of immigration more subtly (and strikingly) elides the history of European migration to North Africa, and its intimate connection to the onset and expansion of French and Spanish colonialism. The presence of European migrants in the country was scarce until the end of the eighteenth century. However, the decision of Sultan Sidi Mohammed Ben Abdellah to open the empire to the world paved the way for the emergence of European communities, particularly in Tangier (López García 2008), reconverted in 1856 into Morocco's diplomatic capital (Therrien 2002). For most of the nineteenth century, North–South migration flows remained limited in scope and spontaneous in nature. At the turn of the century, however, the increasing political and economic influence exercised by European powers over Morocco increased the presence of European migrants and tourists in Moroccan urban centres (Pack 2019). Tangier is a chief example of this phenomenon: by far the most cosmopolitan Moroccan city at the time, in 1909, it counted 9,000 European residents over a total population of 45,000 people (López García 2008). Although Morocco was never a settler colony like neighbouring Algeria, the formal establishment of the Protectorate in 1912 accelerated the flow of people from Europe to French and Spanish-controlled areas, and to Tangier, placed under international rule in 1923: soldiers, colonial bureaucrats, and travel writers, but also people of modest means – shopkeepers, artisans, construction workers, day labourers, all leaving the metropole to find fortune in the colony (Pack 2019). As the number of European residents in Morocco doubled from 44,576 people in 1913 to 98,191 in 1920, the urban architecture of Moroccan cities started acquiring a distinct European trait (López García 2013). This was not only the result of the establishment of cafés, hotels, and entertainment venues founded or run by Europeans and with European-sounding names, like the Gran Teatro Cervantes in Tangier (López García 2014) or the Café de France in Marrakech (Peraldi 2018). In the areas under French rule in particular, the colonial administration promoted deliberate politics of infrastructural reform determined to separate the locals, residing in the *medina* (the old city), from French colonisers and Europeans more broadly, residing in the *ville nouvelle* (the newly built quarters) (Radoine 2012; Wagner and Minca 2014) (see Figure 4). But Morocco did not only host military and civilians making a living out of the colonial venture: during the years of the Spanish Civil War (1936–39), Tangier and the areas under French control became a safety hub for Spanish refugees, mainly republicans escaping conflict first and the dictatorship of Franco later (López García 2008). After the independence of Morocco in 1956, the presence of European residents substantially decreased, but never fully disappeared (Escher and Petermann 2013; Mouna 2016; Therrien and Pellegrini 2015).

Empire, and its legacy, did not only encourage the immigration of Europeans in Morocco, but distinctively shaped the magnitude and direction of Moroccan emigration. Although Moroccans have emigrated since pre-colonial times, the establishment of colonialism in North Africa significantly boosted international emigration from the country. Moroccan workers and soldiers were moved across the Spanish and French colonial empires, both directly – for example, through the recruitment of Riffian soldiers to fight in the Spanish Civil War in Franco's troops (Madariaga 2002) – and indirectly – as poor Moroccans moved to neighbouring Algeria to seek employment in French colonial farms (de Haas 2003, 2005; Pack 2019)[2]. Even after Moroccan independence, European neo-colonial influence continued bearing significant weight in steering the direction of emigration flows. In the early 1960s, Western European countries started actively recruiting North African and Middle Eastern

---

[2] This latter phenomenon is very well described by novelist Mohammed Choukri in one of the most well-known pieces of Moroccan contemporary writing, *For Bread Alone*. In this autobiographic piece, Choukri recalls the history of his family's migration first to Tangier, at the time of the Rif famine in the 1920s, then to Oran, in North-Western Algeria, to work in a farm owned by a French family (Choukri 1980).

Figure 4 Colonial architecture in Tangier, summer 2017. Photographed by the author.

workers to support the post-war reconstruction effort and the economic boom that had followed. The number of Moroccans emigrating to France, Belgium, and the Netherlands skyrocketed in the 1960s and 1970s, and continued increasing afterwards (de Haas 2005). Despite the tightening of European borders since the 1970s, Moroccans have continued migrating to Europe either through family reunification schemes or through irregular channels (Arab 2009; Chattou 1998).

Describing Morocco as a recent country of immigration for 'sub-Saharan migrants' seems to give disproportionate attention to one specific form of mobility characterising contemporary North Africa (Peraldi 2011). From the 1960s onwards, an intense migration corridor emerged between Sahelian Africa and Libya. The labour shortages created by the Libyan oil boom attracted workers from Arab countries, and to a lesser extent, from Sahelian Africa. These movements gave renewed vitality to trans-Saharan routes (Bredeloup and Pliez 2005; Pliez 2006). In the 1990s, the movement of people along these corridors increased. This evolution did not emerge from a social and political vacuum, nor was it driven solely by migrants' aspiration to reach the European 'El Dorado'. On the one hand, the disastrous effects of Structural Adjustment Plans rendered the already fragile social and economic conditions of many African countries even more precarious. Many people therefore decided to seek alternative livelihood strategies outside their own communities and countries (Bredeloup and Pliez 2005). On the other hand, the African diplomacy pursued by Ghaddafi in the 1990s transformed Libya into a pole of attraction for workers from Sahelian Africa. The increase of trans-Saharan mobility was simultaneous to the closure of European borders. European policymakers thus began to see North Africa as a place from where Moroccan, West, and Central African nationals would cross irregularly to reach European shores (de Haas 2008).

In public discourse, the presence of West and Central African migrant people in Morocco has always tended to be qualified as 'transit migration', as if to imply that migrants were temporarily present on the territory of the state while heading to Europe (Düvell 2006). After the announcement of the new migration policy in 2013, policymakers and civil society organisations have increasingly marked a discursive separation between 'transit migrants' and 'settled migrants', the latter expression being used to refer mainly to people who have been regularised and who have decided to integrate in Morocco (see, for example, Mourji et al. 2016). Both 'transit' and 'settlement', however, are fictitious terms because they convey the biased message that patterns of mobility can be mutually exclusive. As for 'transit migration', migrants do not necessarily plan rationally and a priori to move from A to B passing through C (Bachelet 2016; Düvell 2006).[3] Although less theorised, 'settlement' is also a category fraught with prejudice, as there is no clear, or a priori, distinction between migrants who want to stay and those who want to

---

[3] Collyer and Alioua suggest reframing the debate in terms of "fragmented" (Collyer 2007, 2010) and "staged" (Alioua 2011b) migration respectively to

leave. People granted refugee status might still hope to be relocated abroad (see Chapter 5). Others, despite living in areas close to the borders, might decide to remain on a longer-term basis in Morocco and regularise their position after being offered a new employment opportunity (see Abena Banyomo 2019).[4] Even people signing up for the IOM's voluntary return programme may envisage coming back to Morocco, and see the return as a transitory stage, as a way to move back home to fix family affairs or to accumulate resources (Bachelet 2016).

In any case, dynamics of transit and settlement of West and Central African migrants constitute but two of the forms of immigration that characterise contemporary Morocco. Although the number of Europeans residing in the country has considerably decreased since the Protectorate, European migrants still populate Moroccan cities (Boudarssa 2017; Lachaud 2014). The key role played by tourism in the country's economic development plan, and the boom of the low-cost flight industry in the past two decades, has determined an exponential growth in the number of European visitors to the country. In 2019, Morocco recorded the arrival of 7 million foreign tourists – of these, almost 2 million were French, 880,000 were Spanish, and a further 1.8 million came from the United Kingdom, Germany, Italy, Belgium, and the Netherlands (Ministère du Tourisme, de l'Artisanat, du Transport Aérien et de l'Economie Sociale, n. d.). Posters portraying colonial Rabat, Tangier, or Fes form part of the stock of memorabilia invariably present in shops catering to European tourists in Morocco's urban centres, durably written in a marketing strategy selling "colonial nostalgia" to the tourist masses (Minca and Borghi 2009).

But Europeans are not only tourists in Morocco: as much as they might perceive their presence as transient, thousands of migrants from the Global North move to Morocco for lengthier periods of time for a variety of reasons, including for family, a desire of "elsewhereness" (Therrien and Pellegrini 2015), a better lifestyle in a country where the cost of living is cheaper and the weather is sunnier, or for work. Europeans who have moved to Morocco for employment reasons include those who were offered a better job opportunity than in their home countries, and those whose company delocalised production to Morocco. It also includes

account more faithfully for journeys that are not always "planned in advance but one stage may arise from the failure of a previous stage, limiting future options and draining resources" (Collyer 2010, 275).

[4] Fieldnotes, November 2016 and September 2017.

people who moved in the wake of the 2008 financial crisis, and who engage in relatively precarious jobs for a living (Mouna 2016; Peraldi and Terrazzoni 2016). During my fieldwork, my own whiteness faded in the background of upper-class neighbourhoods of major Moroccan cities. But when I stepped into lower-income neighbourhoods, my presence went much less unnoticed. *"Le noir, c'est ton mari?"* (The black man, is he your husband?) asked the driver of a collective taxi that I had hopped into after meeting with a Cameroonian friend for a coffee in a migrant-populated neighbourhood of Rabat.[5] *"Sbaniula?"* (Are you Spanish?) an older Moroccan man asked me, while sitting in a café in a low-income neighbourhood of Tangier, nodding towards the community centre across the street. I knew why he thought I was Spanish. The community centre he was pointing to had been built with Spanish aid money two decades before and was peopled by Spanish aid workers for most of that time. My whiteness led people to think that I, too, might have been a European aid worker (see Gazzotti 2021).[6]

Although Europeans receive considerably less media and political attention than people racialised as 'sub-Saharans', they are not exempted from the irregular practices of mobility. It is well known, in fact, that many European citizens live and work in the country as tourists, taking advantage of a legislative gap in the Moroccan immigration act which allows them to enter and exit the country every ninety days to renew the stamp on their passport (Khrouz 2016a; Zeghbib and Therrien 2016). It is also documented that European and North American citizens play with the boundaries of migration law, overstaying the ninety days allowed by law or working as a tourist without encountering much trouble with Moroccan authorities (Gazzotti 2021).

Both South–North and North–South migration carry weight in the composition of the Moroccan immigration landscape (see Table 1). In 2014, foreign residents represented approximately 0.25 per cent of the total Moroccan population. Out of 84,001 foreign residents, 22,545 were from another African, non-Maghreb country, while 33,615 were Europeans (Haut Commissariat au Plan 2017c). These data should technically include undocumented foreigners, but are generally considered to either exclude or to severely underestimate them.[7] Estimates of

---

[5] Fieldnotes, June 2019.   [6] Fieldnotes, September 2017.
[7] The documents accompanying the 2014 Moroccan census highlight that the records capture the "legal population," defined as "the ensemble of people residing in the Kingdom whatever their national and situation of stay is: 'regular

Table 1 *Evolution of the number of foreign residents in Morocco 1994–2014*

Demographics	1994	2004	2014
Total population	26,073,717	29,891,708	33,848,242
Total foreigners	50,181	51,435	84,001
- *From Europe*	/	Ca 23,609 (45.9%)	33,615 (40%)
- *From Maghreb*	/	Ca 12,293 (23.9%)	11,142 (1.3%)
- *Other African countries*[9]	/	Ca 5,348 (10.4%)	
- *Sub-Saharan Africa*			22,545 (26.8%)
% foreigners over total population	0.19%	0.17%	0.25%

Source: Haut Commissariat au Plan (HCP).

undocumented migration vary, ranging between 10,000–30,000 (European Commission 2016) and 25,000–40,000 (Moroccan Ministry of Interior, in Médecins du Monde and Caritas 2016). Despite being commonly used by most aid agencies, it is not clear how these figures about irregular migration are produced, whether they incorporate the 23,000 foreigners who obtained residency permits during the 2014 regularisation campaign (MCMREAM, 2015 in Benjelloun 2017b),[8] and whether they also include European irregular migrants. In 2015, French

or irregular'" (Haut Commissariat au Plan 2015, translation by author). There is therefore room to think that at least part of the undocumented migrants residing in the Kingdom have been included in the census.

[8] According to data disseminated by the CNDH, 28,400 people applied for a residency permit during the 2017 regularisation campaign (Jeune Afrique 2018). During an interview, however, a human rights activist suggested that many of the people that applied for regularisation in 2017 had already benefitted from the 2014 regularisation campaign, but their residency permit had expired in the meantime (Interview with Selma, human right activist, Rabat, June 2019).

[9] The study published by the HCP about the 2004 census specifies that the share of migrants coming from "other African countries" indicates African nationals not originating from other Maghreb countries (Haut Commissariat au Plan 2009). The study focusing on the 2014 census refers to 'sub-Saharan Africa' to indicate the same category of foreigners (Haut Commissariat au Plan 2017b).

authorities counted almost 49,000 French people as stably residing in Morocco, and a further 20,000 living there for at least a part of the year. In 2013, almost 7,400 Spanish migrants were registered with their consular authorities in Morocco (Mouna, 2016; Therrien & Pellegrini, 2015). Given that the 2014 census counted 33,615 European residents, it is reasonable to suppose that at least 22,000 French and Spanish migrants were not captured in official Moroccan records (otherwise, French and Spanish migrants alone would account for 67 per cent of all foreign residents in Morocco).

One fact risks being overshadowed by this migration number game: that immigration has little demographic relevance in Morocco. According to Moroccan censuses, the number of foreign residents in Morocco decreased from 529,000 individuals in 1952 to 51,435 in 2004. The number rose once again up to 84,001 in 2014. Although the census does not account for all the foreigners living in the country, I agree with Natter that "even higher estimates of around 200,000 migrants do not challenge the overall conclusion that immigration remains a minor phenomenon in Morocco – especially when considering the size and continuous growth of Morocco's emigrant population, estimated at 4 million in 2012" (Natter 2018, 7) and – I would add – when considering that Morocco counts an overall population of over 33 million people.

Narrating the 'Immigration Nation'

The construction of a regime of truth which manufactures Morocco into an 'Immigration Nation' relies on discourses that, as natural as they might appear, are produced according to rules of formation that are politically and historically situated (Foucault 2002). In fact, most reports, websites, or leaflets produced by aid-funded organisations begin with statements along these lines: "2013 marked a turning point in the migration policy of Morocco – a country which over the last 20 years has increasingly become a transit and host country for immigrants and refugees" (GIZ n.d.). In a similar vein, the European Commission states that "Morocco is characterised by the fact that it is at the same time a country of emigration, transit and, more recently, of asylum and settlement for migrants" (European Commission 2016, 3, translation by author). The Swiss Cooperation defines the moment in time when this transformation occurred: "Morocco [...] has always been a transit country [for migrants heading] towards Europe. The closure of European borders transformed Morocco into a host country for an increasing number of irregular migrants, asylum-seekers, and refugees" (Confédération Suisse 2015, translation by author). The website of the Monaco Development Cooperation states "Due to its strategic position and following the deterioration of the political stability and socio-economic situation of many countries in sub-Saharan Africa and the Arab World, Morocco became a point of transit, even of settlement by default, for many asylum seekers and for economic migrants on their way to EU countries" (Principauté de Monaco 2017, translation by author). Again, the European Commission states:

The population of foreigners in Morocco is estimated around 86,000 people (according to the Haut Commissariat au Plan), including foreigners, expatriates residing in Morocco, and irregular migrants. For what concerns the irregular migrants, mostly sub-Saharan nationals, estimations varied (before the regularisation campaign) between 25,000 and 45,000 people [...]. Otherwise, the unstable situation in the Middle East and notably the war in Syria [...] has [sic] generated an increase of the flow of people coming from the region and potential candidates for refugee status in Morocco. (European Commission 2016, 3–4)

The production of these discourses are pervaded by "notions of development and evolution: they make it possible to group a succession of dispersed events, to link them to one and the same organizing principle, [...] to discover, already at work in each beginning, a principle of coherence and the outline of future unity" (Foucault 2002, 24). Donors, NGOs, and IOs share a very consistent and selectively historicised idea of Morocco's migration profile and transition. According to their accounts, immigrants appeared in Morocco between the late 1990s and the early 2000s, when the consequences of European border control policies transformed the Alaouite Kingdom into a spatial overflowing of the Old Continent. Implicitly, immigration in Morocco is therefore reduced to the presence of people moving from what policy-makers have resorted to call 'sub-Saharan' Africa towards Europe.

In *The Anti-Politics Machine*, James Ferguson remarks that development organisations often produce simplified portrayals of the realities that they intervene in. Like the descriptions of Morocco which I previously evoked, the ways in which aid agencies simplify the economic, social, and political context of a country tend to repeat a similar model, with "mistakes and errors [that] are always of a particular kind, and they almost invariably tend in predictable directions. The statistics are wrong, but always wrong in the same way; the conceptions are fanciful, but it is always the same fantasy" (Ferguson 1994, 55). What we could easily dismiss as poor knowledge production is, upon closer inspection, not coincidental, but rather politically productive. Ahistorical representations of reality allow aid agencies to avoid engaging in politically sensitive discussions about political responsibilities for processes of predatory accumulation, dispossession, and inequality (Ferguson 1994). As Timothy Mitchell writes in his book on techno-politics in Egypt, international development reports do not only tend to leave politics aside, but also tend to leave out the political role played by the very agencies that produced the report in the first place (Mitchell 2002). The production of a sanitised portrayal of economic development in aid-recipient countries is instrumental to carving a space for aid agencies' operations. Development expertise, which portrays itself as technical and non-political, steps in to fix problems that are technical and not political. For problems to be technical, politics needs to be left out of the representation (Ferguson 1994; Mitchell 2002).

The migration reports reproduced above, however, do not leave politics entirely out of the picture, but rather selectively bring it in. Stating that the presence of migrants in Morocco is a 'recent' or a 'new' phenomenon means reducing the experience of immigration in Morocco to the 'transit' and 'spatial entrapment' of those migrants who want to reach Europe crossing the Spanish–Moroccan border. This discourse is oblivious to the North–South migration that accompanied colonialism, as well as to the population of European immigrants that currently live in Morocco. In other words, the history of immigration in Morocco is modelled according to the history of migration securitisation in Europe: Morocco became a country of ('sub-Saharan') immigration when irregular migration became a problem in Europe (Peraldi 2011).

The representations of migration in Morocco conveyed by the migration industry are at odds with the existing statistics on the presence of foreigners in the country that I presented in Table 1. Interestingly, however, donors' reports do not ignore existing figures about immigration in Morocco. The data on migrant presence in Morocco are produced and used by European, EU, and Moroccan institutions precisely to contextualise and justify their actions in the field of migration control. In 2016, the European Commission quoted figures from the 2014 census and sources estimating that 25,000–40,000 irregular migrants live in the country as part of its Executive Decision to allocate a €35 million budget support to Morocco for the implementation of the new migration policy (European Commission 2016) (see Chapter 1). When continuously confronted with the numbers, it is not unusual for institutional actors to admit that the number of immigrants in Morocco is quite low. In a booklet distributed to the Conference for the Third Anniversary of the National Strategy of Immigration and Asylum, the Moroccan Ministry of Migration itself stated that "regular migratory flows increase [in Morocco] [...], even if the volumes remain weak" (MCMREAM 2016, 15). A former employee of the IOM Morocco stated that after the organisation started looking into the situation in the borderlands in 2012, they realised that the number of migrants in Northern Morocco was quite small.[10]

Asking why such an image of immigration in Morocco has been produced despite statistical evidence is misleading. Data, to put it simply, are not neutral. The interpretation of statistics by policymakers is situational and inherently political, as data are produced and manipulated within pre-established power structures (Leite and Mutlu 2017). Data are read in order to fit an established discursive practice around immigration in Morocco. This, of course, does not mean that I believe that there are statistical standards against which a certain country can be declared as an 'immigration' country or not. Rather, the use of the label of 'immigration country' in Morocco is linked to the presence of a population group considered 'threatening' to European borders. Discussing the quantitative mismatch between migrant presence and the political salience of migration in Morocco, Fabrice, an academic and senior development consultant whom I interviewed in July 2016, commented:

I mean in purely objective terms, when you look into Africa the migration potential is so huge that it is scary, I mean in the sense ... for everybody, whichever establishment you have, you see what is happening with 1 million Syrians arriving in Europe? I mean 1 million! Nigeria alone every year has a 5 million population increase, so it is not so difficult imagining 5 million arriving ... and the only way to avoid it is to have tight borders and

---

[10] Interview, former officer of the IOM Morocco, Skype, October 2017.

cooperating with neighbouring countries and then, because of this, does it make sense to mobilise so many resources for a few thousands who are there? *No, it is not for those few thousands, it is for the many millions that are behind [them].* This – and you can accept it or not – makes sense somehow.[11]

The representation of Morocco as an 'Immigration Nation' has not been produced by ignoring the numbers, but by interpreting the numbers in an extremely securitised way. Enduring stereotypes about an incipient "invasion" (de Haas 2008) seem to be a determinant in structuring the orientation, workings, and priority areas of the migration apparatus in Morocco. Concerns about the 'migration potential' of Africa merge with an equally enduring "myth of transit" (Cherti and Grant 2013), which considers African foreigners in Morocco as a potential group of clandestine migrants en route to Europe. During an interview, an officer of the EU delegation in Rabat stated bluntly that concerns over transit were at the basis of the EU–Morocco cooperation over the implementation of the new migration policy:

The fact that Morocco has launched the National Strategy on Immigration and Asylum means that [the country] is taking a big responsibility. They consider that the issue is of their concern, and this means sharing the vision of the EU, which says to origin and transit countries "this concerns us all". Morocco is one of the very few countries that takes this responsibility and this budget support is a political response which means *"we know that these migrants were heading to Europe and therefore we want to contribute"*.[12]

In this securitised puzzle of migration control, the need to transform 'sub-Saharan migrants' into a sector of intervention in their own right is not based on the number of migrants *actually* living in Morocco, but on the number of migrants who *could* arrive – and, implicitly, who could move to Europe. Racism and xenophobia permeate the way (white) decision makers interpret facts and evidence concerning black people and charge them with political meanings and feelings of 'threat'. This does not happen because evidence and facts are overlooked, but because they are interpreted "within a racially saturated field of visibility" (Butler 1993, 15). This transforms the relation between the

[11] Interview with Fabrice, development consultant, place withdrawn, July 2016, emphasis added.
[12] Interview, officer of the EU delegation in Morocco, October 2016, emphasis added.

privileged and those impacted by the system, those armed and those unarmed, the perpetrators and the victims. A court can feel entitled to judge a black man beaten by the police while seemingly unarmed and unreactive because he is visualised as a potential offender (Butler 1993). Spanish policemen can feel legitimised to shoot a group of black people swimming towards Spanish shores to avert the risk of migrant 'invasion' (Butler, in Artigas and Ortega 2016).[13] In the same way, aid agencies transform a security concern originating in Europe into a hegemonic representation of immigration in Morocco. This occurs through a racialised manipulation of facts and figures. In this way, policymakers attribute more political salience to estimations of 'sub-Saharan' presence in the country due to a presumed 'transit', or 'potential', 'future' magnitude. The 'threat' is therefore never real but is always considered as incipient. And it is the blackness of the 'potential migrants' that justifies and normalises the construction of a migration industry, based on concerns over migrants who are not there, but who might be.

Performing the 'Immigration Nation'

Manufacturing Morocco into an 'Immigration country' is not only a matter of discourse, but is also largely a matter of performance (Foucault 2002). Discourses about immigration in Morocco as a 'sub-Saharan' experience feed into a series of material practices which give this idea substance and form, stabilising it over a protracted period of time. The construction of the political through its performance is the product of the overlap between mundane and spectacular acts, "articulated through institutions, signifiers and services that materially constitute and discursively (re)produce political authority" (Martínez and Eng 2018, 237). The performances subsuming political infrastructure should not, however, be understood as pre-emptively arranged. Performativity is led by "improvisation," "a form of individual adjustment of pre-given scripts in order to suit the needs of a particular context" (Jeffrey 2013, 35). The securitisation of migration is

---

[13] This happened during what has become tragically known as 'the Tarajal case': on 6 February 2014, the Spanish Guardia Civil used teargas and shot rubber bullets to prevent a group of migrants from swimming towards the Spanish enclave of Ceuta. Fourteen migrant people died in these circumstances (Caminando Fronteras 2017; El País 2017; Lucas 2017).

a highly performative – and improvised – process. The following two sections will highlight how two events (the Ceuta and Melilla events in 2005 and the announcement of the new migration policy in 2013) durably structured the migration industry according to conceptions about immigration in Morocco as a 'transit', and then as a 'settlement' phenomenon.

The Ceuta and Melilla Events, and the Production of Transit

The Ceuta and Melilla events in 2005 constituted a key step in the construction of a public spectacle and awareness of 'sub-Saharan' migration in Morocco (Peraldi 2011). From knowledge available to specialised humanitarian organisations (MSF 2005; MSF España 2003) or to militant and advocacy groups (La Cimade and AFVIC 2005; Maleno Garzon 2020), the presence of West and Central African migrants in Morocco, and the institutional repression enacted against them, became information within the public domain. The public exposure of suffering and violence triggered not only the solidarity of activist groups, but also the response of aid agencies (Peraldi 2011; Valluy 2006, 2007a). The Ceuta and Melilla events thus transformed 'transit' into the formative principle organising the development and humanitarian apparatus in Morocco – both in terms of its targeted beneficiaries and of its areas of operation.

Donors, NGOs, and IOs explicitly identified 'transit' migrants as a group of beneficiaries in project titles, fact sheets, and official communiqués (Khrouz 2016a; Peraldi 2011). For example, the International Federation of the Red Cross and of the Red Crescent got funding from the EU to implement a project focusing on "Improving the protection and living conditions of international migrants (pushed back or *in transit*) and of those made vulnerable by migration in North Africa" (Europe Aid 2008, emphasis by author). Between 2011 and 2013, the EU funded another project called "Reinforcing the protection of the rights of migrants in a *transit* country, Morocco" and implemented by the INGO Terre des Hommes in partnership with the Moroccan NGOs GADEM, and Oum El Banine (Khrouz 2016a, emphasis by author). In the section on 'Context and Beneficiary Population', the 2006 Country Operations Plan of UNHCR Morocco specified that:

... due to its geographic location as well as vast borders, Morocco has become a point of *transit* for many asylum-seekers as well as for economic migrants heading for Europe, mainly from Sub-Saharan countries, of which many are affected by conflict situations.

(UNHCR 2005a, 2, emphasis added)

In this first phase, development and humanitarian organisations limited their programmes and projects to emergency operations. Donors, NGOs, and IOs focused on temporarily responding to migrants' most urgent needs, rather than facilitating their integration in the country. This approach, which implicitly treated the presence of immigrants as temporary rather than structural, was influenced to a large extent by the attitude of Moroccan authorities vis-à-vis migration. At the time, the state refused to portray itself as a destination country for migrants and refugees (Natter 2014). Any activity supporting a possible long-term settlement of migrants, refugees, and asylum seekers – be it access to schools, support to labour integration, or similar activities – was explicitly considered a taboo (see Chapters 4 and 5). The UNHCR mission in Rabat, for example, encountered multifold problems with its activities: the government feared that anything durable "may make the country a magnet for sub-Saharans in search of a better life" (American Consulate of Casablanca 2006). The Moroccan authorities resisted granting official recognition to the UNHCR mission in Rabat, and did not seem keen on allowing refugees recognised by the UNHCR to stay in the country (American Embassy of Rabat, 2006a, 2006b).[14] In conversation with US diplomats, the UNHCR admitted fearing that even issuing plastic cards to refugees and asylum seekers would be perceived negatively by the government "as an indicator of a lengthy stay for the refugees and a permanent presence for UNHCR" (American Consulate of Casablanca 2006).

Similarly, an officer of the Swiss Development Cooperation argued that between 2007 and 2013 "the engagement [of Switzerland in the field of migration in Morocco] was purely humanitarian [...]. Our logic was a logic of substitution because there was no public migration policy, and it was some NGOs that assisted migrants ...."[15] The officer of a drop-in

---

[14] This pushed the UNHCR to speed up the creation of a resettlement programme (American Embassy of Rabat 2006a, 2006b).

[15] Interview, two officers of the Swiss Development Cooperation, Rabat, July 2016.

centre for migrants operating in one of the main Moroccan cities recalled how this situation affected the services that the charity was able to offer:

Interviewee: The access to rights was extremely limited, the children could not go to school, access to healthcare services was extremely limited, there was a whole parallel system, and everything relied on NGOs, mostly on people's self-improvisation . . .

Lorena: So, you offered much more emergency assistance . . .

Interviewee: Yes, for example, there is something that is very telling, another NGO and we offered classes for children. Children could not go to school, but we started from the principle that we could not leave the kids at home and bah, *tant pis pour eux* [too bad for them], they must stay at home and in the street. There were spaces so that the children did not have to spend the day at home and could follow something that looked like a school curriculum.[16]

From a spatial point of view, the presence of development and humanitarian actors gradually came to include all the crucial migration points in the country. Between 2002 and 2008, assistance programmes were launched in Oujda, the gate to Morocco for migrants entering irregularly from Algeria and the first city that migrants could reach after having been deported by the Moroccan police in the desert; Rabat and, to a lesser extent, Casablanca, the two main economic centres in the country which host the majority of West and Central African migrants living in Morocco (Alioua 2011a); Tangier and Nador, the two main points of departure for migrants heading to Europe by sea through the Mediterranean or by land through the two Spanish enclaves of Ceuta and Melilla.

By the early 2010s, "the political fiction of the 'sub-Saharans in transit'" (Peraldi 2011, 11) was then solidly set: it included a set of targeted beneficiaries (the so-called 'transit' migrants), activities aimed at relieving their alleged temporary presence in the country (humanitarian assistance), and places of operation at the main migration stopovers in Morocco.

The New Migration Policy and the Production of Settlement

The announcement of the new migration policy marked a break in the way migration was approached, imagined, and governed in Morocco.

---

[16] Interview, two NGO officers, August 2016.

This policy shift, and especially the two regularisation campaigns, allowed for the conceptualisation of 'sub-Saharan migrants' as no longer a transitory presence, but rather as a settled population. The fiction of transit gave way to the fiction of settlement in Morocco, casting attention on the figure of the 'regularised migrant'.

The policy shift from 'transit' to 'settlement' has put the migration industry on a completely new track and revolutionised the limits of permissibility of the development and humanitarian apparatus. Before 2013, donors, NGOs, and IOs had to limit their mandates to emergency assistance. After 2013, donors, NGOs, and IOs were allowed to expand their operations to promote initiatives facilitating the integration of migrants in Morocco. This meant focusing on the promotion of access to public services (see Chapter 4) and to the labour market (see Chapter 5), and on enhancing the capacity of civil society organisations and state authorities in supporting integration (Chapter 3). Programmes focusing on migrant integration have proliferated, and so have the Facebook pages, communication campaigns, and round-table discussions promoting the fight against xenophobia and sponsoring professional training courses for migrants and refugees. In 2015, the EU launched a programme called "Promoting the integration of migrants in Morocco." From promoting basic assistance to "stranded migrants,"[17] the EU started allocating funding for healthcare coverage for regularised migrants (€2 million), the promotion of access to education (€2 million), the facilitation of healthcare assistance for vulnerable migrant women (€1.4 million), and the integration of migrants into the labour market (€3 million)[18] (EU Delegation in Rabat 2016).[19]

The announcement of the new migration policy also produced a new spatialisation of 'presumed settlement' and 'presumed transit in Morocco'. As a document produced by the European Commission in the framework of the EU Trust Fund for Africa argues:

Schematically, transit migrants would be attracted by border zones (mainly the [region of the] Oriental and the North) while settled migrants and migrants "temporarily" settled will likely be located in the big cities

---

[17] Interview, officer of the EU Delegation, Rabat, October 2016.

[18] This part of the project was implemented in 2017 according to a project-based approach with partnering NGOs, UN agencies, and Moroccan authorities (EU Delegation in Rabat 2017a; European Commission 2017).

[19] The remaining €1.4 million were allocated for technical assistance to the MDMCREAM (EU Delegation in Rabat 2016).

(Rabat, Salé, Kenitra, and Casablanca etc.), while new areas of settlement are developing (Fes, Agadir etc.).

> (European Commission n.d.c, 2, translation by author)

This division is, again, fictitious, as it is constantly challenged both by migrants and by the state itself. Migrants living in marginal neighbourhoods of Rabat and Casablanca move to these cities to rest and earn money, and then move on to Tangier or Nador to attempt to cross the border (Bachelet 2016). Moroccan authorities, instead, displace migrants from the borderlands to cities in the Centre and the South, further increasing the circulation between the borderlands and the rest of Morocco.[20]

After the announcement of the new migration policy, the performance of Morocco as a 'transit country' officially gave way to the representation of Morocco as a 'settlement country'. This included a new set of targeted beneficiaries (the so-called regularised migrants), activities aimed at integrating them in the country, and imagined geographies of settlement coinciding with cities where the migrant presence was tolerated by the authorities. From discourse to practice, Morocco had officially become an 'Immigration Nation'.

Conclusion

In the past decade, Moroccan and foreign scholars published two edited volumes about the diversity of immigrant communities in Morocco – the first one edited by Michel Peraldi in 2011, the second one by Nadia Khrouz and Nazarena Lanza in 2016. The two volumes were written with the specific purpose of dismantling mainstream, albeit deceitful, conceptions about immigration in Morocco as a 'sub-Saharan' fact (Khrouz and Lanza 2016; Peraldi 2011). The introduction to the volume edited by Nadia Khrouz and Nazarena Lanza

---

[20] Although the spatialisation of 'transit' and 'settlement' conveyed by donors might not faithfully follow migrants' own life trajectories, they certainly reproduced the limits of spatial permissibility imposed by Moroccan authorities to migrant mobility. Rabat, Casablanca, and Kenitra are the areas where the authorities allow migrants to stay without being under the constant threat of arbitrary arrest, detention, and internal réfoulement. Nador and, at times, Tangier and Tétouan are areas where all migrants are presumed to be 'potential border crossers' by the authorities, and therefore denied freedom of movement (see Chapter 7).

situates the intervention within 'a particular context of reassessment of the modes of perception and management of foreigners in Morocco, accompanied by the announcement of a new migration policy in September 2013' (Khrouz and Lanza 2016, 1–2, translation by author). That scholars felt compelled to write not one, but two edited volumes to complexify the dominant discourse about Morocco as an 'Immigration Nation' is emblematic of the extent to which the figure of the 'wild man at Europe's gates' (Andersson 2010) has become hegemonic in Morocco.

The aid industry participates into the construction of Morocco into a 'new', 'black', 'irregular', 'transit' 'Immigration Nation' through discursive and non-discursive practices. On the one hand, development and humanitarian actors diffuse and normalise narratives reducing processes of immigration into Morocco to the rise of 'transit' migration in the early 2000s, and neglect to place this migration within a broader history and geography of intra- and inter-continental mobility. I have argued that these narratives are charged with racial categories and inscribed within racialised relations of power, transforming 'sub-Saharan migrants' in Morocco into a mobile 'threat' on their way to Europe. On the other hand, the politicisation and racialisation of migration discourse in Morocco was also fostered by practices that structure the workings of the migration industry around notions of 'transit' and 'settlement'. The Ceuta and Melilla events in 2005 and the announcement of the new Moroccan migration policy in 2013 were the pivotal events in this process: they first traced and then revolutionised the limits of permissibility and the spaces of action of the aid industry. By providing emergency assistance along the main migrant stopovers, development and humanitarian organisations entrenched the idea of Morocco as a transitory place of migration in aid practice. After 2013, emergency assistance gave way to activities aimed at favouring migrant integration. The next five chapters will examine how the aid industry has engaged into Morocco's integration project.

3 | *Fund, Divide, and Rule*

The upper floor of the City Hall of Tangier offered a clear view over the periphery of the city, whose skyline was neatly visible in that sunny but breezy morning. Christine, another European migration researcher, and I had taken a cab together to the building to attend a migration conference organised by an aid-funded organisation. The event gathered civil servants, aid workers, and civil society representatives from various European, African, and Middle Eastern countries. After completing the registration procedure, we headed towards the lunch buffet, where a few early participants were already helping themselves to food. We served ourselves and then backed off, standing with our plates by the door. Our conversation was soon interrupted by Thérèse, a Senegalese woman and an acquaintance of Christine. Thérèse seemed to know most people in the room personally, and she addressed all of them with a frank and direct tone. After chatting to Christine, Thérèse asked who I was, and I returned the question. "I have an NGO, it's called *MarocAfrica**. I also did a movie ..." she said. The movie in question was a documentary about migration in North Africa, that I happened to have recently watched. I congratulated her and assured that I had really liked it. Thérèse spotted two aid workers that she wanted to talk to, and left us. Christine then took me aside. "It's not true that she made that documentary," she whispered, containing her laughs, "she makes it up, she is a bit ..." and then shook her head, rolling her eyes as if to say that Thérèse tended to exaggerate her role in certain things.

Throughout my fieldwork, I kept on bumping into Thérèse at other events organised by aid-funded organisations. Her position as a civil society leader was helping her to secure invitations to various meetings, workshops, and conferences. At all these meetings, she networked and distributed her contact details, seemingly looking for organisations to partner with and obtain funding from. Although Thérèse seemed to be a stable presence in the migration industry, *MarocAfrica** never seemed to come up in my list of organisations receiving funding from European donors for migration-related projects. I ended up casually talking about Therèse with Sherylin, a European aid worker. Sherylin had recently started managing a project which had to rely on other local organisations for the delivery of assistance to migrant people. The search for local partners, however, had been more difficult than she expected. After Sherylin mentioned the organisations that she was considering partnering with, I told her I felt that – in certain Moroccan cities – funding was always being channelled through the same organisations, leaving many migrant NGOs on the side. "Lorena, I understand what you mean, but I need reliable partners," she blurted out. "I cannot partner with someone like *MarocAfrica**! And then, I don't even understand, everybody is introducing me to this woman as Therèse, but I am sure that the first time I met her she introduced herself as Aminata."

Therèse's story speaks to the unequal and racialised power dynamics structuring the Moroccan aid market. The explosion in funding attributed to migration-related projects in the past twenty years has generated economic opportunities for NGOs and IOs working with migrant, refugee, and asylum-seeking people in Morocco. As the president of *MarocAfrica**, Therèse appears to be more and more integrated into the aid industry – she is invited to conferences, she knows aid workers, and she tries to use her connections to obtain international funding. Therèse, however, navigates the aid industry in a clear position of disadvantage. Despite her networking efforts, *MarocAfrica** does not seem to receive funding. Aid workers like Sherilyn, who are reliant on local organisations to implement their projects, dismiss her as not conforming to their parameters of 'reliability' (in this case, having the impression that she introduces herself to people under two different names). Researchers like Christine, whose access to aid-funded conferences is facilitated by their privilege and institutional backing, are also quick to exoticise and mock Therèse as an 'exaggerated' character.

This chapter looks at the actors inhabiting the migration industry, focusing particularly on the effects that funding injections produce on the relations among civil society organisations. I argue that funding injections shake the Moroccan aid market. This happens because aid creates different and conflicting civil society subjectivities vis-à-vis border control policies: some organisations are keen to collaborate with donors, others are sceptical and try to take the distance from the

aid system, others again aspire to become aid recipients but are prevented from doing so. Funding injections create inequalities and conflict between civil society organisations, thus limiting their capacity to
take a unified stance in favour of or against the border regime.

The three sections composing the chapter show that funding injections for migration-specific purposes shape civil society relations by
triggering three different processes: co-optation, when organisations
decide to accept donors' funding (Lecadet 2016a); distancing, in case
they refuse or distance themselves from aid in the fear of being enlisted
into border control policies; and subordination, in the case of organisations, like MarocAfrica*, which aspire to be part of the aid market,
but navigate it in a position of disadvantage (Magallanes-Gonzalez
2020). These dynamics, in turn, create as many kinds of civil society
subjectivities: newcomers, non-specialised NGOs that decide to engage
in migration activities; radicals, who fear co-optation into border
control policies and that decide to refuse aid or to carefully incorporate
it within their own militant strategy; and those remaining on the
doorstep, organisations that would like to receive donors' funding
but are differentially included in the aid market along racial lines. Aid
thus creates conflict among civil society organisations, fracturing them
into "a collection of separated individualities" (Foucault 1979b, 201),
with differentiated stances vis-à-vis the border regime.

Co-optation – On the Newcomers

The most evident consequence of funding injections into the Moroccan
aid market has been the co-optation of civil society organisations into
donors' externalisation policies. Migration, in fact, has not always
been a sector of the aid industry in Morocco. In the early 2000s, MSF
was the only organisation with a structured programme dedicated to
migrants (Maleno Garzon 2004) (see Chapter 7). Aside from MSF,
vulnerable foreigners were given sporadic assistance by several small,
Moroccan and faith-based organisations, operating with very limited
capacity and mostly on a volunteer basis (see Del Grande 2007; Rachidi
2016). The arrival of European funding shook the Moroccan aid
market, attracting NGOs and IOs into migration work.[1] The

---

[1] Migration scholars argue that aid transforms NGOs and IOs either into direct
    local implementers of exclusionary migration policies produced in the Global

expansion of the migration industry to its current size was facilitated in particular by two critical funding junctures, which created space for Moroccan and international NGOs, as well as for IOs, to implement projects in the field of migration. The first relevant funding injection dates back to the early 2000s, shortly before the Ceuta and Melilla events. In 2002, the EC launched the first call for proposals for the preparatory action B7-667 (Centre for Strategy and Evaluation Services, n.d.), the first EU budget heading specifically devoted to migration, replaced in 2004 by the AENEAS programme (Europe Aid 2006). After the Ceuta and Melilla events in 2005, the number of aid-funded organisations assisting 'sub-Saharan migrants' increased (Guerini 2012; Natter 2014; Peraldi 2011). In the wake of the border "crisis," the Swiss Development Cooperation ramped up its interest in migration-related projects, the IOM expanded its operations and activity portfolio, the UNHCR rushed the appointment of a new mission chief (Collyer 2012; Valluy 2007c),[2] and NGOs that had never worked in migration before reconverted their activities to assist 'sub-Saharan migrants'.[3] The second main funding injection was the announcement of Morocco's migration policy. Following the King's announcement in 2013, Moroccan authorities actively exhorted European actors to play a role in the implementation of the new migration policy. On 11 September 2013, the departments of Interior, Foreign Affairs, and Justice issued a communiqué stating that:

... the partners of Morocco, in particular the EU, are equally concerned in the first instance by the new migration scenario. They have to demonstrate a more concrete engagement in their support to the implementation of this new Moroccan immigration policy. (MAP 2013a, 3)

Donors' response did not fall short of expectations. Existing donors confirmed their engagement in the field of migration in Morocco,

---

North (Bartels 2017; Geiger and Pécoud 2010), or into brokers that mediate the relation between Northern and Southern country authorities (Lavenex 2016; Wunderlich 2012). In this chapter, however, I use the term 'co-optation' in a looser way, not so much to point to the outsourcing of specific border functions to NGOs and IOs. Rather, I adopt it to gesture towards the formation of a civil society sector linked to European donors through funding allocation, and being allocated the task to loosely assist Morocco in managing migration in a context where border containment has been pushed South.

[2] Interview, former officer of the UNHCR Morocco, Skype, October 2017.
[3] Interview, officer of a Moroccan NGO, Rabat, July 2016.

transforming their action from 'assistance to stranded migrants' to 'favouring migrant integration'. As I said in Chapter 2, in 2015, the EU granted Morocco a 4-year budget of €10 million under the SPRING allocation to promote the integration of migrants in Morocco (EU Delegation in Rabat 2016). The following year, the EC approved and granted Morocco a further €35 million budget support[4] for the implementation of the new National Strategy on Immigration and Asylum, focusing on law implementation, capacity-building, voluntary return, and social assistance (European Commission 2016).[5] Since 2015, the German Development Agency (GIZ) and the Belgian Development Agency (Enabel) have accounted for €12.9 million (GIZ n.d.) and €4.6 million (Enabel n.d.) respectively for projects supporting the implementation of the new migration policy. As a respondent from the MDMCREAM commented, "Now a panoply of actors want to help Morocco implement the new migration policy."[6]

As had happened in 2005, this second funding juncture attracted more organisations to work in migration (see Rachidi 2016). *SudSud**, a European NGO specialising in rural development, started working on migration, closing its office in the rural centre of Morocco and opening a new one in Oujda, to better suit the geographical relocation of its activities.[7] *The Association pour la Culture et le Developpement Nador**, a Moroccan NGO that had long been involved in campaigns against Moroccan irregular emigration in the North of the country, started cooperating on projects on the fight against xenophobia and assistance to 'sub-Saharan migrants', recycling some of the material and infrastructure used for previous projects.[8] Fatoumata, a Cameroonian woman member of a migrant-led NGO active in the field of women's rights, told me during an interview in the summer of 2019 that she had recently met with the Moroccan branch of a large INGO to discuss migration issues in Morocco. "But they do not work on migration here – do they?" I asked. "No, they don't, *mais la*

---

[4] The program was divided into €28 million for budget support and €7 million for technical support (European Commission 2016).
[5] Chapter 4 will further highlight how the European Union and Switzerland adjusted their strategy to support Moroccan authorities more directly in the implementation of the new policy.
[6] Interview, officer of the MCMREAM, Rabat, September 2016.
[7] Interview, officer of an INGO, Rabat, September 2016; Interview, officer of an INGO, Oujda, November 2016.
[8] Interview, officer of a Moroccan NGO, Nador, November 2016.

migration, ça commence à leur plaire (migration, it is starting appealing to them)" she answered.[9]

Although the appearance of new organisations working in the field of migration is evident, newcomers would rarely justify their entry into the world of migration as a strategic reorientation of their activities as a result of funding opportunities. At the time of the interview, Claudia was tasked with project writing and development for *SudSud**. In her own account, the shift of the NGO towards working on migration was mainly due to her own interest on the topic:

The reason that you asked me at the beginning [why did you start working on migration] is because I like migration, in case you had not noticed [laugh]. For a long time, I also thought about doing a PhD on migration; I studied it and I invested a lot myself to transform it into a sector of intervention for us [as an NGO] as well. Everybody mocks me and says "ah, now everybody throws himself on migration because there is funding available," but in my case it was a long time that I was trying and now let's say that we managed.[10]

Rosa works for *Solidaria**, a European NGO that had historically focused on education and youth engagement in urban areas. In the early 2000s, the NGO started implementing projects focusing on Moroccan migrants, especially around the theme of diaspora communities. At the time of the interview (April 2016), the organisation had recently started a project on 'sub-Saharan migration'. Although this was the first project of the kind that her NGO had been implementing, Rosa did not describe it as a deviation from the work that her organisation had historically done:

We tend to [implement] continuous projects; even when donors change we try to follow a durable line [of action], not to implement spot projects. Our migration programme started in 2003, but it never ended. What happened in the meantime is that in Morocco the migratory pressure changed, so what is of public interest now is the phenomenon of the returning migrant rather than the migrant that leaves [...] we are working a lot – I am talking about the past two years – on a phenomenon that up to a few years ago seemed science-fiction [...] that is the integration of non-Moroccan migrants in Morocco, or the wave of sub-Saharan, Syrian, etc., that transit through Morocco and that in many cases want to stay here.[11]

---

[9] Interview with Fatoumata, officer of a migrant-led NGO, Rabat, June 2019.
[10] Interview with Claudia, officer of an INGO, Rabat, March 2016.
[11] Interview with Rosa, officer of an INGO, Rabat, April 2016.

For Rosa, starting to work on migration was simply a way for her organisation to keep up with the shifting dynamics of public interest, rather than to follow funders' priorities. As she argued, migration was a programme of action that the NGO had been developing for a decade. Background data induced me to take these statements with a pinch of salt, however: the date when Rosa's organisation first started working on migration (early 2000s) coincides with the approval of the first EU budget lines in the field of migration. However, in her narrative, shifting the focus of attention from one migrant population to the other was not seen as a contradiction in the organisation's line of action, but more as the natural evolution of their work.

For other organisations, the evolution of priority areas was intimately connected to the evolution of Moroccan public policies. Driss is a Moroccan man who works for a large Moroccan NGO, quite close to Moroccan authorities. He describes the choice of the organisation to start working on 'sub-Saharan migration' just after 2013 as a rhythm imposed by the transformation of the state's boundaries of permissibility:

We are auxiliaries to public powers [. . .]. Before, in Morocco, migration did not occupy a priority position on the political agenda, and there was no question of regularisation. We, as an organisation, cannot transgress our patron; our priorities are the priorities of state authorities . . . and on top of that, migration was a political topic, and we forbid ourselves to engage in politics. But when migration was included in the Moroccan political agenda, then we started being able to work on a few things . . . .[12]

In other cases, forming an NGO was justified by civil society representatives as a way to ensure a form of institutional protection for an activity that emerged out of solidarity. This was the case for *Maroc Accueil Intégration**, a Moroccan NGO operating in a small city in the Moroccan interior. The NGO was run by Malika, a Moroccan woman in her 40s with previous experience in civil society activism in the area. As she explained to me, a couple of years earlier she had started assisting migrants begging at the traffic lights of the town, where they had been dropped off by Moroccan authorities during the internal displacement campaigns that had pervaded the country since 2014. Conscious of the potential risks she could incur in assisting

---

[12] Interview with Driss, officer of a Moroccan NGO, Rabat, September 2016.

migrant people, Simo, one of Malika's acquaintances, advised her to form an NGO, which would provide her with a legal framework through which to carry out her activities. Malika followed his advice, got other friends onboard, and included Simo on the NGO commit-tee. *Maroc Accueil Intégration** was still running on donations, and on limited funding provided by local authorities, but was actively trying to bid for funding from larger donors to sustain the activities of the organisation.[13]

In her work on racism and inclusion policies in higher education, Sara Ahmed argues that frontline bureaucrats resort to different sense-making strategies to justify their engagement in the implementation of policies which are matters of contestation. One of these is "building a social justice framework for themselves" (Ahmed 2007, 241), where participating in the functioning of the policy is instrumental to achieve social progress in a broader scheme of social justice. *SudSud** started working on migration because Claudia thought it was an important topic to address. Rosa and Driss perceive working on migration as a necessary step to fulfil the duty of their respective organisations, namely, to accompany the state in the implementation of public pol-icies. Malika believes donors' financial assistance is a necessary avenue to pursue in order to keep on assisting migrant people in distress. This attitude is very different from a naïve "buying into" security policies: the normalisation of security is mediated through the appeal to a sentiment of care (Bastani and Gazzotti in press) (in this instance, for the theme of migration in the case of Claudia, for the advancement of public policies in Morocco in the case of Rosa and Driss, for the well-being of migrant people themselves in the case of Malika).

Funding injections shake the aid market by increasing the number of organisations involved in migration-related work, to the point of creating a migration sector within the aid market. Co-optation into aid-as-border control policy, however, does not happen purely as a consequence of a corporate-driven rationality adopted by civil society organisations. Civil society representatives normalise their involvement into the implementation of security policies by appeal-ing to a sentiment of care towards the object of policymaking.

---

[13] Interview with Simo and Malika, officers of a Moroccan NGO, place withdrawn, July 2019.

Distancing – On the Radicals

The availability of funding from European donors to work on migration-related projects is not unanimously welcomed by civil society organisations. Critical organisations are often wary of accepting donors' funding, as they fear that accepting aid might co-opt them into the European migration control project. In an institutional environment where funding for civil society organisations is scant, organisations face a difficult choice: accepting or refusing aid for migration-related projects?

During fieldwork, I found that distinct organisations adopted different strategies to deal with this conundrum. The first strategy consists in rejecting donors' funding. Selma works for a Moroccan organisation which is quite vocal about the human rights violations committed by both Moroccan and European authorities. She explained to me that the organisation just counts on volunteers. "Our referential is the international referential of human rights," she pointed out. Later in the conversation, talking about organisations working with funding from the state and from European donors, she sarcastically commented that "if you have a double referential [the international referential of human rights and donors' priorities], then it becomes complicated."[14] An NGO that has accepted donors' funding can also decide to change its mind halfway through, if the priorities of the organisation and those of the donors irreparably clash. Emblematic was the case, in 2006, of the dispute between the UNHCR, the French NGO La Cimade, and the Moroccan NGO AFVIC, the two latter both active in the field of migrant rights. In 2005, the two NGOs had agreed to implement a capacity-building project for civil society organisations operating in Morocco, funded at 75 per cent by the UNHCR (La Cimade and AFVIC 2006a, 2006b). The establishment of this collaboration had not been straightforward. La Cimade and AFVIC's desire to obtain funding from UNHCR, and their simultaneous fear that they might be co-opted into the European externalisation policy, created a conflict between them and other NGOs active in the field of migration in Morocco. Despite the conflict, La Cimade and AFVIC decided to accept the collaboration, and started training sessions for civil society organisations operating in the field (Valluy 2007b, 2007c). The project

[14] Interview with Selma, officer of a Moroccan human rights organisation, Rabat, June 2019.

included a training component, and cascading funding element, to allow local NGOs to create centres for the assistance of migrant people. With time, however, the two implementing organisations realised that the UNHCR seemed more eager to fund centres that would assist exclusively its population of concern, namely asylum seekers and refugees (La Cimade and AFVIC 2006b, 40). Given the pervasive violence against all migrant people in the country, La Cimade and AFVIC considered that this objective clashed with their own mandate, and therefore decided to cease its partnership with the UNHCR (La Cimade and AFVIC 2006b).

Alternatively, interviews revealed a second strategy of resistance to aid: "juggling," which means, accepting donors' funding, but at conditions that would ensure the strategic independence of the organisation. Karim is a Moroccan man who is a member of a local human rights organisation that operates in the field of migrants and refugees' rights. He explained to me that the organisation does not completely refuse European state funding, but carefully tries to strike a balance between funding needs, the organisation's agenda and independence:

We participated in several projects; one of these was funded by the EU. Basically what we did is that we transferred certain themes on which we were already working to the project. I have to say that the EU delegation respected our autonomy [. . .] at the end of the day, the European Union for us should not just be a donor, but a partner to work with. Then after some negotiations we started working with another donor; we transferred activities that we were already doing, because they work according to a different logic, they support us. They work by cycles of strategic identification, and then they were working already with a drop-in centre for migrants, so they knew that there was too much border violence against migrants. [. . .] we decided not to have a donor funding us for more than 50%.[15]

Rejecting or juggling with funding does not necessarily mean that organisations critical of the border regime work in complete disconnection with aid-funded NGOs and IOs.[16] Officers belonging to both worlds often share the same professional circles. The conference for the

[15] Interview with Karim, officer of a Moroccan NGO, Rabat, July 2016.
[16] European state donors are not the only sources of funding for organisations like Karim's. Funding bodies like the Open Society Foundation, the Fund for Global Human Rights, or the Rosa Luxembourg Foundations give critical civil society organisations an alternative, less conflicting source of income to fund their activities.

Third Anniversary of the SNIA, that I mentioned in the Introduction, was attended by donor representatives, officers of the IOM and the UNHCR, as well as by people qualifying themselves as activists. During an interview with Junior, an Ivorian man and member of a labour union engaged in the defence of foreign workers, and not receiving funding from donors, I noticed that the notebook that he held between his hands had an IOM logo on top. Other IOM brochures were spread in the office. This suggested that Junior had attended an event organised by the IOM, where the organisers had distributed promotional material to the participants.[17]

Organisations with a more radical position about migration control policies clearly see European aid as an instrument of border surveillance. Accepting aid therefore constitutes a political dilemma to which these actors can respond in two ways: rejecting donors' funding; or juggling, which means strategising aid in a way that does not clash with the values and politics of the organisation. Distancing from aid, however, does not mean that civil society organisations completely extricate themselves from the aid industry. The radicals, in fact, still interact with aid-funded organisations, either by participating in the same events or sharing the same social spaces.

Subordination – On Those on the Doorstep

Thérèse's organisation, whose story I started this chapter with, exemplifies a category of actors that is increasingly taking space within the aid industry: migrant-led civil society organisations. The emergence of a migrant-led civil society movement goes back to the years immediately following the Ceuta and Melilla events. The deterioration of migrants' treatment in the country led foreigners of different origins to organise and publicly denounce the abuses committed by the state (see Chapter 1). These organisations often lacked official recognition by Moroccan authorities (Bachelet 2018). However, migrant-led NGOs have managed to organise public demonstrations, publish press releases and join transnational networks of border activists, like the Migreurop network. Alioua defines the start of migrant militancy as a "shift to politics" for migrants in Morocco. Migrant grassroot organising, in fact, stopped being just a means to regulate and support

---

[17] Interview with Junior, officer of a trade union, Rabat, summer 2019.

migrant existence in a difficult context, and started becoming also a tool to claim rights from state and non-state actors involved in the militarisation of the border (Alioua 2009).

The political environment surrounding migrant activism significantly changed after 2013. In the conclusions to its report *Foreigners and Human Rights in Morocco*, the CNDH explicitly exhorted Moroccan authorities to involve civil society organisations in the elaboration and implementation of migration policy reforms. The report specifically stated that "the integration of organisations of migrants in this process is fundamental, as is the regularization [. . .] of the situation of certain organisations assisting migrants [. . .]" (CNDH 2013, 6, translation by author). The collaboration between migrant organisations and Moroccan authorities was sanctioned by the SNIA, which includes an action specifically targeting the "support to migrant networks in the elaboration of economic co-development projects in Morocco and in their origin countries" (MCMREAM 2016, 96). The MDMCREAM devised three strategies to operationalise the partnership between the state and civil society in the implementation of migration policies: the creation of a permanent system of concertation with civil society; the implication of civil society organisations in the regularisation campaign; and the allocation of funding for projects related to migrant integration.

These political gestures created an environment conducive to the formation of migrant-led civil society organisations, and their co-optation into the integration policy formulated by the state. Before the announcement of the new migration policy, there were "only about ten" migrant NGOs active in Morocco. In March 2016, the National Council for Human Rights estimated that the number had risen to "over twenty" organisations (MCMREAM and CNDH 2016, 134). By September 2016, thirty-two migrant-led civil society organisations had received official recognition by the Moroccan authorities (MCMREAM 2016, 96).

The migration industry quickly adapted to the new political environment. Migrant-led NGOs became a stable presence at events organised by aid-funded organisations. NGOs and IOs started delivering pedagogical workshops providing migrant NGO leaders with notions of project development, of the legal background regulating the freedom of association,[18] and of best practices in the field of migrant protection

---

[18] Fieldnotes, October–December 2016.

and vulnerability,[19] among others. In at least one case across my interviews, this top-down political momentum appeared to have been central to the creation of a migrant-led organisation. In June 2019, I interviewed Sheila, a European aid worker employed by an IO operating in Rabat. Towards the end of the interview, Sheila suggested I contacted Eric, a Liberian man that she described as "the president of our NGO." Then, she quickly corrected herself, "No I mean, of the NGO that we supported throughout their constitution."[20] I contacted Eric, who agreed to meet in a café in central Rabat. As Eric explained to me, the creation of the NGO came out of a donor-funded workshop animated by a delegation of an INGO. During the workshop, the facilitators asked participants about the problem of migrants and refugees in Morocco, inviting them to propose possible solutions. "Based on the findings, we formulated recommendations, and then we started thinking – rather than just being aid beneficiaries, why not being actors [of change] ourselves?" Eric then showed me pictures of activities that the NGO had organised or participated in, most of which had taken place either with the support of or in the framework of broader events that Sheila's IO had organised.[21] Given the strong involvement that Sheila's IO had played in the constitution of the Eric's organisation, it is not surprising that Sheila had inadvertently called Eric "the president of our NGO."

Even though the institutional environment after 2013 had encouraged the emergence of a vibrant migrant civil society sector, these NGOs always seem to remain on the doorstep of the migration industry (Magallanes-Gonzalez 2020). Migrant-led organisations, in fact, become part of the aid market, but in a subordinated position: they operate as subcontractors for bigger organisations, as beneficiaries of cascading funding, or simply as beneficiaries of training provided in projects implemented by INGOs or IOs, like the IOM. Chief among the factors causing this liminality is recognition by the Moroccan state. For certain NGOs, regularisation had been quite straightforward. Babacar, the president of *Drari dial Ifriquiya** [Kids of Africa, in Moroccan Arabic], a migrant-led organisation supporting West and Central African children and young people,

---

[19] Fieldnotes, September 2017.
[20] Interview with Sheila, officer of an IO, Rabat, June 2019.
[21] Interview with Eric, officer of a migrant-led NGO, Rabat, June 2019.

proudly stated that his organisation had been the first one to be regularised after the announcement of the new migration policy.[22] Other organisations, however, had encountered multiple obstacles while trying to obtain paperwork. During the training sessions of a capacity-building project implemented by *SudSud**, officers of participating migrant NGOs lamented that the law regulating the constitution of associations was unevenly applied over the national territory. Local authorities of different cities requested different documents to register the organisations, thus creating delays and challenges for associations wishing to formalise their activities. Being critical about the behaviour of Moroccan authorities vis-à-vis migrant rights in Morocco seemed to be an element that can further push migrant-led NGOs into a legal limbo. Stéphane, for example, is a Congolese man who has been on the board of a vocal migrant-led NGO for several years. At the time of the interview, the NGO had not been able to secure recognition by the state. "We have always been associated with NGOs that have bad relationships with the authorities, so it is not easy for us to be recognized [by the State]," he explained to me.[23] Lack of formal recognition significantly affects the capacity of migrant-led civil society organisations to operate autonomously. In virtue of its regular status, *Drari dial Ifriquiya** had managed to partner with several institutions and to receive funding from multiple donors. This was not the case for other organisations. "At the moment we do not have the definitive authorization," Eric explained to me during our interview. "We cannot apply to the calls for projects launched by the EU, Enabel, etc."[24] Stéphane confirmed that the lack of official and finalised paperwork prevented his organisation from receiving funding from certain donors:

Lorena: And is it an issue for you, the fact that you do not have the definitive authorisation?

Stéphane: Well yes, because if you do not have one you cannot open a bank account, and you have to rely on other NGOs to receive funding. The donors, they often do not accept this, because they want the financial autonomy . . . .[25]

[22] Interview with Babacar, officer of a migrant-led NGO, Rabat, June 2019.
[23] Interview with Stéphane, officer of a migrant-led NGO, Rabat, June 2019.
[24] Interview with Eric, president of a migrant-led organisation, Rabat, June 2019.
[25] Interview with Stéphane, officer of a migrant-led NGO, Rabat, June 2019.

Migrant-led civil society organisations do not passively experience their subordination in the migration industry. To the contrary, they enact strategies of resistance, by voicing their criticisms on social media (Tyszler 2019) or by addressing them directly to aid-funded organisations. In some instances, these criticisms can lead funding providers to find measures to patch the inequality structuring the aid market. The project managed by *SudSud**, for example, included a cascading funding component, accessible only to migrant-led organisations that had attended the training module on financial management. Mario, one of the officers working on the project, explained to me that *SudSud** had decided to include a cascading funding component after migrant-led NGOs had requested to participate more equally in funding allocation:

One of the problems that emerged in other projects, or when you tried to involve migrant-led organisations [in this project] is that they would say "you come and see us to get data [from the field], but then we do not directly participate in the management of funding" ... so we had the idea to train them to the point of launching a call for projects within the same project.[26]

The announcement of the new migration policy fostered a political environment formally favouring the formation of migrant-led civil society organisations. Although the institutional discourse praises the involvement of migrant NGOs in migration management, migrant NGOs remain on the doorstep of the aid market. The lack of formal recognition, and the subsequent difficulties in achieving financial autonomy, confine these civil society organisations to the role of subordinated actors.

Conflict

Aid shakes the Moroccan civil society sector, transforming it into a conflictual environment. Two series of cleavages emerge: a conflict between actors accepting aid and actors distancing themselves from donors' funding; and a conflict between donor-funded organisations and actors who aspire to be aid-recipient, but that are structurally left on the outskirts of the aid market. The increase of actors working in

[26] Interview with Mario, officer of an INGO, Rabat, April 2016.

migration sparked criticism among activists and organisations historically engaged in migrants' protection. The people I interviewed found
this development concerning in many ways. First, the rising number of
Moroccan and migrant civil society organisations conducting work on
migration was believed to be just nominal. The newly founded NGOs,
some of my interviewees thought, were not really operative. During an
interview, Said, a young Moroccan development consultant operating
in Tiznit, told me that he had heard that a local NGO working on fair
tourism had started conducting actions benefitting 'sub-Saharan immigrants'. "To be honest, I never saw them doing anything about fair
tourism," he confessed to me, shaking his head. "I know they have
contributed to a distribution organised in favour of sub-Saharan
migrants, but I do not think they do much concrete action. They
work on migration only on paper."[27] Pierre-Marie, instead, is
a Cameroonian man that works for a faith-based organisation providing assistance to migrants in a city in the Moroccan interior. While
talking, he insisted on tracing a difference between "organisations
working on migration" and "organisations working in the field,"
with real activities and real contact with beneficiaries:

Lorena: So you're the only one working with migrants here, right?
Pierre-Marie: No, there are more than 40 NGOs.
Lorena: 40 NGOs? But you mean in general, not working with
    migrants, right?
Pierre-Marie: No, I mean that work with migrants. Well, I mean, then
    they are virtual, because on the field, it is just us.[28]

In their accounts, Said and Pierre-Marie suggested that the apparent
presence of a vibrant civil society movement active in migrant assistance was deceitful: many organisations *claimed* that they worked on
migration, but few of them were actually engaging in the field.

A second point of concern raised by experienced aid workers and
human rights advocates related to the capacity of newcomers to navigate the migration world and deliver quality work. Sara, a European
human rights activist with a long experience in migration, told me that
her organisation had recently received an invitation to participate as
a beneficiary in a project on capacity-building for NGOs operating in

[27] Interview with Said, development consultant, Tiznit, July 2019.
[28] Interview with Pierre-Marie, officer of a faith-based charity, city in the
    Moroccan interior, July 2019.

the field of migration. The project was implemented by an INGO that was new to the migration world. "I don't know if they are your friends or not ..." Sara commented, giving me a strange look. "I wanted to reply that they are the ones that need capacity-building! They have never worked in migration before."[29] Sara clearly felt sceptical about the capacity of this newcomer NGO to navigate the field of migration, and even more so given that they seemed to be unable to differentiate between newly born civil society organisations (and that would more likely need capacity-building) and those, like Pauline's, that have been active in the field for years. The coexistence between experienced organisations and newcomers is therefore uneasy: a hierarchy of purity and professionalism has been established between the two, as first-comers do not recognise the newcomers as legitimate actors in the field of migration (Natter 2018, 10). The subtle hostility increases the distance between them, fostering a form of partisan politics ("I don't know if they are your friends or not ...").

A third concern that emerged in the interviews was the risk of co-optation of newcomers into the border control policy enacted by the EU and its member states. Julia, a French aid worker based in a big Moroccan city, considered that non-specialised organisations were particularly exposed to the risk of becoming "partisans of European priorities" (Soukouna 2011, 38, translation by author):

There are NGOs that are not at all specialised in this field that embark on huge programmes in regions that are a bit complicated ... in any case, we cannot read the Moroccan context without putting it in perspective with the bilateral relations with the EU ... really, there is a business of migration, there are actors that emerge and that have nothing to do with migration, it's super visible. This can be counter-productive, because if someone does not know, then the programme will be very general, it will be something very complacent that will not tackle the entirety of the situation ....[30]

According to Julia, the lack of professional capacity of newcomers is not only detrimental to their capacity to deliver quality work, but also to their ability to apprehend the political complexity of the field that they inhabit. Co-optation into border control, therefore, is not necessarily considered a matter of political orientation of an organisation,

[29] Interview with Sara, human rights activist, Tangier, December 2016.
[30] Interview with Julia and Nicole, NGO officers, August 2016.

but also as a direct consequence of the level of professionalism and knowledge of the field displayed by newcomers.

A second, important cleavage that emerged during interviews is that between migrant civil society organisations that struggle to access funding, and aid-funded NGOs and IOs. Despite the resistance strategies that they enacted, migrant leaders clearly felt being confined in a subordinate position within the migration industry. During the interview with aforementioned Fatoumata, she complained about the dearth of funding available, and about the scarce consideration given to migrant-led organisations by donors, INGOs, and UN agencies:

The organisations, they do not give you even a cent – the EU has money that they need to give away. The ministry of migration had launched a call for projects, but their eligibility criteria were impossible to comply with; you needed to have years of experience, a head office, [enrolment in] the National Fund for Social Security ... and then if you ask Moroccan NGOs, they want to be the ones leading the project. Even [international] NGOs, they always want to go towards the Moroccan NGOs. We do not see ourselves as winners in this framework.[31]

Actually, the subaltern position of migrant-led organisations in the distribution of aid money was reflected in my research work as well: migrant civil society leaders, in fact, did not feature prominently in my interviewee list until late in my work, because their organisations did not tend to appear on the lists of funded projects published by donors. In the attempt of unravelling the workings of the migration industry, my research risked ignoring those actors remaining on its doorstep.

That migrant-led organisations do not equally participate in the division of migration money did not mean that they were not considered as crucial in borderwork. At the beginning of our conversation, Fatoumata had highlighted how "being in the field" was one of her main comparative strengths. Later, however, she pointed out that other actors seemed to expect her to share her knowledge, in a very unequal exchange:

The Mutual Aid calls us to know the amount of [migrant] people in this and this situation ... and I give them a number, and the guy is seated in his office ... but I am not the National Institute of Statistics! We have to do the

---

[31] Interview with Fatoumata, officer of a migrant-led NGO, Rabat, June 2019.

fieldwork and then … even researchers come to ask us things! To be honest, just me, I must have supervised at least a hundred students.[32]

Within the aid market, the proximity of migrant-led organisations to members of migrant communities was recognised as a form of expertise, as an advantage that migrant-led organisations had in comparison to Moroccan or International NGOs. In her work on the localisation of aid work, Pascucci argues that locally-recruited aid workers are entrusted with "tasks that mobilize their 'native', subaltern knowledges and gendered emotional and affective capacities" (Pascucci 2018, 745), which are deemed by INGOs and IOs as essential for conducting "actual field operations and securing access to hard-to-reach areas" and populations (Pascucci 2018, 744). Aid workers, donors, Moroccan authorities, and even researchers clearly see the value of Fatoumata's 'local knowledge' about migrant communities, and seek to take advantage of it as a resource. Their understanding of her knowledge, however, is marred by prejudice about what Fatoumata 'should' know by virtue of her own migrant identity – yet, as she pointed out, she is not "the National Institute of Statistics," and she has to do fieldwork herself to find out. The knowledge exchange happens on unequal terms: Fatoumata is constantly solicited by a number of actors requiring her knowledge, without receiving much in return. The actors willing to access Fatoumata's knowledge are what Ruben Andersson calls "migrant eaters" (Andersson 2014, 33), people that make a profit out of migrant suffering and knowledge, and as Fatoumata points out, active fieldwork, in a system where migrants do not equally partake in the sharing of the resources generated by migration.

Eric also expressed the feeling of belonging to a group publicly portrayed as central in the implementation of the new Moroccan migration policy, but then exploited by larger organisations. He complained that European aid workers and high-profile representatives of IOs publicly showed an interest and inclusive attitude towards migrant-led organisations. Offstage, however, their attitude significantly changed:

Sometimes, we exchange cards, but then you send them an email and they never answer. Then, if you see them at a meeting they tell you that they

---

[32] Interview with Fatoumata, officer of a migrant-led NGO, Rabat, June 2019.

forgot, but I know very well that it is because they do not really consider you. Then, I mean ... I do not need anyone's card, if you want to discuss something, we discuss ... .[33]

As Eric's interview makes clear, the aid industry marginalises migrant-led civil society organisations in a deceitful way. On the one hand, it engages in an onstage spectacle of inclusion, as resource rich-er organisations utilise migrant-led NGOs to foster a narrative of inclusive policymaking ["sometimes, we exchange cards," "if you want to discuss something, we discuss ..."]. On the other hand, this narrative of cooperation is matched by an offstage politics of dismissal and exclusion, as communication with migrant-led civil society organisations is effectively halted ["you send them an email and they never answer"]. Migrant-led civil society organisations are thus subjected to multiple processes of value extraction, in a context that formally praises their 'inclusion' in a 'humane' process of migration policymaking (Magallanes-Gonzalez 2020).

Funding injections create different kind of civil society subjectivities vis-à-vis donors' funding. This, in turn, creates conflicts within the civil society sector. The political character of aid creates a cleavage between actors accepting aid and organisations with a longer, more radical record vis-à-vis the fight for migrants' rights. This establishes a hierarchy of legitimacy, and an attitude of mistrust of the latter towards the former. The structural marginalisation of migrant-led civil society organisations creates a further layer of conflict between them and actors that can easily access donors' funding. Migrant-led NGOs are deemed 'worthy' for migration-related projects by larger NGOs and donors in virtue of their own 'migrantness' – not as peers, but as less-funded or unfunded mediators between the aid world and migrant communities.

Conclusion

Funding injections shake the Moroccan aid market. Civil society organisations are not all equally receptive to donors' intervention, or integrated into the aid market. Three kinds of actors emerge: the newcomers, the radicals, and those that are on the doorstep. The newcomers are organisations that decide to accept donors' funding,

---

[33] Interview with Eric, president of a migrant-led organisation, Rabat, June 2019.

showing a corporate attitude vis-à-vis security policies. Co-optation into border control policies, however, is not perceived as such by interviewees, who normalise the acceptance of security-related money as part of a broader organisational strategy to achieve a greater good. The radicals are those organisations that consider aid money as an attempt by European donors to co-opt civil society actors into their externalisation strategy. Scepticism pushes these organisations to be careful about the relation they have to aid: some of them decide to simply distance themselves from it, while others try to juggle financial and political independence while accepting donors' money. Those who remain on the doorstep are migrant civil society organisations. They are discoursively portrayed as central to the new migration policy and solicited for "field information" by other aid-funded actors, but they significantly struggle to access funding.

By generating dynamics of co-optation, distancing, and subordination, aid entrenches inequalities and creates conflict within the civil society sector. The different stances that organisations assume or are forced to assume vis-à-vis migration money generates a situation where "everyone bickered with everyone" (Andersson 2014, 53). Radical actors criticise those who accept funding. Those who accept funding joke about the critical posture of radicals. Migrant-led civil society organisations criticise those who manage to obtain donors' funding but refuse to share equally, and so on and so forth. The end product of this is a civil society landscape that regularly comes together (at meetings, ceremonies, training workshops), but that is very fragmented within. Whether donors were conscious of this or not at the beginning, funding injections have managed to divide civil society around the issue of migration-related work in Morocco, preventing it from having a unified stance against – nor in favour of – the border regime (see Anderl et al. 2019).

4 | *Excluding through Care*

"Hi Lorena."I glanced distractedly at the WhatsApp notification on my phone, which I had left by the sink while washing the dishes. I was in a house in the Fes suburbia, where I had rented a room for the week to be able to do interviews with NGOs operating in the Fes–Meknes area. As my phone kept vibrating, I rinsed my hands, and I unblocked the screen with my little finger. The message was from Sandra, a friend of mine from the United States who was teaching English to West and Central African kids in Rabat. I dried my hands on my trousers and grabbed the phone to read more carefully. "A friend of mine is currently homeless and begging," the message continued. "He's a minor. Would you know of any organisations or any of your European friends in Rabat that would be able to help him?." The friend that Sandra was trying to support was Bénoit, a young Cameroonian guy that she had met through her work. Bénoit had been looking for work, as a cleaner, in restaurants, but without much luck. After enquiring a bit more about the case, I told Sandra that I did not know of any NGO specifically working with foreign minors in Rabat at that time, but that I would make some calls to enquire. I later recalled an organisation that ran emergency shelters for unaccompanied minors. I wrote to Sandra, advising her to direct Bénoit there. "The problem is … he is not actually a minor," she told me. "I am telling people he is because this might make them more eager to help him. He went to the drop-in center and told them his real age [20], so they did not help him." After making a quick recap, I realised that all the NGOs I could think of would have been more likely to help Bénoit if he was under eighteen. 'Unaccompanied minors', in fact, constituted one of the categories most likely to be classified as vulnerable by aid-funded organisations.

As the case of Bénoit shows, aid produces an elusive form of migrant marginalisation. Since the early 2000s, aid-funded NGOs and IOs have been at the forefront of care provision for migrants, refugees, and asylum seekers living in Morocco. This parallel apparatus of social assistance sits in the interstices of multiple processes of exclusion. The funding it relies on depends on the border externalisation interests of European donors. The people it assists are endangered by migration control policies, and they are often excluded from public service provision in Morocco. But despite their role as care providers, aid-funded organisations are also producers of marginalisation. NGOs and IOs, in fact, have the authority to ultimately decide who can and who cannot access care. They do so by establishing thresholds of eligibility. As an adult, Bénoit is not considered vulnerable enough to be eligible for support, but this does not make his position any less precarious: Bénoit remains homeless – too poor not to ask for support, but too bureaucratically old to be eligible for it.

This chapter explores the ambivalent nature of aid-funded assistance to migrant people in Morocco. I argue that the aid-funded network of migrant care plays a double function of relief and segregation, care and domination. Aid-funded NGOs and IOs, in fact, provide a form of fleeting relief to migrant communities in a context where state-funded support is lacking. However, aid supports a structure of care provision that is *rooted in* and *conducive to* migrant marginalisation. The very presence of migrant people in need of assistance, and the availability of funding for projects focusing on migrant relief, is tied to European donors' political interests in containing 'sub-Saharan' mobility in the Western Mediterranean. Furthermore, the capacity of aid-funded organisations to provide care is intimately linked to their obligation to turn down assistance requests from migrants, refugees, and asylum seekers not deemed 'eligible' for support. Care and abandonment are not mutually exclusive. Rather, they are co-constitutive of a system of donor-sponsored regulations of migrant lives operating in tandem with the spectacular workings of border violence.

This chapter retraces the production of migrant exclusion through mechanisms of aid-funded care. I first identify patterns of state disengagement and (discoursive) engagement in migrant integration, connecting them to the evolution of migration policy in Morocco. I then explore how the state formally and informally outsources the costs for service provision to migrant people onto civil society organisations. I examine donors' engagement in the funding of migrant assistance and how border politics affects their funding strategies. The next section investigates the bureaucratic strategies that NGOs and IOs adopt to filter the assistance requests received. The last section explores how aid workers make sense of migrants' criticism of the aid system. I argue that these actors process migrants' complaints by enacting sense-making strategies through which they distance themselves from their role in the production of migrant marginalisation.

State (Dis)Engagement from Migrant Care

Despite the rise of migration to the top of the political agenda in the early 2000s, the Moroccan state has fundamentally disengaged from the direct provision of basic services to migrants and refugees. Until 2013, state disengagement was part of a broader security-oriented attitude towards migration control, aimed at deterring migrants from both crossing into Europe and settling in Morocco. As a result, migrants had a hard time accessing state services. They were completely left to find solutions to their daily problems through their own *débrouillardise* (improvisation) (Alioua 2011a, 416), relying on migrant networks of mutual assistance and on the support of local and international NGOs (Bachelet 2016). The launch of the new migration policy in 2013 seemed to upset the established order. In a break with a past of marked and purposeful disinterest towards migrant integration, the state committed to a major engagement in this field. The SNIA, in fact, mentions "facilitating the integration of regular migrants" as its first objective. This includes easing access to education and culture, programmes for youth and leisure, healthcare, accommodation, social and humanitarian assistance, professional training courses, and employment (MCMREAM 2016).

The shift, however, has been more rhetorical than practical. Official discourses about migrant access to state-supported services are largely inconsistent with the implementation of the integration strategy. Healthcare provides a case in point. In principle, migrants have access to medical care in Morocco. In order to limit the spread of transmissible diseases, a circular distributed in 2003 by the Ministry of Health allowed medical structures to provide health services to irregular migrants (MSF 2013c). The Hospital Internal Regulation issued in 2011 reiterates that "foreigners, whatever their status, are admitted and treated in the same way as Moroccan citizens" (MCMREAM 2015, 22). However, access to healthcare is *financially* more problematic. Basic medical assistance is provided free of charge to anyone in Morocco in the *centres de santé* (healthcare centres). According to the MDMCMREAM, between September 2016 and June 2017, 13,485 migrants were treated in primary healthcare centres in the areas of Rabat-Salé-Kenitra, Tangier-Tétouan, and in the region of the Oriental (MDMCMREAM 2017).

Secondary and tertiary medical care, however, comes at a cost. Moroccan authorities have given contradictory signals concerning their intention to make migrants eligible for applying to the Regime of Medical Assistance (RAMED, in the French acronym), the system subsidising healthcare for low-income citizens. In October 2015, the Ministry of Economy and Finance, the Ministry of Interior, the Ministry of Foreign Affairs, and the Ministry of Migration signed a convention allowing regularised migrants to benefit from the RAMED (PNPM 2017b; Qacimi 2015). In March 2017, the Medical Agency for National Insurance (ANAM, in the French acronym) and the Ministry of Migration signed another convention to deliver RAMED cards to migrants (LesEco.ma 2017a). Despite these highly publicised and performative events, however, the two conventions are de facto inoperative. Some regularised migrants tried to apply to the RAMED, but their attempts proved unsuccessful because there are no procedures in place to operationalise the conventions (PNPM 2017b). Hesitation about the expansion of the RAMED to migrants is not surprising. In fact, the open attitude of the state vis-à-vis migration has not been met with a decisive increase of financial resources for this purpose (GADEM 2018a). Between 2013 and 2017, the budget of the MDMCREAM has increased from 383.4 million dirham (€35 million) to 587.7 million dirham (€53.7 million). However, out of a total budget of 530 million dirham (€48.5 million) for the year 2016, only 45 million dirham (€4.1 million) were flagged for the implementation of activities specifically related to the integration strategy (European Commission 2016).

In this situation of institutional stalemate, migrants remain de facto excluded from the provision of basic health services. Research conducted by the Université Internationale de Rabat uncovered that out of a sample of 1,453 'sub-Saharan migrants' surveyed in the cities of Rabat, Casablanca, Mohammedia, Salé, and Tangier, 420 people declared having fallen ill in the previous 4 weeks. As many as 147 respondents stated they did not seek medical assistance, and around 25 per cent of them stated a lack of financial means as their main reason not to. Of those who had sought medical assistance, almost half of them paid over 100 dirhams (€9.10) for the visit, and 8 per cent paid a bill ranging from 500 to over 1,000 dirhams (from €45.70 to over € 91.40). These costs are onerous for most of the migrants surveyed, many of whom earn considerably less than the average Moroccan monthly income (2,413 dirham, i.e. €220.60). As I will further detail in Chapter 5, close to 58 per cent of all respondents from the same study declared earning less than 2,500 dirhams (€228.50) a month, and almost half of them earned less than 1,250 dirhams (€114.20). Considering that 85 per cent of all respondents do not have any sort of medical coverage (Mourji et al. 2016), it is unsurprising that many migrants do not seek medical help in case of illness. If not on the basis of racial discrimination, vulnerable foreigners risk being excluded from healthcare services because of their precarious economic situation. Marina, a European NGO officer working on an EU-funded healthcare project, told me:

The access to the building is guaranteed, they will not kick you out ... but then you don't have the money to pay for treatments, so if you don't have an NGO behind you that can pay ... well, the doctor can be really nice, but he can't make the diagnosis because you don't have the money to pay the X-rays.[1]

Despite adopting a discursive attitude that appears to be extremely proactive in the inclusion of migrants into welfare provision, the state reinforces the financial exclusion of poor foreigners from social assistance. This lays the basis for the delegation of care responsibilities to non-state actors (Natter 2018; Norman 2019).

Outsourcing Care to Non-State Actors

In a context of state disengagement, NGOs, IOs, and the donors supporting them are therefore at the forefront of care provision. In practice, they substitute the existence of public healthcare coverage for

---

[1] Interview with Marina, officer of an INGO, Rabat, September 2016.

vulnerable foreigners. The number of migrants claiming NGO support to pay for healthcare fees can be considerable. In the study conducted by the International University of Rabat previously mentioned, Mourji et al. (2016) state that, of the seventy-nine migrants who declared having been hospitalised, 24 per cent of them managed to pay for their medical treatments thanks to the support of an association. In their 2017 report, the MDMCREAM stated that between January and September 2016, 2,350 migrants had received financial assistance for their medical bills from Caritas, a Catholic organisation at the time funded by Switzerland and Germany. Between April and December 2016, the same organisation subsidised the rent of 1,000 migrant people and hosted 130 vulnerable people in emergency accommodation (MDMCMREAM 2017, 58–65). In the period 2017–18, the UNHCR subsidised pharmaceuticals for 2,600 people, assisted 689 refugees needing a long-term or onerous medical treatment, and put in place a 24/7 emergency number for refugees needing immediate medical attention (MDMCMREAM 2018). In 2019, the UNHCR's annual budget for healthcare expenses of their population of concern was 541,119 USD.[2]

Throughout the 2000s, the state obstructed the action of organisations engaged in the assistance and the defence of migrants' rights, obliging them to operate with great discretion and, at times, denying them legal recognition (Natter 2018). In 2013, the attitude changed, with the state actively incorporating non-state actors into its own integration strategy.[3] Moroccan authorities, in fact, have adopted formal and informal methods to outsource the costs of welfare provision to NGOs and IOs (PNPM 2017a, 2017b). One of the most direct and comprehensive measures is the support of state-civil society partnerships in the implementation of the new migration policy. Since 2013, Moroccan authorities have engaged directly with NGOs working with migrants, inviting an even more active participation of civil society in the governance of migrants' welfare. The importance of involving NGOs in the elaboration and implementation of the new migration policy is constantly emphasised by politicians (LesEco.ma 2017b; MCMREAM and CNDH 2016), members of human rights

---

[2] Email communication with a UNHCR officer, June 2019.
[3] As the interview with Stéphane in Chapter 3 suggests, though, the State seems to still ostracise the legalisation of civil society organisations that are critical of the State (Interview with Stéphane, officer of a migrant-led NGO, Rabat, June 2019).

institutions, and promotional texts produced by the Ministry of Migration (MCMREAM 2015, 2016). Between 2013 and 2017, the Ministry of Migration launched multiple calls for projects addressed to civil society organisations. Project proposals could target different areas of migrant integration, such as access to employment, language teaching, and social assistance (MCMREAM 2015, 81). Between 2013 and 2015, the Ministry of Migration funded 130 projects with a budget of 31.5 million dirhams (€2.8 million) (MCMREAM and CNDH 2016).

The state also adopts informal tactics to outsource the cost of migrants' welfare onto non-state, aid-funded actors. State-run hospitals, in fact, either refer patients directly to NGOs or try to convince civil society organisations to negotiate 'conventions' to cover medical costs incurred by migrant people (PNPM 2017b, 12, translation by author). In a recent report, the PNPM complained that healthcare institutions seem to apprehend NGOs as substitute providers of healthcare insurance for foreigners (PNPM 2017b). During our interview, Marina explained that "it's civil society that now takes care of all fees [for migrant healthcare], due to the lack of the RAMED or whatever, it's civil society – or actually it's the donors – that takes care of this, it's super expensive."[4]

By outsourcing public services to non-state actors, Morocco follows a regional trend. In fact, most countries in the Middle East and North Africa started dismantling their welfare state during the neoliberal reordering in the 1970s and 1980s. The welfare state in Morocco has never been as robust as in other countries in the region (Catusse 2010). The presence of NGOs in social assistance has been a constant element in Moroccan pre- and post-independence history. In the 2000s, social issues rose to the top of the political agenda, and the state started re-engaging in social services (Bono 2008; Catusse 2010).[5] This, however, did not coincide with the expansion of traditional welfare programmes. The government and the Palace – the

---

[4] Interview with Marina, officer of an INGO, Rabat, September 2016.
[5] This shift in intervention is not only in line with the rise of a new global sensitivity to the issue of poverty and inequality. It is also motivated by the state's perceived need to reaffirm its primacy in an increasingly competitive domestic political scene, with Islamists openly engaging in actions of social assistance (Hibou and Tozy 2015).

Makhzen[6] – opted for addressing the rampant share of poverty and inequality affecting the country through neoliberal tools. The most emblematic of such instruments is certainly the National Initiative for Human Development (INDH, in the French acronym). Since the early 2000s, the INDH has channelled funding for social, economic, and cultural interventions through local NGOs (Bono 2008; Catusse 2005). Delegating social protection to non-state actors should not be understood as an obliged path imposed by a lack of state funding. A recent report from the Economic, Social, and Environmental Council, a Moroccan public consultative body, called for a "change of paradigm" in the Moroccan system of social protection. The report subtly reprimanded the state for spending less money on welfare than public finances would allow (Conseil Economique, Social et Environnemental 2018, 11, translation by author).[7]

Since migration escalated to the top of the public agenda in Morocco, the state has outsourced social assistance for migrants to aid-funded NGOs and IOs. This pattern has become particularly evident after 2013, when Moroccan authorities started directly and indirectly delegating the financial efforts to cover migrant care to non-state actors. Outsourcing seems part of Morocco's strategic choice to rationalise resources by purposefully delegating care for migrants to non-state actors (Norman 2019, 43). The rise of aid-funded NGOs and IOs as social assistance providers is therefore rooted in a logic of abandonment, whereby the state decides to deny

---

[6] By "Dar Makhzen" I refer to a restricted circle composed of the King and to his closest advisors (Claisse 2013, 285). Throughout the book, I draw a distinction between the government and the Palace, or Makhzen, because the King detains an undeniable amount of power in Moroccan polity. As Ferrié and Alioua have it: "The most important policies are, first of all, conceived within the entourage of the King and, then, entrusted to the ordinary actors of public action, ministers, members of parliament, civil servants" (Ferrié and Alioua 2017, 20–21).

[7] French scholar Béatrice Hibou understands the outsourcing of state functions not as symptomatic of a loss of state sovereignty, but rather as a (cheaper) mode of government in its own right (Hibou 1999, 2004; Hibou and Tozy 2015). Historically, governing through outsourcing has allowed Morocco not only to rationalise government costs, but also to incorporate more firmly non-state actors within state outreach, and to gain international legitimacy by securing the financial and political support of donors, ready to praise Morocco as a model of "democratic participation" for its support to civil society organisations (Bono 2007; Catusse and Vairel 2010).

care to migrant communities that have already been pushed to the margins by border externalisation policies.

Donors and the Politics of Integration

European aid constitutes the backbone of the system of non-state assistance available to migrants in Morocco. Since the mid-2000s, the EU and, until 2019, Switzerland have been the two most prominent funders of projects concerned with migrant assistance. Between 2014 and 2018 alone, the EU allocated over €32 million to projects targeting the 'protection' and 'socio-economic integration' of migrants (European Commission 2018b). Between 2006 and 2019, Switzerland granted at least 9.7 million CHF[8] (€9.03 million) in projects including activities of direct assistance to migrants, refugees, and asylum seekers in Morocco. The strategy of funding allocation pursued by the two donors, however, evolved with time in line with their changing political priorities.

Before the new migration policy, both the EU and Switzerland acknowledged that Moroccan authorities viewed the presence of migrants as temporary and refused to support any sort of long-term integration policy (see Chapter 2). From the mid-2000s until 2013, both donors therefore channelled aid for migrant relief exclusively through NGOs and IOs[9]. In 2013, the announcement of the new migration policy pushed donors to reconsider their funding allocation strategy. They thus opted for a change in approach and resolved to channel aid for migrant assistance also through the state. An officer of the Swiss Development Cooperation recalled:

In 2013, Morocco announced this new migration policy. We therefore thought that it was no more appropriate to continue [working] in a logic of substitution [...] We wished [...] to go towards an approach of institutionalisation.

---

[8] This figure was calculated by analysing the project information available on the website of the Swiss Development Cooperation in Morocco (www .eda.admin.ch) and on the website of the UNOCHA Financial Tracking Service (https://fts.unocha.org).

[9] Interview, two officers of the Swiss Development Cooperation, Rabat, July 2016; Interview, officer of the EU Delegation in Morocco, Rabat, October 2016.

An EU officer similarly remembered:[10]

What changed is that after 2013 Moroccan authorities decided to become responsible for service provision to regularised [migrants] – and also some services to non-regularised [migrants], like access to school. We thought it was no more appropriate to work with a substitution approach. However, Moroccan authorities were not ready yet [to provide services directly to migrants] and migrants were not confident enough in addressing public services directly. We decided therefore to support this triangle between civil society and the state.[11]

In the words of both Swiss and EU aid workers, the new migration policy marked donors' shift from a logic of 'substitution', where aid was used to fund projects that substituted the action of the state, to a logic of 'institutionalisation', where development projects did not replace state services but rather supported Moroccan authorities in expanding public services to migrant people. Donors thus interpreted the launch of the SNIA as the promise of a substantial readjustment of duties between the state and civil society. Both the EU and Switzerland thought that the Moroccan state would reappropriate most of the functions fulfilled by NGOs. Civil society organisations would then focus only on monitoring and mediating the implementation of the new migration policy. Both donors seemed to believe that aid would merely be a temporary instrument to support Morocco's integration policy, as the long-term social assistance for migrants would be covered by the state. Certainly, in the case of the EU, these expectations were influenced by the fact that the donor clearly perceived the SNIA as a sign of a major commitment of Morocco in border control cooperation. "The fact that Morocco has implemented the National Strategy for Immigration and Asylum means that Morocco is taking a responsibility [in border control cooperation]," the aforementioned EU officer explained. "They [Moroccan civil servants] consider that the [migration] issue concerns them and this means sharing the vision of the EU, which says to the countries of origin and transit, 'this concerns us all'." As the same EU officer commented during the interview, "It is important for Morocco to be manifestly supported with substantial [funding] support and budget support by the EU." The officer also

[10] Interview, two officers of the Swiss Development Cooperation, Rabat, July 2016.
[11] Interview, officer of the EU Delegation in Morocco, Rabat, October 2016.

added, with a certain impatience, "but now they [Moroccan author-
ities] should be able to do this without us [the EU]!" The shift in the EU
funding strategy should therefore be read as a diplomatic exercise (den
Hertog 2016). Allocating Moroccan authorities' funding for migrant
integration and for the implementation of the new migration policy
writ large is a way for the EU to materially express its support to
Morocco for its commitment in border control cooperation. This
financial support, however, is delivered with the expectation (and
political impatience) that Morocco will soon be in a position to autonomously deliver services to foreigners.

The donors' decision to rely more on the state and less on civil society
organisations was not unanimously welcomed by organisations operating in the field. The officers of a charity providing direct assistance to
migrants complained:

The EU [...] told us that now the funds were oriented to the reinforcement of
Moroccan services. They therefore didn't want to pass through NGOs anymore, but through the state. Voilà, this was the message. Now the EU is
coming back on it a little bit, but at a certain moment we were a bit at risk
because the donors decided that they wanted to work with the Moroccan
authorities because there is this new migration policy ... that has not been
translated [into practice] and that addresses an extremely limited public [of
beneficiaries]![12]

The respondents might have, of course, been critical due to the funding
shortage that this redirection of donor funding was likely to create for
their organisation. However, their concern also seemed of a practical
nature: channelling funding through the state at a moment when the
implementation of the Moroccan migration policy seemed to be
unclear risked restricting the material assistance available to vulnerable
foreigners. These concerns would prove to be very accurate. In 2018,
the EU announced a new €6.5 million programme, *Assistance to
Migrant People in a Situation of Vulnerability*, funded through the
Trust Fund for Africa. The funding is aimed at supporting social
assistance projects implemented by civil society organisations in collaboration with state authorities. The programme factsheet justifies the
action by arguing that "despite a strong engagement, the system in
place struggles to sufficiently ensure access to essential basic services for

---

[12] Interview, two NGO officers, August 2016.

the vulnerable migrant populations" (European Commission 2018c, 4, translation by author). This change in strategy allows the EU to avoid straightforwardly criticising the implementation of the SNIA by continuing to frame aid as a temporary measure to support the migration policy transition.

The disengagement of the state from migrants' assistance and the outsourcing of care onto non-state actors has always intersected with the presence of donors in the migration aid market. After the announcement of the new migration policy, donors tried to retreat from their engagement towards NGOs and IOs with the view of assisting Morocco in becoming an autonomous care provider for migrants. The turn that the implementation of the new migration policy has taken, however, has maintained donors, and their diplomatic stakes, at the heart of the system of social assistance for migrant people made precarious by border control.

Producing Bureaucratic Exclusion

Processes of border externalisation, outsourcing of state services, and aid politicisation transform NGOs and IOs into frontline providers of assistance for migrant, refugee, and asylum-seeking people in Morocco. This, however, does not mean that these aid actors are able to respond to all the assistance requests that they receive (see, for example, PNPM 2017b; Terre des Hommes – Espagne 2014). Aid-funded organisations, in fact, operate with budgets and beneficiary benchmarks pre-emptively defined together with donors. Projects are audited according to an accountability structure that essentially responds to donor requirements and that does not aim to provide universal care. NGOs and IOs thus have to regularly turn down people demanding assistance. The duty to help is thus intimately tied to the duty to deny help (Harrell-Bond 2002).

As providers and deniers of care, aid-funded organisations are in the position to decide who can and who cannot access assistance. These decisions are made through a variety of bureaucratic strategies aimed at filtering the number of migrants that can access the aid system. Labelling is a prominent option among such techniques. Aid-funded projects, in fact, rarely address the entire migrant population. Rather, they target a well-defined category of beneficiaries (Capelli 2016). As an example, the Tamkine-migrants project, funded by the EU and

Switzerland between 2015 and 2018, addressed "migrant women in
a great state of vulnerability." The project, "Protection and Promotion
of the Rights of Migrants in Morocco: Domestic workers and human
trafficking victims, Tetouan," also funded by the EU between 2015 and
2017, identified migrants categorised as "domestic workers" and
"human trafficking victims" as its target group (EU Delegation in
Rabat 2016). Interviewees justified the reliance on categorisation as
instrumental in establishing boundaries of action between each organisation and in preventing aid agencies 'from stepping on each other's
feet'. Julia and Nicole, that I mentioned in Chapter 3, explained that
their organisation does not assist refugees in order to avoid interfering
with the work of the UNHCR:

> We do not work with refugees, this can result in people being frustrated [...]
> it is a bit complicated because it is not that we do not want to take care of
> them, but it is the field of action of another partner [the UNHCR], so we will
> take care of people that are asylum seekers, until they get refugee status and
> then some people, I don't know if someone wants to continue their psycho-
> logic therapy with our psychologist here, ok, but normally once someone gets
> refugee status we pass the case to the partners of the UNHCR.[13]

The firm separation between 'migrants' and 'refugees' thus determines
different pathways to social assistance for poor foreigners. If a person
has refugee status, they can access a system of assistance managed by
the UNHCR. The IO determines the population deserving assistance
under its mandate, ensures the financial endowment of the programme,
and then establishes partnerships with relevant NGOs. If a vulnerable
foreigner does not have refugee status, they must seek assistance from
other organisations providing help to 'irregular migrants' and 'regularised migrants'. These organisations include local and international
NGOs, faith-based organisations situated in different Moroccan cities,
operating with funding provided directly by donors to the organisation
or channelled by donors through the IOM.

To further screen their beneficiaries, development and humanitarian
actors apply certain criteria of deservedness, the most widespread being
'vulnerability' (Bartels 2017). Vulnerability is an uncertain category.
Most often, it is used to refer to "womenandchildren" (Turner 2018,
119) as a vulnerable population (see also Turner 2017). In my

---

[13] Interview with Julia and Nicole, NGO officers, Rabat, August 2016.

interviews, however, it became clear that the aid workers dealing directly with migrant people requesting assistance had a large margin of manoeuvre to decide who was "actually" vulnerable (and therefore eligible for assistance) and who was not. Julia and Nicole went on to explain that their organisation leaves room for social workers to carry out more individualised assessments of people's vulnerability:

Julia: When people arrive for the first time, we welcome them through an initial interview. We evaluate their needs, because our main criteria in a centre like ours is vulnerability, we really try to help the most vulnerable people, so there is a first interview . . .

Lorena: And how do you define vulnerability?

Julia: This is the difficulty, we work with our staff over that . . .

Nicole: This is their expertise, the people that work in this centre most of them are migrants themselves, so they have experienced a mobility pattern, they know the difficulties that someone that is in a mobility pattern in Morocco faces. Their expertise, as social workers, is to express a judgement to see if there is room . . . voilà, it is subjective of course.[14]

The IOM also uses the vulnerability framework to screen beneficiaries for voluntary return (ISPI 2010). The organisation defines vulnerable people as "all individuals who fall into one of the categories of humanitarian assistance (women, minors, elderly, and ill persons) plus victims of slavery and/or human trafficking" (ISPI 2010, 35). Richard, an IOM officer, explained that the IOM utilises a mix of fixed categories and individualised assessment by the Voluntary Return team to decide whether migrants can benefit from return assistance:

The priority is really to allow vulnerable people to leave – unaccompanied minors, victims of human trafficking, elderly people, ill people, but then, you could tell me, how is it possible that the vast majority [of beneficiaries of Voluntary Return] are young men between 18 and 35? Good question, are they also vulnerable? We always check, if there is a migrant that is in front of our door, he sleeps day and night in front of our door it is a vulnerable case, you can see that, then there are others that arrive with a smartphone . . . it depends, this is why there is the interview, this is why our teams are trained . . . .[15]

---

[14] Interview with Julia and Nicole, NGO officers, Rabat, August 2016.
[15] Interview with Richard, IOM officer, Rabat, August 2016.

Although presented in technical and professional terms, assessing vulnerability relies on a large margin of discretion on the part of the agency's staff. Frontline workers are required to go beyond appearances when assessing the vulnerability of people who are not systematically categorised as vulnerable. Commodities such as smartphones are depicted as a sign of economic sufficiency by humanitarian actors, influencing whether they perceive migrants as destitute. In order to receive assistance from a particular organisation, migrants therefore have to fulfil the eligibility criteria characterising the target group. Fulfilling these criteria not only relies on one's status, but also by the capacity to portray oneself as vulnerable – and being recognised as such by the street-level operator (see also Maâ 2019).

Even when portrayed in a technical way, the labelling and filtering of beneficiaries is an exclusionary process. It is experienced as violent and unfair by people on the receiving end. Daouda, for example, is a Cameroonian man that I met in a small city in the Moroccan interior in the summer of 2019. When I met him, Daouda was ostensibly in a precarious condition: he was unemployed, homeless, and was begging at a traffic light. He had moved from one Moroccan city to the other in search of a job, without much success. He had also been forcefully removed from northern to central Morocco by state authorities on multiple occasions. While speaking, Daouda mentioned to me that he had spent a period living in Tetouan. As his living conditions were very precarious there as well, he had requested help from a local faith-based organisation. The person he had spoken to had declined his request because his case was not deemed vulnerable enough to be assisted. "He [the charity worker] was so mean!" Daouda recalled. "He started shouting to me when I insisted, he told me that he could just help people that were injured very badly."[16] The charity worker justified his behaviour by implying that Daouda is not suffering enough to be eligible for help, seemingly invoking a form of rough vulnerability assessment. Daouda, however, experienced this refusal as simply malevolent and the tone of the charity worker as somewhat violent. Turner argues that assistance policies tend to apprehend women and children as axiomatic vulnerable subjects, thus systematically leaving behind young men (Turner 2017). The stories of Daouda – and of Bénoit in this chapter's introduction – reveal that not conforming to certain

---

[16] Interview, a Cameroonian citizen, city in the Moroccan interior, July 2019.

parameters of vulnerability ("he could just help people that were injured very badly" or "[he] told them his real age [20], so they did not help him") confines them in the category of people who are too distressed not to demand help, but too bureaucratically in good shape to deserve it.

As frontline implementers of projects assisting migrants, aid-funded NGOs and IOs are at the forefront of migrant *inclusion* and *exclusion* from care. The delivery of assistance to precarious foreigners in Morocco is carried out according to strategies that decrease the number of people deemed eligible for help. Such strategies include labelling and vulnerability assessments, among others. The implementation of both these strategies is shifting, contingent, and subjective. It relies both on fixed categories and on the discretionary capacity of street-level aid workers to identify certain people as 'vulnerable enough' to receive help. Although framed in technical terms, bureaucratic filtering produces marginalisation in ways that are perceived as unfair by the people on the receiving end.

Who Is Responsible for Migrants' Suffering?

The exclusion of migrants from care is the product of a larger architecture of control with which racialised foreigners must interact. The frontline position that NGOs and IOs occupy, however, transforms them into the visible and reachable edge of the long marginalisation production chain. Aid-funded organisations thus often become the target of migrants' grievances. In its 2017 report, the PNPM complained that by outsourcing service provision for migrants onto civil society organisations, the state also externalises the responsibility to deny care and to deal with complaints:

Since 2015, the services of certain NGOs providing assistance to migrants regularly receive people referred by CHU [Centre Hospitalier Universitaire, University Hospital Centre], that told them that this association could pay their bill. It is therefore NGOs that have to deal with people's frustration if after the evaluation of their situation no aid can be granted.

(PNPM 2017b, 16, translation by author)

As Barbara Harrell-Bond argues, the relation between displaced people and humanitarian workers is an asymmetrical one, where the latter (who give) have way more power than the former (who receive).

Wittingly or unwittingly, NGOs and IOs interacting directly with migrants are therefore transferred "the *power* to decide who *deserves to receive*" from their sponsors (Harrell-Bond 2002, emphasis in original).

When confronted with these expressions of dissent, however, aid workers tend to enact mechanisms of sense-making in order to not perceive themselves as responsible for migrants' suffering.[17] The first of these strategies of sense-making relies on the dissociation between individual and collective responsibility. Aid workers that I interviewed tended to consider that they were not to be held responsible for failing to assist migrants or for causing migrants' suffering. Rather, other more powerful actors were to be blamed, including donors, European governments, and Moroccan authorities. During an interview, I asked Moncif, a Moroccan man working as a senior officer for a Moroccan NGO, why the organisation he worked for only focused on refugees. He answered "Well we do not make differences, but the donors do. If someone comes and they are not a refugee, there is nothing we can do for them."[18] Louise, a French woman who used to intern for an NGO providing legal assistance to asylum seekers in Morocco, mentioned the difficulty in communicating the role and limits of the organisation to asylum-seeking people in situations of distress:

Louise: Sometimes, they [asylum-seeking people] do not manage to make the distinction between us and the UNHCR, they think we are the same thing ... so then they tell us, "I do not understand why you rejected me [my asylum application]" ... but I did not reject anything ...

Lorena: [...] And how do you manage these cases?

Louise: I just try to tell them that it is not me, that it is like that and that we do not really have a choice, we can appeal but then if the appeal does not work there is nothing we can do [...] then they understand that it is not us. Some have the impression to speak to Macron or

---

[17] The reaction of institutional actors towards more organised expressions of dissent can escalate to completely unsympathetic forms of reaction. In 2009, the UNHCR alerted Moroccan authorities to a protest happening outside its headquarters. The demonstration was dispersed by the harsh intervention of the police (Scheel & Ratfisch 2014). This happened at a time of institutional violence against migrants, and calling the police could have potentially led some of the protesters to be arrested and deported to Algeria.

[18] Interview with Moncif, officer of a Moroccan NGO, Rabat, July 2016.

Merkel ... when they understand that I am European, some tell me, "You must say to the European governments that ... ." Yes of course, I go home and tell this to them! [Laughs][19]

Maria is an Italian woman who works for a European NGO that has implemented various projects related to migration in the past few years. When I asked her about the difficulty she encountered in her job, she mentioned a quarrel that occurred during the launch of a project assisting migrants in different areas of the country:

During the launch of the project, one migrant in the public raised his hand and asked, "So what have you done so far to help migrants?" We said we had done nothing yet because the project was being launched on that day. Then he kept on asking, "Why do you just help migrants, and not for example refugees?" But again, our project is about migrants and not refugees and we are not obliged to do everything for everybody ... . I understand he was frustrated, but he was placing his frustration on the wrong people.[20]

Maria seemed sympathetic to the man speaking from the audience and to the issues he raised. However, she could not help but think she was the wrong target for his complaints. Neither she nor the organisation she worked for, she thought, had a duty to provide care for the entire migrant population. Louise tries to solve this situation by communicating more clearly about her role and its limits. Differently from Maria, Louise seems to understand that migrant people are pushed towards making demands that might seem excessive or misplaced because they conflate the frontline worker's privilege (being White, being European, being in a position of power) with the privilege of more powerful decision makers. By depicting migrants' complaints as misplaced, Moncif, Maria, and Louise highlight the panoply of actors that contribute to the production of migrant exclusion. At the same time, however, this technique allows them to downsize their own role in the border control system.

Besides drawing a line between individual and collective responsibility, aid workers distanced themselves from the production of migrant exclusion by emphasising the technical character of vulnerability frameworks. Irene, a Southern European woman who used to intern

---

[19] Interview with Louise, intern of a Moroccan NGO, Agadir, July 2019.
[20] Interview with Maria, officer of an INGO, Rabat, September 2017.

for the social team of a Moroccan NGO, was among the people who had to make decisions about assistance requests. She recalled the moment when the team responsible for social assistance had to communicate to their beneficiaries that they had to leave the accommodation in which they were hosted:

We would normally allow people to stay for a month, a month and a half maximum . . . there were times in which people did not want to leave because otherwise they would have been homeless and live in the street . . . we tried to avoid these situations and mediate, trying from the beginning to help them find a house. But I remember that once there was this person that arrived one day in the office, he was extremely angry, and started screaming, "Where will I go, where will I go if I leave the house?"

While recalling the decision-making process to evaluate assistance requests, Irene explained, "I mean, we tried to do what we could, but if you do not fit the criteria we had to say no . . . at the end of the day, the organisation was not a bank."[21] Irene's testimony shows that assistance denials are not apprehended as a political act of marginalisation. Rather, they are framed as the result of a bureaucratic process that *technically* defines who deserves and who does not deserve assistance. This process allows Irene to legitimise her actions by highlighting their technical character, thus framing the discussion in terms of adherence to a protocol rather than engagement into politics or injustice. But technical decisions *are* political. As Hibou argues, "the production of indifference is, first of all, a social production." By supporting the "selective rejection of those who are arbitrarily defined as different, out of their place, excluded from community" (Hibou 2012, 121, translation by author), bureaucracy legitimises the order of things established in society.

A third mechanism through which aid workers distance themselves is by developing racist discourses that depict migrant people as 'undeserving' and 'manipulative'. This was certainly the case of Maxine, a French woman who used to work as a frontline NGO officer in a big Moroccan city. Maxine's job included conducting distributions of food, medicine, and clothes in key areas of the city. She was also in charge of providing financial assistance to migrant people struggling to pay rent or medical bills. During the interview,

---

[21] Interview with Irene, former intern of a Moroccan NGO, phone, October 2018.

Maxine mentioned that she conducted food distributions using her own car. However, some of the migrant people she met implied that the organisation that she worked for had paid for her car, thus implicitly accusing Maxine of enriching herself through her migration work. She also recalled that during the food distributions, some migrant people had justified their assistance requests by stating that "you [Maxine] are European, you [Europeans] stole from us, so now you have to pay [us] back." In so doing, migrant people traced a relation between past colonial exploitation in Africa and the present unfairness of the aid system. These statements are quite similar to the interactions described by Louise and Maria. But while Louise and Maria described migrants' accusations as "misplaced," Maxine posited them as evidence depicting migrants as ungrateful and undeserving. Maxine clearly inhabited her role as a frontline worker through binary categories dividing migrants into 'good' and 'bad' people. During the entire interview, Maxine continued to describe migrant people as an impossible 'problem' to manage. She also labelled them as "all liars" because she had found out that the people she had been distributing clothes to had decided to resell the garments rather than wear them. Towards the end of the conversation, she brushed off stories about sexual violence against migrant women in Morocco by stating that "at the border they [migrant community leaders] send the women first so they can play with the border guards." She then concluded that these situations were not "actually rape, but it is a transaction, it is strategic."[22] The misogynist and racist discourse upheld by Maxine naturalises and minimises sexual abuse against migrant women by depicting them as complicit in the production of the violence that they suffer (Tyszler 2019). The description that Maxine provided of the people she 'assisted' perfectly retraces the stereotype of the 'bad' refugees, which is quite pervasive in the discourses of humanitarian actors prone to see 'beneficiaries' as "thankless, ungrateful, cheating, conniving, aggressive, demanding, manipulative, and even dangerous persons who are out to subvert the aid system" (Harrell-Bond 2002, 58). According to Harrell-Bond, the figure of the 'bad refugee' is likely to be mobilised by aid workers to intervene in situations where their power is threatened

---

[22] Interview with Maxine, former NGO officer, place withdrawn, July 2019.

(Harrell-Bond 2002, 58). By alternating between general racist statements about how 'bad' migrant people are and anecdotes from her own work, Maxine recrafted her own professional encounters with migrants into evidence for her argument. Criticising the aid world, or using aid-funded supplies for purposes that Maxine did not consider legitimate, were, in her view, actions that further justified her vision of migrants as manipulative people.

The dispersed character of the border transforms aid-funded organisations into the visible and reachable targets of migrants' grievances. Aid workers develop different strategies to make sense of migrants' complaints. Moncif, Louise, and Maria frame the suffering of migrants as the product of other more powerful border control actors. Irene justifies decisions over assistance requests as inevitable because they are the result of technical frameworks of eligibility. Maxine, instead, rebukes claims over her own involvement in historical structures of exploitation by framing them as evidence of migrants' 'bad' character. These tactics do not spark solidarity or lead aid workers to question their own positionality into broader architectures of border control. Rather, sense-making strategies work as coping mechanisms that help aid workers downsize their perception of their own responsibilities in the production of migrant marginalisation. Moncif, Louise, and Maria feel legitimised to carry on with their work *because* they are not the most powerful actors in the production of the border regime. Irene is reassured about the fairness of her assessments *because* she respected the eligibility criteria. Maxine does not doubt herself *because* the accusations are made by people that she qualifies as manipulative and ungrateful anyway. Because they downsize aid workers' role in border control, these mechanisms of sense-making transform the production of marginalisation into what Povinelli labels "quasi-events." Contrary to spectacular forms of violence, quasi-events are injustices that slip through, that vanish in the "ongoing flow of the everyday." Migrant marginalisation that is produced and reproduced through the aid industry does not reach "the threshold of awareness and theorization" (Povinelli 2011, 133) that would allow aid workers to *actually* reflect on the structures of inequality that migrants' grievances highlights. Complaints do produce reactions – aid workers do record and analyse them. However, these reactions are not enough to destabilise the status quo. Sense-

making mechanisms downsize aid workers' perceptions of complaints, making grievances disappear into the background.

Conclusion

Aid-funded organisations occupy an ambivalent position in the regulation of migrant care in Morocco. On the one hand, they are often
the sole consistent providers of assistance to West and Central
African people living in precarious situations. On the other hand,
however, the care they provide is *rooted in* and *conducive to* marginalisation. Assistance is rooted in marginalisation because the
presence of migrant people made vulnerable by border control, and
the availability of funding for projects related to migrant assistance,
are directly tied to the interests of European states in controlling
mobility in the Western Mediterranean route. But care is also, and
more elusively, conducive to marginalisation. In fact, aid-funded
organisations are rarely in the position to fulfil all assistance requests
that they receive. Their position as frontline care providers transforms them into decision makers, endowed with the authority to
declare who deserves assistance and who does not. The exclusion
of migrants from care provision is produced through a bureaucratic
process that frames claimants as "eligible" or "ineligible" for assistance through technical procedures such as labelling and vulnerability assessment. Despite their technical character, the screening and
filtering of assistance requests produces marginalisation that can be
experienced as violent by those people on the receiving end of exclusion. This merging between care and abandonment is particularly
effective in blurring the boundaries of border containment because it
prompts mechanisms that disperse responsibilities for the production of migrant marginalisation. Confronted with migrants' dissent,
frontline aid workers enact three strategies to make sense of their
own involvement in broader architectures of border control. They
dissociate between individual and collective responsibility. They
invoke the technical nature of screening frameworks. They portray
migrants' complaints as part of broader racist discourses depicting
them as 'bad' people. These sense-making mechanisms allow aid
workers to distance themselves from responsibilities over the production of migrant marginalisation. In this way, migrants' dissent
does not manage to trigger mechanisms to address the injustice and

power imbalances pervading the border control system writ large. Rather, sense-making mechanisms blur the boundaries of responsibility. They transform complaints over injustices into misplaced accusations, inevitable consequences, or evidence of the 'bad' character of people on the receiving end of border externalisation policies.

5 | *Making Migrants Work*

During one of my fieldtrips in Morocco, I audited the sessions of a professional training course run by *Construire nos demains** ["Building our tomorrows", in French], a small Moroccan NGO operating in a large Moroccan city. Managed by two young NGO officers, the professional training project was funded by a European donor. The course was attended by around fifteen people, all from West and Central Africa and in different administrative situations (some of them were irregular, others were asylum seekers, others again had refugee status). One of the participants was Mamadou, a young Malian man who had received refugee status a few years prior. One day, a few minutes after the beginning of the session, Mamadou entered the class, out of breath. "Sorry for being late" he apologised. "I had another training and we finished late". The training workshop Mamadou had attended had taken place in another neighbourhood of city, approximately fifteen minutes away by taxi. "Another training course?" I asked him, while Clara, one of the two project managers, started introducing the content of the new session. "But how many trainings are you doing?" The young man started laughing, a bit sarcastic. "Lorena, you don't even know how many training programmes I've been doing in the past few years". As I would later find out, Mamadou had completed several training courses, in fields very different from each other, without any resulting in a job. When I asked Mamadou why he was doing so many training courses given that he was so frustrated about them, he answered "Lorena, you know, a training is always better than nothing, when you have nothing better to do". I would remember this conversation a few months later when, in the premises of another Moroccan NGO, I met Roméric, a young Cameroonian man, who told me that he had recently completed a training course in hairdressing. Prior to that, he had done a course in mechanics. Neither of the two training courses that Roméric had attended, however, had been successful in helping him find stable employment.[1]

The many training workshops that Mamadou and Roméric had attended attest of a specific juncture in Moroccan migration history. Sometime between 2014 and 2016, favouring migrant labour integration became a top priority for all the actors involved in migration governance in Morocco. Moroccan authorities included "vocational training" and "employment" into the sectoral programmes of the SNIA (MCMREAM 2016; MDMCMREAM 2017), recognising labour integration as a tenet of the ambitious project of migration policy reform launched in September 2013. Donors, IOs, and NGOs promptly deployed their energies and funds to put this policy in practice. As Richard, the IOM officer mentioned in Chapter 4, told me succinctly in 2016, "suddenly you have people with a residency permit ... very well, but now you need to give *these people* something to do".[2] The stories of Mamadou and Roméric, however, suggest that labour integration projects were not achieving the expected result of reducing migrant unemployment. If this is the case, why were Mamadou and Roméric still attending training course after training course? What other functions are aid-funded labour integration projects fulfilling? What do they *politically*, if not practically, do?

This chapter explores the social and political life of aid-funded efforts to facilitate migrants' and refugees' access to the Moroccan labour market. I argue that labour integration projects filter border containment power on the ground by functioning as sites of disciplinary power: they do not coerce migrant people into settling in Morocco. Rather, they subtly push them into internalising the need to engage into labour integration (Foucault 1979a). In the empirical sections, I will show that labour integration projects give aid workers a discursive instrument to entrench the narrative of Morocco as a "possible integration country" among migrant people, and to push the latter into internalising the responsibility of solving their own unemployment. Focusing on the case of asylum-seeking and refugee people, I show that the structures of power at work in the aid market push displaced individuals to either proactively engage into, or distance themselves

---

[1] Interview with Roméric, Cameroonian citizen, Tétouan, date withdrawn.
[2] Interview with Richard, IOM officer, Rabat, August 2016, emphasis added.

from, training workshops in order to fit certain presumed models of refugeehood.

The chapter first analyses patterns of migrant employment and unemployment in Morocco, situating them within the broader political economy of labour in the country. It then analyses the emergence of labour integration activities for migrants and refugees, identifying them as market-centred development tools. I highlight that the proliferation of neoliberal poverty reduction strategies in Morocco belong to a political trend to promote a quick fix solution approach to structural unemployment problems. I move on to show that labour integration activities struggle to reduce migrant unemployment. They, however, manage to achieve other objectives. I explain how implementing actors transpose a political understanding of "working migrants as immobile migrants", thus producing an equation between employment (or job search) and settlement. In the last two sections, I describe two forms of disciplinary power produced by labour integration initiatives. First, I look at how the implementation procedures and assessment language of these projects depict labour integration in Morocco – a country with a high and structural unemployment rate – as a feasible endeavour. Second, I examine how labour integration activities spark fears of spatial and economic immobility among asylum seekers and refugees, pushing them to shape their participation into professional workshops as a way to perform a certain model of refugeehood vis-à-vis the UNHCR.

Migrant (Un)Employment in Morocco

The labour situation of many West and Central African migrant and refugee people in Morocco is quite precarious. According to the quantitative study conducted by the International University of Rabat mentioned in Chapter 4, only 57% of the migrant people surveyed were employed, with a large incidence (67%) of the sample working in the informal sector. Out of a total of 1,453 respondents, 28% earned less than 1,250 MAD (€123) per month and 30% between 1,250 MAD and 2,500 MAD (€114–€228), which is just around or less than the average income in Morocco (2,413 MAD – €220/month) (Mourji et al. 2016). Other research has shown that, while some migrants manage to set up their own small business, many others have to take up poorly paid, highly precarious, and physically demanding jobs in constructions sites, shops, and stalls in the market. This category of workers has little to no capability to negotiate with their employers and are at a high risk of exploitation (Edogué Ntang and Peraldi 2011). When they are unable to find employment, migrants are forced to beg, an activity that they often consider shameful (Edogué Ntang and Peraldi 2011). Many women are obliged to use their bodies as an economic and protection resource (Pian 2010; Tyszler 2019). Vis-à-vis this weak economic situation, most migrants interviewed by the International University of Rabat expressed a feeling of dissatisfaction in relation to their daily life, characterised by job instability and discontinuity, economic insecurity, and difficulties saving. This translated into anxiety and mental health problems (Mourji et al. 2016).

Foreigners in the country face barriers to their inclusion in the labour market. Since 2004 the Moroccan labour legislation imposed a criterion of national preference. This allows employers to hire a foreigner for a certain position only if it is demonstrated that no other Moroccan national can cover the said post (Khrouz 2015; PNPM 2017b).[3] Furthermore, the position of foreign workers is rendered even more precarious by the lack of clarity surrounding the procedure through which the National Agency for the Promotion of Employment and Skills (ANAPEC, in the French acronym) rules over labour authorisations, the rigidities of immigration law vis-à-vis the timing and practicalities for obtaining a work visa or residency permit, and the stricter application of the national preference option since 2012 (Khrouz 2016a). The new migration policy has not really contributed to improving migrants' access to the formal labour market. Although Moroccan authorities announced that they would lift the criteria of national preference in 2014, this statement was never confirmed by an official implementing procedure (PNPM 2017b). The data disseminated by the MDMCMREAM are telling. Between 2015 and 2016, the Ministry of Labour and Social Affairs validated the labour contracts of

---

[3] It seems, however, that justifying the recruitment of 'some' foreigners is easier than for others. During fieldwork, a European aid worker told me that one of her first jobs in Morocco was as a communication officer for a private company. The contract she had signed, however, did not state her real professional position within the company, but stated that she was a 'language teacher'. As the company had explained her, it would have been easier to demonstrate to the ANAPEC that there were no Moroccans available to fill the position if the job involved teaching a language she was a native speaker of rather than communications (fieldnotes, autumn 2016).

only twenty-seven regularised migrants (MDMCMREAM 2017). Considering that the MCMREAM declared that over 23,000 migrants received a residency permit during the 2014 regularisation campaign (Benjelloun 2017b, 51), this number is minimal, and it reflects the difficulties that integrating migrants into the formal labour market entails.

Morocco's Labour Politics

The working conditions endured by migrants speak to a broader story of structural labour devaluation affecting the Moroccan labour market, characterised by high rates of unemployment and a stark incidence of informal activity (Kettani and Peraldi 2011; Khrouz 2015). According to the HCP, in the last term of 2017, 10.6% of the active population in Morocco was unemployed, with a much higher incidence in urban (15.1%) than in rural areas (4.3%). Most job seekers (71.1%) had been out of employment for over twelve months (Haut Commissariat au Plan 2017a). However, unemployment statistics might conceal the real unemployment share, because they underestimate underemployment (LO-FTF 2018). The Danish trade union council for international development cooperation (LO-FTF) estimates that, in 2013, half of the total labour force in Morocco were employed informally. As a consequence of the high incidence of the informal labour market, "75% of Moroccan workers do not have access to the existing pension systems and 85% are excluded from healthcare insurance" (LO-FTF 2018, 18).

The current state of the Moroccan labour market is the product of the economic development trajectory of the country, and in particular of its subordinated integration into the world economy (Berrada 1986; Berrada and Saadi 2013). With the establishment of the Protectorate in 1912, Morocco became an area of production of goods to export and trade in France. The productive structure of the country became mostly centred on agriculture and extraction (Capello 2008; Swearingen 2016), neglecting the development of the industrial sector (Piveteau et al. 2013). The expropriation of land from local farmers to make room for colonial agricultural production accelerated internal migration from the countryside to the cities. This supported the creation of an urban working class, which would become a primary source of cheap labour for the colonial economic apparatus. Measures regulating labour conditions (such as the introduction of a minimum salary and the basis of a system of social security) did not substantially contribute to an improvement of life conditions for Moroccans, as they aimed at ensuring the expansion and reproduction of colonial capital (Berrada 1986; see also Catusse 2010). The economic and social strategy undertaken by Morocco after independence presented numerous signs of continuities with the colonial era (Capello 2008). The Moroccan development strategy in fact remained centred on the export-oriented agricultural, extractive, and service sectors. Attention to industrial policy remained scant (Bogaert 2011; Vermeren 2016) and only regained momentum after the rise in price of raw materials in the 1970s. Throughout this decade, Morocco associated the nationalisation of the economy with the attraction of foreign capital and the development of the export industrial sectors. Together with the natural resources, cheap labour remained a key pillar of the Moroccan economic development strategy (Fernández 2018). Some improvement in the protection of workers occurred in the years immediately following independence. However, the expansion of the social protection system was prevented, and salaries were kept low so as not to increase industrial production costs (Berrada 1986). The drastic reduction of phosphate prices in the late 1970s and the contraction of the European economy were detrimental to the health of Moroccan finances (Vermeren 2016). The imposition of the Structural Adjustment Plan (SAP) in 1983 entailed the reduction of public expenditure, the liberalisation of the economy, the privatisation of state-owned companies – and therefore the reduction of public employment – and the development of export-oriented sectors (Emperador Badimon 2010; Malki and Doumou 2013). SAP-related economic reforms laid the basis for the expansion of foreign capital in Morocco, especially in the form of delocalisation of industrial production (Cairoli 1998; Jiménez Álvarez 2003). The position of Morocco in the global economy as an export-oriented country further increased by virtue of the fiscal advantages given to foreign companies investing in certain areas of the country – such as the Free Zone in Tangier (Rothenberg 2015) and, first and foremost, the cheap cost of labour (Berrada 1986; Berrada and Saadi 2013). As Alami argues, these transformations increased structural unemployment, the expansion of informal labour activities, especially in sectors such as services and trade, and the casualisation of employment (Alami 2000).

Migrants' integration into the Moroccan labour market does not happen in a political or economic vacuum, but rather in a context where unemployment and informality are structural parts of a political economy of labour devaluation. Unemployment, under-employment, and informality are therefore not recent, easily amend-able shortcomings of the Moroccan labour market. They have been a central and constitutive feature of the country's economic develop-ment for the past century.

Old Solutions to New Problems

After 2014, donors, NGOs, and IOs have joined their efforts to ensure that all actors, including migrants, civil society organisations, and state institutions, work together to achieve the objective of migrant labour integration. In 2017, the European Union launched a €4.4 million call for projects on "pathways towards the professional integration of migrants in Morocco" funded within the framework of the Mobility Partnership (see Chapter 1). The initiative aims at supporting 2,200 regularised migrants to enrol in professional training programmes and to access waged labour or to set up a small business. The programme also aims at reinforcing the capacity of Moroccan authorities to pro-mote migrant labour integration (EU Delegation in Rabat 2017b). In the same period, Belgium (Enabel n.d.) and Switzerland (El Aissi 2018) signed contracts with the Mutual Aid[4] to execute projects promoting the capacity of public institutions and civil society organisations to support the economic integration of migrants. Besides large, medium-term projects, a myriad of micro-initiatives have emerged to favour migrant economic subsistence. Labour integration activities supported in Morocco mainly fall into two categories: support to self-employment, labelled as facilitation of income-generating activities (IGAs)[5]; and employability and professional training courses for 'easily marketable' jobs. In academic development jargon, these are called

---

[4] The *Entraide Nationale* (Mutual Aid) is a public institution under the tutelage of the Ministry of Family, Solidarity, Equality and Social Development. It is in charge of providing assistance to destitute populations.

[5] There is not a clear-cut definition of IGAs. UNICEF states that IGAs "cover initiatives as diverse as small business promotion, cooperative undertakings, job creation schemes, sewing circles, credit and savings groups, and youth training programmes" (UNICEF 1994). In her study of the INDH in Morocco, Bono recalls that INDH booklets define IGAs as "an activity which consists in

"market-centred development programmes", because they are rooted in the belief that the market (not structural, state-led economic reforms) can provide solutions to economic marginalisation. Both pathways generally end up favouring migrants' integration into fairly unskilled labour activities. IGAs allow migrants to set up small snack bars or shops. Professional workshops, instead, generally train migrants in cooking, mechanics, hairdressing, or dressmaking. The kind of training pathways proposed do not vary much. This generates some irony among civil society organisers. Fatoumata, the NGO officer that I quoted in Chapter 3, told me that her organisation had partnered with a Moroccan NGO to train migrant women to become assistant nurses. "You need to vary" she explained, "everybody does catering, braids, sewing . . . but it is not possible to have everybody trained to do braids!" she concluded, rolling her eyes in exasperation.

In light of the structural weaknesses of the Moroccan labour market, "favouring migrant labour integration" sounds like a challenging endeavour, which can potentially question the structure of the Moroccan economy and labour market, the welfare state available to the unemployed, and the very position of Morocco within international political economy. After examining the content of labour integration projects for migrants, one realises that to the 'new' problem of migrant unemployment, donors, development agencies, and NGOs have resorted to 'old' solutions. In fact, market-centred development tools became first fashionable and then globally mainstream in the early 1990s, when the deleterious effects of SAPs pushed state and non-state actors to look for alternative pathways to development. Informal labour, self-employment, and market-attuned, unskilled jobs became a new development poverty-reduction formula centred on the capacity of the poor to fight "against their own poverty" (Bogaert 2011, 142; see Elyachar 2005). The engine of this approach to poverty-reduction is not a political aspiration to eradicate poverty and inequalities. Rather, these instruments are driven by a security-

producing goods or services and/or in transforming products in order to sell them", while the Moroccan Development Social Agency defines IGAs as "very small economic activities, led by poor and vulnerable populations, that produce a regular income" (Bono 2010, 27, translation by author). In interviews, development and humanitarian workers used the word "IGAs" in a much tighter sense, and exclusively to talk about self-employment, not to refer to professional training and employability courses. For consistency, I will adopt this distinction throughout the chapter.

generated need to identify avenues to manage and 'patch' social malaise to avoid its degeneration (Delcourt 2009; Hibou 2012). Market-centred development tools are what Denyer Willis and Chandler call "quick fix" solutions to social problems because they level off the consequences of inequality rather than addressing its underlying, structural causes (Denyer Willis and Chandler 2019).

Morocco has solidly engaged in neoliberal poverty-reduction strategies since the early 2000s. Rather than pushing for economic and social reforms decisively reshaping the country's productive and redistributive strategy, the government and the Palace adopted poverty reduction tools based on supporting the poor in providing their own needs through small, mostly unskilled, entrepreneurial activities (Bono 2008). Informal labour started being praised by public authorities as a flexible resource which could play a decisive role in overcoming the crisis of the Moroccan labour market (Alami 2000, 93). At the same time, the Ministry of Labour and its partners began directing job-seeking graduates towards the private sector, rather than towards state employment (Emperador Badimon 2010). The INDH became the linchpin through which Morocco raised market-centred development interventions as the way out of poverty and unemployment (Bono 2008). IGAs and labour training courses have been included in programmes targeting a panoply of marginalised social groups, such as single mothers (Capelli 2016), women living in poor regions (Soleterre Onlus 2017), as well as groups considered more problematic for internal and international security – including disenfranchised youth, alternatively conceptualised as 'potential migrants' or 'potential terrorists' (Gazzotti 2018). A few years later, the same techniques for labour integration were applied to foreigners in the country. Daniele, the development consultant that I mentioned in Chapter 2, sarcastically put it in our interview, "before you did embroidery with Moroccan women, now you do it with sub-Saharan women".[6]

Thus, labour integration activities for migrants and refugees in Morocco are part of an established trend of policymakers and development planners to "patch" the weaknesses of the Moroccan labour market through tools relying on the poor's capacity to exit poverty by themselves, rather than through structural reforms promoting social security and wealth redistribution.

---

[6] Interview with Daniele, development consultant, Rabat, March 2016.

Working Migrants, Immobile Migrants?

As I have explained in Chapter 2, the migration industry has historically contributed to the construction of a political performance of migrant 'transit' (pre-2013) and 'settlement' (post-2013) in Morocco. Labour integration projects are integrally part of this settlement spectacle. Although never explicitly depicted by donors as a border control strategy, labour integration activities for immigrants and refugees are rooted in a perceived connection between employment status and migrant spatial stability over a given territory.

Labour has always played a central role in border control strategies. Building on a sedentary and colonial approach to human development and well-being (Bakewell 2008; Landau 2019), donors perceive aid as an instrument to combat irregular migration by spurring the development of sending and 'transit' countries.[7] In this way, donor countries would manage to settle 'potential' migrants by providing them with an economic alternative to migration, or so the rationale goes (Rodriguez 2015; Tazzioli 2014)[8]. Since the early 2000s, donors, NGOs, and IOs have on many occasions resorted to labour integration programmes to immobilise different categories of migrants, or 'potential' migrants, in Morocco. Cooperation projects favouring the promotion of IGAs, vocational training, and support to

---

[7] Preventive strategies to migration containment include a wide array of approaches, including the attraction of diaspora investments and the incentives for the 'productive' investment of migrants' remittances (Charef and Gonin 2005; Geiger and Pécoud 2013; Kapur 2004), the concentration of economic development projects in regions with high emigration rates (Caillault 2012; El Qadim 2015), the creation of temporary recruitment programs (Arab 2009), and incentives to foreign companies to hire local workers (Vives 2017b).

[8] The idea that aid (and development more broadly) can be effectively used to curb immigration seems to persist among policymakers although academic research has proven that this approach has no real scientific foundation. However, the very absence of a basis of evidence for this policy approach highlights a third function played by aid: the symbolic and performative illusion of state control. As Oeppen argues in the case of public information campaigns in Afghanistan, these tools allow the state *to be seen doing* something about migration (Oeppen 2016, 64). The intended audience of much developmental efforts on migration control are not local communities in sending and 'transit' countries, but donors' constituencies (Oeppen 2016). Political pressure in donors' constituencies thus constitutes an influencing factor in shaping policy responses to migration, to the point that the production of knowledge on migration becomes entrenched in "signalling the legitimacy of policies or policymakers, rather than [being] a resource to help inform the substance of policies" (Boswell 2011, 21).

employability have been developed to favour the reintegration of Moroccan migrants forcefully or voluntarily returned from Europe (International Organisation for Migration 2016; Istituto Meme 2008; Vianello 2007). They have also been deployed to prevent the mobility of 'potential irregular migrants', a category which profiles young males living in areas deemed 'at high migration propensity' (Marín Sánchez 2006; Vacchiano and Jiménez 2012). All these programmes were based on the (simplistic) belief that employment, often in the form of precarious jobs, could alone constitute an alternative to emigration (Caillault 2012; INAS and UNICEF 2010).

In the specific case of the control of 'sub-Saharan' mobility, labour integration became an integral part of the SNIA because the Moroccan state started thinking of migrants as a settled, rather than a transit, population. Before 2013, only a handful of organisations were offering professional training courses and financial support for IGAs – mainly in Rabat and Casablanca (see Pickerill 2011). After the announcement of the new migration policy, programmes promoting training courses, workshops, internships, and financial assistance for migrant labour integration have boomed. The promotion of labour integration activities did not only coincide with the state's acceptance of migrant presence on its territory, but also with the idea that migrants who seek – and obtain – a job are those who are no longer interested in crossing the border. Carmen is a Spanish woman working in a drop-in centre for migrants in Tangier. She explained that her team had decided to rearrange the centre's programmes according to "migrants' psychological time", understood as the time that the migrants expected to spend in Morocco. The centre's initiatives were therefore divided into "short, medium, and long-term permanence". Labour integration activities characterised the 'package' offered to those migrants aiming to spend a long time in Morocco. Carmen told me that this group was very small, especially compared to the number of migrants considered as short- and medium-term permanence. At the time of the interview (September 2017), her organisation had supported the creation of only 5 IGAs for a total of over 1,200 beneficiaries.[9] This distinction, of course, was not airtight, as employment is not an equivalent for immobility.

---

[9] Interview with Carmen, officer of a faith-based organisation, Tangier, September 2017.

In his ethnography of a migrant-populated neighbourhood of Rabat, Bachelet argues migrant shopkeepers did not really fear the competition of other West and Central African stall-keepers, as they knew that sooner or later the latter would close their activity to travel to the borderlands and try to cross (Bachelet 2016).

Critical aid workers and human right activists sense the existence of a link between labour policies and migrants' perceived spatial mobility. This triggers their suspicion vis-à-vis the fervour of donors in generating local employment possibilities for migrants and refugees. In an interview, two aid workers started making sarcastic comments about all the attention being paid to integration projects:

Interviewee 1: Now integration is the new referential leitmotiv.
Because *ça passe vachement bien* [it passes quite easily] for Europe to approve projects to fix populations [in Morocco]

[...]

Interviewee 2: Most donors ... we have difficulties making donors accept a programme in its entirety. Most of them want to fund education, or labour integration, things that are really focused on integration ... it is really difficult for us ... to [help migrants] pay rent, to reimburse transportation ... there is no donor that wants [to reimburse] these invoices ....[10]

Suspicion towards labour integration also targeted donor-funded projects implemented by Moroccan authorities themselves. In 2015, the EU launched a twenty-four-month project, funded within the framework of the Sharaka programme[11] to support the ANAPEC in the labour integration of regularised migrants (MCMREAM 2016; MDMCMREAM 2017). "All this question of the European Union wanting to upgrade the ANAPEC honestly sounds quite strange to me" I was told by a Moroccan human rights activist in December 2016.[12] "I have the feeling that Europe wants to use Morocco as a big centre to upgrade migrants'

---

[10] Interview with two NGO officers, August 2016.
[11] The Sharaka programme is an EU-funded initiative aimed at facilitating the implementation of the EU–Morocco mobility partnership signed in 2013 (see Chapter 2). For more information, see the website www.sharaka.ma/le-projet/presentation/
[12] Informal conversation with a Moroccan human rights activist, Rabat, December 2016.

skills and then select just the ones that European countries want. Otherwise, why so much effort trying to upgrade the ANAPEC?"[13] According to the two aid workers mentioned above, labour integration, like education, is part of an 'integration' package that is seen by donors as instrumental to "fix populations", to facilitate migrants' settlement in Morocco. The human rights activist interviewed goes further, implying that the EU's interest in upgrading the state capacity to provide labour integration courses not only fits into the broader European border externalisation strategy, but also into a plan to further filter the sourcing of manpower. For all respondents, the interest in labour integration is not genuine, but is part of a politicised border control plan.

"What Are All These Trainings Useful For?"

That labour integration activities have proliferated in Morocco does not mean that everybody is convinced about their usefulness. As I said in the introduction, Mamadou had been attending training course after training course, without improving his chances in finding a job

---

[13] It must be highlighted that in the late 2000s the ANAPEC had fulfilled precisely this function: selecting just the migrants that European countries wanted in order to send them to Europe. In 2006, the ANAPEC had been involved in a circular migration programme managed by the municipality of Cartaya, in Southern Spain, and funded by the EU through the AENEAS programme. The project aimed at favouring the recruitment of Moroccan seasonal workers to pick strawberries in farms in the province of Huelva, taking advantage of the possibility, provided by Spanish migration law, to recruit seasonal workers directly in their countries of origin. In this framework, the ANAPEC was tasked with selecting the women who would otherwise have been recruited in Spain. The seasonal workers were mostly Moroccan women from rural areas with a low level of literacy and often with family and children at home. Their profile corresponded to the well-studied criteria of precariousness, dependency, and patriarchal subjugation, which, according to Spanish and Moroccan bureaucrats, made these women more likely to return home, rather than illegally remain in Spain. These characteristics were essential not only to ensure successful return rates, but also the low negotiation capacity of the workers (Arab 2018a; Hellio 2014; Vacchiano 2013). This "win-win-win" labour migration policy also resulted in objectionable excesses. The fact that the labour permit was tied to the labour contract – in turn, limited to a specific employer – and the lack of a firm trade union protection exposed the women to exploitative working conditions and to the abuses of their own employers (Arab 2018a, 2018b; Hellio 2014; see also Hellio and Moreno Nieto 2018).

afterwards. That he was not the only sceptical person became apparent a few weeks later. Towards the end of the training course, Rabia, a Moroccan aid worker employed by the IO partner of the project, showed up in the premises of *Construire nos demains** to discuss the next stages of the project with the two project managers, and the beneficiaries themselves. This visit was clearly unexpected. The atmosphere in the room was tense. The project managers were annoyed that the IO had not alerted them to the fact that Rabia would be coming. The people attending the training session viewed Rabia with suspicion. Rabia herself did not seem to feel at ease as she obviously sensed that her presence was not particularly welcomed. What followed was a two-act argument. "So well, I am here because you need to start making plans to liaise the beneficiaries with possible employers" Rabia said, addressing the project managers. The latter rebutted the proposition. "It is not our job to do this . . . we are trainers, we can advise [the project beneficiaries] but we don't have the time to contact possible employers. This should rather be the job of your organisation". Then, Rabia turned her attention to the asylum-seeking and refugee people present in the room, reminding them that, as 'people of concern' of the UNHCR, they could use the employability services offered by the agency. She therefore invited them to see a "career consultant", to conduct a "skills assessment" and to survey the possible options for their employment. The discussion heated up immediately. "What are these training programmes useful for?" asked Mansour, a Cameroonian man attending the course, visibly upset. "We are overwhelmed by training courses which never lead to anything. I did a lot of workshops and nothing ever came out of this" he added. Several other participants nodded in approval.

The grievances and disillusionment described are not simply anecdotal. Data about the success rate of labour integration programmes for migrants and refugees in Morocco exist, and are not encouraging. In 2016, the Monaco Development Cooperation carried out an evaluation of the Programme for the Economic Integration of Urban Refugees in Morocco (PISERUMA). The project was launched by the UNHCR in 2007 to favour the local integration of refugees in the country and therefore reduce their dependency on the financial assistance of the UN agency.[14] The programme offered both support for

---

[14] Interview, UNHCR officer, Rabat, November 2016.

IGAs and enrolment in professional training courses. The evaluation of the project revealed that, since the inception of the project in 2011, 151 refugees had benefitted from professional training courses. However, just 21 (14 per cent of the total) had subsequently found employment (AMAPPE 2016). The IOM project "Professional training and subsistence opportunities for regularised migrants in Morocco", which ran from July 2014 to February 2017, did also not offer encouraging results. The project had targeted 198 participants in total – 130 women had benefitted from professional training courses and a further 68 women from courses to support the development of small enterprises. The project evaluation states that the evaluators had not found enough evidence that the training courses "had necessarily improved the chances of regularised migrants to access the job market" or that there was a "link between professional training of regularised migrants and their access to employment opportunities" (IOM 2018, 5, translation by author). In particular, of the over 123[15] women that had enrolled on the professional training courses sponsored by the programme, only 25 had finished the course and just 1 had found a job afterwards. Of the over sixty-eight women that had enrolled on the course supporting prospective small entrepreneurs, only fourteen had completed the course and five had an enterprise open and running at the time of the evaluation (IOM 2018, 15).

Under anonymity, development practitioners themselves recognised the low impact and cosmetic character of labour integration projects on migrants' employment rate. Very telling is the account of Irene, the NGO worker that I quoted in Chapter 4, who recalled that her organisation would systematically refer beneficiaries to a labour integration programme when, even after careful examination, no form of economic support could be granted. As she explained:

There were people that, after we would try and suggest to pursue a professional training or to look for work, would reply angrily, as to say "I tried this, and this, and this, do you realize that you are trying to tell me to do things which I have already done and that have not worked so far?" At the end, the reaction changed a lot depending on how long the person had been in the country, if they had just arrived, they were angrier, as to say, "there is

---

[15] There is a discrepancy in the report within the number of women that had joined these courses.

nothing going in the right way", if they had been there longer they were more resigned.[16]

Irene kept on suggesting to migrant people to engage in labour integration activities. This, however, did not mean that she believed they worked – actually, she was constantly reminded of the contrary by the beneficiaries themselves. The reason why she kept on advising people to consider these pathways was one of protocol: in case the person was ineligible for financial assistance, labour integration was the option that the NGO pushed for. In Irene's account, time, practice, and knowledge of the system did not allow beneficiaries of the labour integration programmes to find a job. Rather, it allowed them to recognise – and, somehow, accept – the limits of the system. Gabriel, a senior aid worker working for a European donor, similarly pointed out that the obsession of the migration industry for labour integration activities was living a social life of its own, disconnected from the very question of results:

We will train associations, we will train everybody, everybody will be trained and over-trained, but nobody will find legal employment because it's impossible. So first everybody (the donors) supported professional training, then they turned to self-employment, the creation of economic activities ... [...]. Training is easy ... [...]. We will do feasibility studies, we will support business creators, we will support IGA, we will do it, whether it's successful or not. This is easy, we can spend thousands and thousands [of €] on it, and even more ... [...] it is more difficult to really find employment, and legal employment. Informal, black work, this is easy to do, they (the migrants) get away with it, and they got away even before. Switching from IGA to a real company that hires people, that is structured, that is recognised and that values skills ... this is more difficult as well.[17]

Interestingly, Gabriel pointed out that the labour integration activities sponsored by donors were "easy": they were activities that were easy to manage and that attracted an important amount of money. The momentum that these activities were experienced seemed, however, to be unjustified vis-à-vis the reality of the ground. While funding projects was "easy", obtaining real results was "difficult". Disillusionment about labour integration activities is widespread

---

[16] Interview with Irene, former intern of a Moroccan NGO, phone, October 2018.
[17] Interview with Gabriel, officer of a European donor, Rabat, September 2016.

also in other contexts of border externalisation. In his work on the migration industry along the Western Mediterranean route, Andersson evokes the story of the CIGEM, an EU-funded labour integration centre in Bamako. The CIGEM aimed at favouring the labour integration of Malian 'potential' emigrants as well as return-ees – to prevent the former from emigrating and the latter from re-emigrating. The job centre, however, was never able to provide many jobs to its target population, to the point that Andersson baptised it as "the Jobless Job Center" (Andersson 2014, 241).[18]

Although gaining large consensus by donors and implementing agen-cies, evaluation reports and testimonies by migrant people themselves suggest that labour integration activities did not fulfil their stated objective: increasing the chances of beneficiaries to find a stable and dignified job in Morocco.

Labour Integration as a Site of Disciplinary Power

A Country of "Possible Integration"

Even though the results were deceiving, labour integration projects were *doing* something. The first political function they played was that of entrenching the idea of Morocco as a 'possible country of integration' among displaced people. During the training sessions run by *Construire nos demains**, Mansour, Mamadou, and their col-leagues complained about the apparent uselessness of training work-shops, as they had not been able to get a job after attending them. Rabia, the IO officer, seemed to have a different opinion. "You are not obliged to follow training workshops", she replied. "If you are doing so much training, maybe it would be appropriate to see a career advisor to

---

[18] More broadly, the efficacy of market-centred development tools as poverty-reduction tools has been debunked by academic research. Since the late 2000s, scholars have argued that there is no sound scientific evidence that microcredit had brought about positive impact in terms of poverty reduction, although there were instead proof that in some cases the small-loan formula had damaged the social and economic tissue of the areas where it had been introduced (Bateman and Chang 2012; Lazar 2004; Rahman 1999). Bateman and Chang argue that the success and perpetuation of microcredit as a poverty-reduction strategy is due more to the political appeal that such a project has for neoliberal policymakers – i.e. outsourcing poverty reduction to the poor themselves – rather than to its poverty-reduction impact (Bateman and Chang 2012).

review your professional choices". The reaction of Rabia was some-what surprising. It was abundantly clear to everybody that the Moroccan labour market had an unemployment issue – the same people in the room were exasperated by their inability to find a job. However, Rabia seemed to imply that their lack of chance was *also* due to mistakes that Mansour, Mamadou, and the others were making in their job search. The antidote to this, she suggested, were a number of bureaucratic steps: "seeing a career advisor", "reviewing your professional choices", maybe "doing less training". People in the room started shaking their heads, clearly not convinced. Rabia adjusted the shot, with a more empathic "finding a job in Morocco is difficult for everybody". Before leaving the room, she added "We can sit down and talk and try to find a compromise. For example, a few refugees gathered together and founded a cooperative, now they work as members of the cooperative". People kept on shaking their heads, clearly perplexed. This time, however, they did not voice their discontent as they had done just before. Rabia left the room, that had suddenly fallen into a frustrated silence.

The UNHCR labour integration programme to which Rabia had gestured towards was organised around bureaucratic steps aiming to channel the agency's population of concern towards the labour integration activity with most chances of success. When a refugee decides to participate in the labour integration programme, the career advisors of an NGO partner of the UNHCR conduct an initial skills assessment to evaluate whether the beneficiary is best placed to take up professional training or to create an IGA. Young people between the age of seventeen and twenty-one with minimal previous professional experience and limited social capital are generally oriented towards professional training. Older refugees with a stronger network business capacities, and more clearly feasible plans are instead deemed eligible for support for small entrepreneurial activities.[19] Both pathways to labour integration are constituted by multiple steps, follow-ups and assessments to increase refugees' capacity to conform to market requirements. In the case of professional training courses, after their selection, beneficiaries are enrolled in training centres. To practically apply the skills learnt in class, the training course is then followed by an internship in various companies. Once the training phase is completed,

---

[19] Interview with Brahim, officer of a Moroccan NGO, Rabat, October 2016.

beneficiaries are encouraged to join a course on employability. This provides refugees with the necessary skills to successfully *sell* their professional profile on the labour market. Eventually, the organisation provides support in the job search (AMAPPE 2016).

As Rabia put it, the pathway to (less un-)employment was paved with bureaucratic procedures through which project beneficiaries learn "market mechanisms" (Hibou 2012, 132) and try to comply with market requests, shaping their profile to appear more 'marketable'. Centred around a logic of subjectivation, the rhetoric of Rabia transforms the outcome of the employment search into a responsibility of the jobseeker – and, to a lesser extent, of the organisations mandated to mediate the job search (Emperador Badimon 2010). This neoliberal narrative allows Rabia to move the burden of unemployment resolution from the context to the individual. She thus displaces attention from the structural complexity of migrant labour integration in Morocco to the petty technicalities of job seeking. In this way, Rabia manages to depict a situation that is not hopeless: at the end of the day, she implied, there were things that could be done to improve the success rate of the professional training courses. It was up to the trainers and the project beneficiaries to assume their share of responsibility, and make sure to do everything they could to spur the success rate of the programme. Rabia's narrative makes Morocco a "possible country of integration" *if* migrants learn how to juggle the neoliberal labour integration system. In this way, training programmes filter border containment power (reiterating a narrative of Morocco as a 'possible country of integration') by trying to extract utility from the individuals they try to discipline (they push migrants to conform to neoliberal models of labour integration) (Foucault 1979a, 218).

Labour integration activities per se did not seem to be effective in facilitating participants' integration into the job market. Despite their low success rate, they seemed to be successful in equipping aid workers with discursive arguments to entrench the idea of Morocco as a "possible country of integration". The bureaucratic structure of labour integration programmes, in fact, seems to depict employment in Morocco as a complex, albeit feasible, endeavour, its success or failure relying *also* on the capacity of the unemployed to exploit their skills in the right, marketable way. In the everyday interaction between the institution and those qualified as 'sub-Saharans', this significantly displaces the attention away from the fundamental incapacity of the

Moroccan job market to absorb poor foreign workers in a stable and dignified way, placing responsibility for the success of integration onto migrants themselves.

Being the "Good" Refugee

The second function played by labour integration activities consists in creating and entrenching certain models of refugeehood among training beneficiaries. In fact, binary representations of 'transit' and 'permanent' migration are not only upheld by institutional actors. The perception that the international community has of 'transit' and 'settled' migrants is well known to beneficiaries themselves, who internalise these categories and try to model their behaviour around them.

How this process of internalisation worked emerged clearly the first time that I audited the training sessions given by *Construire nos demains**. On that occasion, I was struck by a debate between the potential participants and the two trainers. The latter were giving an introductory session to people interested in joining the training course. After explaining the different components of the workshops and the degree of engagement requested of the participants, they opened up to the audience for questions. Aissatou, one of the participants, had been recognised as a refugee, and she asked if enrolling in the project would reduce her chances of obtaining resettlement in a third country. Other participants nodded, expressing a similar concern. Quite surprised, the two programme managers asked for clarification. It turned out that quite a few of the participants were either being considered by the UNHCR for resettlement in a third country, or strongly hoped to be soon offered that opportunity. As the number of refugees that the UNHCR managed to resettle in a third country every year was very low, participants feared that engaging in a professional training programme would negatively influence their chances of obtaining it. In particular, they feared that the UNHCR might interpret their participation as proof that they actually wanted to stay in Morocco and not seriously consider them for resettlement. This concern apparently pervaded the whole refugee community, which had developed a certain suspicion towards training programmes in particular and UNHCR as an institution. "People [the refugees] are happy when they [UNHCR and associated NGOs] tell you that you haven't been selected for a training program, even proud!" said Khadija, another lady also present at the session. The two programme managers looked at each other, slightly perplexed. "Well, if it is like this, we need to be informed ...", Clara hesitantly said. They were confused. Were these concerns just the product of overthinking on the part of the refugee people in the room? Or had their desire to build a useful project pushed *Construire nos demains** into an ambiguous larger game?

Under the UNHCR mandate, "resettlement is not a right", the UNHCR Resettlement Handbook states. "There is no obligation on States to accept refugees through resettlement" it continues. "Even if their case is submitted to a resettlement State by UNHCR, whether individual refugees will ultimately be resettled depends on the admission criteria of the resettlement State" (UNHCR 2011b, 36). In Morocco, in particular, the agency considers resettlement in a third country as a residual option. During an interview in 2016, a UNHCR officer explained that resettlement applies only to critical cases, such as LGBTI refugees, unaccompanied minors, or single mothers, "people who face a lot of difficulties here but that could rebuild a life in a resettlement country".[20] At the end of 2015, UNHCR Morocco counted 5,478 individuals under its mandate. During that year, only forty-six refugees had been resettled to a third country (UNHCR 2015). Between 1 January and 30 September 2016, fifty-eight refugees were relocated to other countries (US, Canada, and France) (UNHCR 2016). Resettlement is also a delicate diplomatic issue: when the UNHCR expanded its operations in the country in the late 2000s, Moroccan authorities were conflicted between not wanting to allow refugees recognised by UNHCR to stay in the country (American Embassy of Rabat 2006a) and fearing that the option of resettlement would attract large numbers of migrants from Western and Central Africa (American Embassy of Rabat 2006b). Resettlement opportunities, however, remain scarce, to the point that asylum seekers and refugees have organised a number of protests to claim broader access to it (Scheel and Ratfisch 2014).

Refugee and asylum seekers described the labour integration projects as if they were screens from which the UNHCR could observe their behaviour, or from where they could make their behaviour legible to the UNHCR. In this portrait, labour integration projects look like

---

[20] Interview, officer of the UNHCR, Rabat, August 2016.

a structure akin to the Foucauldian panopticon: an architecture of surveillance that allows the inmate to be seen by the supervisor, who stands in a central tower from which he can observe everything without being seen by the prisoners. The panopticon allows discipline to be exercised to maximum effect and with minimum effort: the pervasiveness of power is ensured not by the figure of the surveillant himself, but rather by a material infrastructure that induces "in the inmate a state of conscious and permanent visibility that assures the automatic functioning of power" (Foucault 1979a, 201). As legal migration opportunities for poor West and Central African people in Morocco were extremely limited, resettlement constituted one of the few legal mobility avenues for refugees living in the North African country. Low resettlement figures, and the political drive sponsoring local migrant integration, pushed refugees and asylum seekers to fear that they could lose access to one of the only legal escape routes out of Morocco if they had shown interest in any of the labour promotion activities.

During interviews, however, aid workers involved in UNHCR-sponsored integration activities consistently stated that all refugees were eligible for labour promotion projects, whatever their future mobility plan was. Brahim, an officer of a Moroccan NGO working on the PISERUMA programme, specified that the UNHCR had stopped sharing with them the list of the refugees who were being considered for resettlement. He explained that a misleading rumour had spread in the refugee community stating that enrolment in labour integration activities would lower their chances of obtaining a relocation. "UNHCR just calls us if they know for sure that someone will be relocated very shortly" he told me. "In that case, it's not worth enrolling them in a professional training course or supporting them in the creation of an income-generating activity".[21]

Based on the different versions given by the people that I interviewed, it is of course impossible for me to establish whether labour integration actually matters for resettlement decisions or not. What these data show with certainty, however, is that it does not really matter: the fear of being "stuck" in Morocco, and the powerful role that UNHCR was playing in the life of refugee and asylum-seeking people, were enough to trigger the latter's suspicion vis-à-vis labour integration programmes. Like in Foucault's panopticon, the surveillant does not

---

[21] Interview with Brahim, officer of a Moroccan NGO, Rabat, October 2016.

even need to be surveilling for power to work: the prisoner, who "is seen, but [...] does not see" (Foucault 1979a, 200), lives in the constant awareness that someone might be looking at them, and is induced to behave accordingly. They are therefore being pushed to monitor their conduct, to refrain from manifesting their wills and their dissent, to avoid any action that might irritate the source of power – that might be observing them, or that might not.

The fear to be seen as 'willing to integrate in Morocco' was not the only concern that asylum seekers and refugees felt vis-à-vis labour integration activities. During the quarrel with Rabia evoked earlier, the latter had made clear that nobody was obliged to follow any training courses. Khadija, visibly irritated by the answer, replied that even if there was not any obligation to follow training courses, she was concerned that the UNHCR would curtail her financial assistance if she refused to take a course she had been advised to take. Others in the room had nodded, expressing agreement. Labour integration activities, therefore, were sites where West and Central African asylum seekers and refugees would project not only their fear of immobility in Morocco, but also their fear of losing the support of the UNHCR altogether.

The UNHCR does not ensure financial assistance to all those falling under its mandate. According to a factsheet compiled by UNHCR Morocco in March 2016, cash assistance was ensured to 1,200 "vulnerable refugees", out of a population of 4,277 refugees/persons in need of international protection. Based on an assessment conducted by UNHCR partners, the UN agency would grant between €80 and €110 on average to people in need of financial assistance.[22] In a country where finding and maintaining a job was such a difficult endeavour, the financial assistance provided by the UNHCR was certainly an essential relief for those who were eligible to receive it. Granting financial assistance to refugees is, however, a contested topic within the history of the UNHCR, due to the shared (and politically situated) belief within the agency that financial assistance could lead to refugee dependency on aid[23] (Crisp 2003). The UNHCR has developed a varied sets of activities and strategies to promote refugees' "self-reliance" (see

[22] Interview with Irene, former intern of a Moroccan NGO, phone, October 2018.
[23] This concern has not always ranked highly in the UNHCR agenda. Rather, the narrative of self-reliance emerged in the 1980s, as the UNHCR started navigating a political landscape characterised by increasing funding constraints,

UNHCR 2005b, 2011a), understood as the "the ability for refugees to live independently from humanitarian assistance" (Slaughter et al. 2017, 1). The PISERUMA project itself was created in the late 2000s as part of the UNHCR's self-reliance package,[24] precisely to reduce refugees' dependence on financial assistance.[25]

The multiple political meanings that beneficiaries attribute to labour integration activities speak to the broader contested relationship between refugees and the UNHCR. During a later conversation, Mamadou explained to me that it was difficult for asylum seekers and refugees to understand exactly how decisions about resettlement or financial assistance were taken. Labour integration activities, therefore, were a platform for them to show the UNHCR that they were "serious":

> You know Lorena, we are just beneficiaries, we do not really know how they work in the inside. The UNHCR, when they suggest you to do a training course, it is not to block you, it is for ... sometimes there are people that enrol to a training course, but then they come once yes, once no ... if you do not take it seriously, how can the UNHCR take you seriously? [...] We cannot know how it is because it is an issue between states, it is closed to the outside, you know.[26]

The relationship between asylum seekers and refugees to the UNHCR is a complex one. The former feel like the agency grants them support ("when they suggest you to do a training course, it is not to block you, it is for ... "), but then feel clearly at the receiving end of an enormous power imbalance ("we are just beneficiaries, we do not really know how they work in the inside") and diplomatic game ("We cannot know how it is because it is an issue between states, it is closed to the outside, you know"). Engaging *seriously* in labour integration activities then becomes a way to prove your own industriousness to the UNHCR ("if

the emergence of populist, anti-immigrant, security-related rhetoric, and a shift in the nature of UNHCR operations (Crisp 2003).

[24] As Turner argues, humanitarian organisations tend to promote normative forms of self-reliance, posing clear boundaries of permissibility to how refugees can try to help themselves. The tendency of Syrian refugees to appropriate available resources in the Jordanian camp of Za'atari and make use of them in ways not allowed by the UNHCR and related organisations was a reason for concern, rather than a symbol of pride, for humanitarian workers (Turner 2018).

[25] Interview, UNHCR officer, Rabat, November 2016.

[26] Interview with Mamadou, Malian citizen, place withdrawn, June 2019.

you do not take it seriously, how can the UNHCR take you seriously?"). In a context where the provision of social assistance is not
ensured as a right, but is discretionarily provided by charities, the poor
start feeling the need to prove their good character "beyond the 'objective' parametres introduced to select individuals eligible for assistance"
(Bono 2014, 148). Labour integration programmes, like other instruments of discipline, exercise the maximum power at minimum costs
because they are "visible" – the behaviour of migrant people is potentially always visible to the aid agencies they interact with – but "unveri-
fiable" – beneficiaries do not know whether someone is actually
checking their attendance or their performance during training workshops, but they have no way to verify it otherwise (Foucault 1979a,
201).

Refugees attributed different political meanings to labour integration activities. On the one hand, they saw it as a way for the UNHCR to
understand their willingness to integrate. On the other hand, they saw
it as a way for the agency to measure the 'industriousness' of their
population of concern. Refugees reacted differently to these two meanings, feeling the need to distance themselves from labour integration
activities, while at the same time feeling obliged to engage in them. This
politicisation reflected refugees' perception of the power imbalance vis-
à-vis the UNHCR, as the agency played a huge – yet unlegible – role in
ordering the present and the future of their lives. Labour integration
activities became the battlefield where the disciplinary power of the
border and of the neoliberal social regime became visible and tangible.
This pushed refugees to assume behaviours that, they believed, would
allow them to navigate a world of evident constraints and limited
agency.

Conclusion

Aid-funded projects do not settle displaced people away from the
European border by offering them economic alternatives to migration.
Much to the contrary, labour integration activities did not seem to be
very effective in facilitating migrant labour integration at all. This,
however, did not mean that these projects did not *do* anything.
Labour integration projects filter border containment power by working as disciplinary mechanisms. They operate in a context marked by
structural constraints (in terms of unemployment, of border closure, of

influence of IOs). These significantly limit the choice that displaced people can adopt, and that therefore 'push' beneficiaries to adopt certain attitudes vis-à-vis labour integration projects.

I have identified two ways in which these programmes deploy this disciplinary power. The first is by fostering discourses portraying labour integration in Morocco as a feasible endeavour. The adoption of market-centred development tools to decrease unemployment displaces the attention away from the structural problems affecting the Moroccan labour market. Rather, the focus is placed on individuals and the organisations assisting them as agents determining the success or failure of labour integration. In this way, unemployment becomes an individualised failure, thus transforming the questionable idea of integrating migrants into a struggling labour market into a feasible endeavour.

Second, labour integration activities become stages where displaced people perform certain kinds of model behaviours to abide to models of refugeehood. Feelings of powerlessness spark anxieties of spatial and economic immobility. These fears induce beneficiaries to either distance themselves from or to overengage in training workshops, in the hope to prove the UNHCR that they are either "not integrated enough in Morocco" – and therefore eligible for resettlement into a third country – or "industrious and diligent in their professional integration" – enough to deserve the financial assistance allocated by the agency.

6 | *Return, Inc.*

It was a sunny summer afternoon, and the heat was almost unbearable. Maria Hagan and I were sitting with Patrick, a Cameroonian asylum-seeking man, in a shady spot in a quiet neighbourhood of Agadir, at walking distance from the seaside. From where we were, we could hear the honking of taxis and chatter of people on the promenade that runs along the beach. Patrick had joined us after Sunday service at the Protestant church, services very well attended by migrant people from various African countries. Some of them, like the pastor, had been living in Agadir for years. Many others found themselves in the city after being forcefully displaced from the North of the country during arrest-and-disperse campaigns. Patrick belonged to this second group of people. At the time of interview, Patrick had been in Morocco for almost two years, and had attempted to cross the border to Spain several times. A few months earlier, the police had arbitrarily arrested him in Tangier and displaced him to Agadir. After sleeping at the bus station for a few months, Patrick had managed to find a job in a factory that paid him 70 MAD (€6.40) per day, each working day stretching from 8 a.m. to 7.30 p.m. Although the working conditions and pay were not good, Patrick did not feel like there were too many other options open to him. "Because now, in Cameroon, there are two crises," he explained. "The English-speaking crisis and ... the effects of Boko Haram". He gave us a questioning look and asked, "Do you know Boko Haram?" We nodded. "This is Cameroon now. This is what made me leave Cameroon". Patrick picked a stone up off the ground and started playing with it, then continued: "If things improve, if the situation gets quieter, it's ok, I can sign my deportation, I can go back to my sister, it's ok. This is what I want now". He then raised his eyebrows. "It is not because we are in Morocco that we are ok. Things for us are really bad".

By "signing his deportation", Patrick did not mean being forcefully deported back to Cameroon by Moroccan authorities. "Signing one's deportation" is an expression recurrently used by migrants in Morocco to refer to the AVRR programme run by the IOM (Maâ 2019). Contrary to deportation, AVRR is a form of removal based on migrants' will to leave the territory of the host country 'voluntarily' (signing one's deportation) (Koch 2014; Webber 2011). First implemented in 2005, AVRR is the longest-running IOM programme in Morocco. With 1,399 returns carried out in 2015 alone, Morocco was the IOM's "eighth largest return mission in the world in 2015" (International Organisation for Migration 2017, 28).

The AVRR is often depicted as the quintessential border externalisation instrument, that allows states in the Global North to push their borders South (Alioua and Rachidi 2017; Caillault 2012). However, a closer look at the functioning of the AVRR in Morocco reveals that the balance of power in the governance of migrants' return is more complex than it seems (Maâ 2019, 2020b). For one, contrary to what some existing academic work implies (Bartels 2017), the AVRR started not as a result of the imposition of the EU, but at the demand of the Moroccan government itself in the early 2000s. Donors do not demonstrate unwavering support of how the programme functions: on several occasions, funding shortages have pushed the IOM to shut the AVRR down, a measure which has led migrants to organise protests and sit-ins to demand it back. The actual implementation of the Voluntary Return programme therefore seems to rely on a number of factors that contradict the alleged normative power of the EU and the IOM: donors' interest in the programme is discontinuous, the commitment of the Moroccan government is very high, and migrants organise protests when the IOM is not able to provide their voluntary repatriation.

This chapter shows how aid elusively expands the deportation capacity of 'transit' countries. I conceptualise the role that aid plays as 'elusive' because the AVRR is not coercively imposed on Moroccan authorities, embassies of countries of origin, or migrants themselves by Northern donors or the IOM. AVRR leverages structural power dynamics that push these different actors to converge towards a specific migration control device, and to cooperate in its implementation. For Moroccan authorities, Voluntary Return constitutes a way to remove undesirable foreigners from the country in a cheaper and diplomatically more acceptable way. For embassies of countries of origin, it is an instrument to externalise the financial costs of diplomatic assistance for a category of citizens that they consider "problematic".

For migrants, it is a way of accessing a last-resort way out of the country in conditions of exhaustion – or so is depicted by IOM officers. In the Moroccan context, Voluntary Return cannot be easily understood as a way through which aid 'buys' the collaboration of states in countries of 'origin' and 'transit' (Korvensyrjä 2017). Rather, different local actors cooperate in the implementation of aid-funded projects *if* these initiatives suit their political agendas or situated needs.

This chapter falls into five sections. I first explain how the Voluntary Return programme functions, and I clarify the role that each actor (the IOM, donors, the Moroccan government, embassies of countries of origin, and migrant themselves) is called to play in its implementation. The following three sections look at the counterintuitive attitude of the Moroccan government, embassies of countries of origin, and migrants themselves vis-à-vis the AVRR. By scrutinising the reasons that push these actors to collaborate in the implementation of the programme, I rescale the alleged normative power of both the IOM and European donors in border externalisation. The last section questions the political use of the category "Voluntary Return" in the Moroccan context. I open the pathway to new research about the social life of the label, and prompt doubts about what it may conceal.

How Voluntary Return Works

The IOM's AVRR programme can be easily classified as the most controversial activity run by the agency, in Morocco and beyond (Webber 2011). As the programme title suggests, the distinctive feature of the Voluntary Return programme is that the return of a given person to their country of origin is voluntary. Migrants must go to the agency's headquarters in Rabat to register their interest in returning to their country of origin. They also have the right to change their mind about return at any moment before departing. Many question how genuine migrants' 'voluntariness' is: the dire living conditions of migrants in Morocco and the possibility of accessing economic resources as part of the reintegration package, in fact, seem to leave many migrants without much option than to plead for Voluntary Return (Caillault 2012; see FTDES and Migreurop 2020, for the case of Tunisia). Likely aware of this critical environment, the IOM is particularly zealous in stressing the voluntary quality of the programme, both in publicly available documents and in interviews. The 2019 Edition of the IOM Morocco activity report lists "return based on the voluntary decision of the beneficiary" as the first of seven essential principles that "transform migrants into the main actors of their return" (International Organisation for Migration 2019b, 19, translation by author). During the interview that I conducted with IOM officers in 2019, the two respondents proactively took the chance to highlight the agency's view on voluntariness in Voluntary Return:

> Interviewee 1: [...] There are two things: first, here we do not do any publicity on Voluntary Return, we do not have posters or mass sensibilisation, the people are referred to us by partners. Second: the response is really axed on the migrant. We highlight that it is really voluntary and that the person can always change his mind.
>
> Interviewee 2: [...] The people come here by themselves and it is one of the solutions that we offer them, and the government here perfectly understands the question of voluntariness – sometimes there are flight cancellations, people that change their minds, and they [the government] perfectly understand this.[1]

Compared to other projects run by the agency, the AVRR is the only direct assistance programme directly managed by the IOM. It is also the most pervasively visible to those visiting the agency's headquarters in Rabat. During an interview in summer 2016, Richard, the IOM officer that I cited in Chapter 4 and 5, pointed at the building next door, 13 rue Ait Ourir. He then told me "the villa next door, number 13 ... they exclusively work on return towards Morocco and also from Morocco, as you can see our beneficiaries are at our doorstep", referring to the people queuing in front of the agency's external door to register for return. At each visit I paid to the IOM for interviews (summer 2016, autumn 2017, summer 2019), a few migrant people were standing on the pavement outside the front door of the villa at number 11 rue Ait Ourir, likely on a break from sitting in the waiting room for AVRR applicants. A sign was attached to the agency's front door and read "The Assistance to Voluntary Return and Reintegration is a service that the IOM provides FREE OF CHARGE. THE IOM DOES NOT USE ANY INTERMEDIARY". During my first visits, the waiting room for migrants waiting to apply for AVRR consisted of a small, dark space behind the security counter. By my last visit in 2019,

---

[1] Interview with two IOM officers, Rabat, July 2019.

another, brand new waiting room had been built on the other side of the courtyard. Contrary to the other small, dark spot, the new room was covered in transparent panels that let the light filter in. A few posters outlining the different phases of the AVRR programme were hung on the walls of the waiting room, where some migrant people sat, some with their luggage, others without.

The way that AVRR operates is more complex than other development cooperation programmes. The first element of complexity is the high number of actors that, directly or indirectly, are involved in its functioning. The IOM directly manages both the financial and the logistical aspects of the projects. Financially, it fundraises for the project and channels donors' funding into support for specific components of AVRR. Logistically, the organisation registers, interviews, and selects its beneficiaries (see Chapter 4). It contacts embassies of origin countries to recognise their citizens and to deliver a travel document to them if they are undocumented (or if they have documents but choose not to use them) (Maâ 2019). It mediates with the Moroccan Ministry of Interior to obtain travel authorisations. It arranges ticket purchase, transfer to the airport, and post-arrival assistance in the country of origin – which is mostly managed by IOM agencies in countries of origin (OIM Maroc n.d.b). Donors, Moroccan authorities, embassies of countries of origin, and civil society organisations all need to be involved in the programme for it to operate. Donors ensure funding. Moroccan authorities allow the IOM to operate in the country, grant travel authorisations for irregular migrants and, most recently, also fund flight tickets. The embassies of countries of origin provide travel documents. Civil society organisations ensure the implementation of assistance activities that are complementary to the exclusive return component of the project: referrals (Institute for Studies on International Politics (ISPI) 2010), provision of emergency healthcare and accommodation (Maâ 2019), as well as pre-departure training. Paradoxically, beneficiary recruitment is the part that requires the least direct involvement of the agency. As the IOM has a very discrete communication policy on the topic, migrants are either referred to the agency by other NGOs or, more frequently, self-refer after having learnt about the programme through word of mouth (Institute for Studies on International Politics (ISPI) 2010; Maâ 2020b).

The second element of complexity is funding. As for most other programmes run by the IOM, the AVRR does not count on continuous contributions from IOM's member states. It rather depends on project-based funding (see Chapter 1). However, where other projects are limited in time, the AVRR has been running since 2005. Formally, the AVRR is still composed of discrete projects, all contributing to the main backbone of the programme (the funding of return), to the reintegration-related activities (pre-departure orientation, professional training courses, and post-arrival assistance package) and the provision of humanitarian assistance in the pre-departure phase[2] (OIM Maroc n.d.a). As the programme is composed of discrete projects, the donors funding the AVRR constantly change. In 2010, the IOM listed Germany, the UK, Belgium, Spain, Italy Norway, the Netherlands, Switzerland, and the EU as funders of the AVRR (International Organisation for Migration 2010). In 2018, instead, it was funded by Morocco, Germany, Spain, Italy, Norway, and the Netherlands (International Organisation for Migration 2018). Funding for the programme is thus discontinuous, and the type of assistance that the IOM can grant to its beneficiaries is not homogenous. Since 2005, the Voluntary Return programme has had to be interrupted in 2010, 2012, and 2016 due to funding shortages (International Organisation for Migration 2010).[3] The level of pre-departure and reintegration assistance provision also varies, depending on the specific conjuncture of AVRR-related projects funded at any specific moments in time[4] and on the beneficiary's country of origin.[5]

Voluntary Return as Moroccan Migration Policy

Moroccan authorities have been central to the establishment, continuation, and everyday operation of the Voluntary Return programme.

---

[2] Interview with two IOM officers, Rabat, July 2019
[3] Interview with Richard, IOM officer, Rabat, August 2016.
[4] Maâ, for example, explains that after the interruption of the programme in 2016, the IOM Morocco resumed registrations for those applicants that accepted to be returned even with the condition that only the flight will be paid for, but not the reintegration package (Maâ 2019).
[5] For example, the FORAS – Enhancing Reintegration Opportunities project provides pre-departure training only to migrants that are voluntarily returning to Cameroon, Côte d'Ivoire, Guinea, Mali, and Senegal (International Organisation for Migration 2019a; OIM Maroc n.d.a). The second phase of the project (FORAS II) expanded eligibility to migrant people from three more countries (Burkina Faso, Democratic Republic of Congo, and Togo) (OIM Maroc 2020).

The Moroccan government, in fact, gave the decisive push to launch the programme in 2005. In October of that year, the IOM freighted a charter flight for 220 Malian voluntary returnees, at the request of both Moroccan and Malian authorities (International Organisation for Migration 2005, 16). At that time, the IOM did not have an office nor solid project portfolio in the country, and the agency's presence was physically reduced to a member of staff operating out of the offices of Mutual Aid. In those first few years, the AVRR operated on a case-by-case approach, being deployed to provide repatriation for specific cases.[6]

Moroccan authorities, however, considered IOM spot assistance to be gravely insufficient. In a conversation with American diplomats, Khalid Zerouali, director of Migration and Border Surveillance in Morocco's Interior Ministry, argued that IOM support was not enough to complement the substantial economic effort that Morocco was making to repatriate irregular migrants (American Embassy of Rabat 2006c). The economic pressure that Morocco sustained was particularly strong because, at the time, the authorities adopted an aggressive deportation policy. The state did not seem keen to allow people who were not in need of international protection to remain in the country. It insisted that "once assessed, those who are economic migrants must then be repatriated to their countries of origin, which Morocco has done in cooperation with the International Organisation of Migration (IOM)" (American Embassy of Rabat 2006c). In 2004 and 2005, Moroccan authorities "voluntarily" returned 2,480 and 4,485 people respectively (MCMREAM 2016, 86), with the IOM stepping in for the repatriation of just 295 migrants in 2005 (OIM Maroc 2019, 4). The first AVRR operation run by the IOM happened weeks after the Ceuta and Melilla events, in a militarised context where Moroccan authorities had escalated arrests of migrant people in the North of the country, their displacement to the desert, and their return to origin countries. It is not surprising that the first group of migrants who the IOM 'voluntarily returned' were Malian: in 2005 alone, Morocco returned 1,289 Malian citizens, and Malian authorities had themselves set up air bridges to repatriate their nationals (Chappart 2015).

As mentioned before, until 2014 the AVRR functioned intermittently, mainly due to funding instability. The IOM faced resistance to

---

[6] Interview with two IOM officers, Rabat, July 2019.

securing funding because donors questioned the efficiency of the AVRR as a border control method (Bartels 2017). Furthermore, European countries felt that funding the programme could potentially jeopardise EU attempts to convince Morocco to sign the readmission agreement (Maâ 2020b). Once again, Moroccan authorities significantly bolstered the implementation of AVRR by integrating it within the country's own migration management strategy. The new migration policy announced in 2013 explicitly incorporates voluntary return as part of the transversal programme named "Management of migration flows and fight against trafficking in human beings", which constitutes one of the eleven programmes structuring the implementation of the SNIA. More specifically, the AVRR contributes to meeting the fifteenth specific objective of the SNIA, namely "mastering immigration flows according to an approach that is humane and respectful of human rights" (MDMCMREAM 2018, 18–19, translation by author).[7]

The financial investment that Morocco has made in the programme reflects the central role that Voluntary Return plays in the government's new policy. Through three successive amendments to the 2007 Memorandum of Understanding between the IOM and the Government of Morocco, Moroccan authorities have agreed to subsidise the return of 1,000 people in 2014, 1,500 people in 2015, and 3,000 people in 2016 (MDMCMREAM 2017, 97), mainly through the purchase of flight tickets. Over those three years, Moroccan authorities contributed 38.5 million MAD (€3.5 million) to the functioning of the AVRR (MCMREAM 2016, 87). Publicly, Morocco explains its involvement in funding AVRR by showcasing an argument that sits between the humanitarian and the pragmatic. As a respondent from the MDMCREAM put it:

The Voluntary Return programme – we do it since 2004, since when there is a Memorandum of Understanding between the Moroccan Ministry of Interior and the IOM that stipulates that the Moroccan state funds the [plane] tickets and the IOM funds reintegration. Now there is even a pre-departure orientation phase, and it is a programme that has a lot of success

---

[7] The other activities included in the programme are: the "reinforcement of integrated border management"; the "implementation of the exceptional operation of regularization"; and the "fight against human trafficking and reinforcement of knowledge of the Moroccan security services" (MDMCMREAM 2018, 71–77, translation by author).

among irregular migrants, because traffickers sell them Eldorado and then when they realise that crossing is difficult ... we give the possibility of regularization to those who want to stay here, and for those who want to go home there is voluntary return.[8]

The Voluntary Return programme therefore meets two objectives of the new Moroccan migration policy. On the one hand, it allows Moroccan authorities, domestically and internationally, to be seen as offering a "humane" solution to migrants stranded in the country due to the closure of European borders and at risk of becoming easy prey for traffickers. On the other hand, it allows authorities to work towards their own objective of controlling the number of irregular migrants in the country ["we give the possibility of regularisation to those who want to stay here, and for those who want to go home there is the voluntary return"]. This second function is central as Morocco seems to display Voluntary Return as a substitute for deportation. As the Moroccan NGO GADEM highlighted in a 2018 report, the SNIA does not acknowledge any of the administrative measures foreseen by Law 02–03 as possible mechanisms to deport a foreigner from the Moroccan territory,[9] and exclusively apprehends the AVRR as a possible return measure (GADEM 2018a). Fabrice, a development consultant working for a European donor, similarly explained that:

First, Morocco doesn't expel any foreigner. [...] They have what they call the *refoulement interne*, [...] but they don't send them to the border anymore as they used to do. So, the reason why they are interested in voluntary return is political; they can't do forced returns, so they prefer paying for voluntary return rather than having irregular migrants more or less settled in Morocco ... so that is basically the idea and what they say is "well, we are ready to co-fund, this is a European problem, so Europe has to pay as well".[10]

Placing Voluntary Return at the heart of the migration policy would therefore not only allow Morocco to avoid the legal constraints and

---

[8] Interview with officer of the MDMCMREAM, Rabat, June 2019.

[9] Law 02–03 distinguishes between *réconduite à la frontière* (return to the border) and *expulsion* (expulsion) as return measures that Moroccan authorities can take against foreigners. The *return to the border* is a measure addressing foreigners that have been residing irregularly in Morocco, and that are returned in virtue of their irregular status. *Expulsion*, instead, is a measure tackling foreigners that are returned to their country of origin because they constitute a "severe threat to public safety" (GADEM 2018b, 7).

[10] Interview with Fabrice, development consultant, place withdrawn, July 2016.

costs imposed by the Moroccan migration act concerning the deportation of a foreigner. It also allows the country to more easily mobilise the financial support of European donors. Morocco's financial investment in the AVRR, however, could also be read as part of the country's strategy to utilise its migration policy to further its African diplomatic agenda (see Chapter 1). By offering citizens of African countries two 'humane' solutions to the suffering of irregular mobility (regularisation or voluntary return), Morocco would show its commitment to establishing fair relations with its African partners, especially after a decade marked by deportations and the systematic abuse of migrant people.

Morocco's transformation into a donor greatly contributed to stabilising the AVRR. In an interview granted to online Moroccan newspaper *Yabiladi* in 2014, the then IOM Chief of Mission for Morocco, Anke Strauss, declared that the IOM was having a hard time raising the €1.5 million necessary to run the programme, which costs €2,600 per returned migrant. Strauss welcomed Morocco's contribution as a fortunate trend inversion: "Up to now, Morocco was offering us the necessary administrative support on issues of return visa, help at the airport . . . this time, it contributes towards a quarter of the sum that we need [to run the programme]" (Chaudier 2014). The increase of incoming funds has expanded the operational capacity of the AVRR. Between 2005 and 2013, the IOM had managed to support the voluntary return of 4,230 people, with an average of 539 migrants per year. Between 2014 and 2019, the number of people returned increased to 8,668 (OIM Maroc 2019) (see Figure 5).

The direct involvement of the Moroccan government in funding the programme is widely regarded by the international community as a sign of Morocco's commitment to border control cooperation. Such a level of involvement in AVRR operations is, in fact, unusual for a 'transit' country. The EU qualifies the specific arrangement for Voluntary Return in Morocco as "without precedent in the region [North Africa]" (European Commission 2016, 7, translation by author). Richard, the IOM officer I interviewed in 2016,[11] pointed out that: "Here we have a privilege that is very rare: that Morocco itself is a donor".[12] The EU Commission supports the

---

[11] Interview with Richard, IOM officer, Rabat, August 2016.

[12] IOM's narrative about "Morocco's exceptionalism" is in stark contrast with the agency's early portrait of the country's involvement in AVRR funding: back in 2006, Brunson McKinley, general director of the IOM, declared that it was

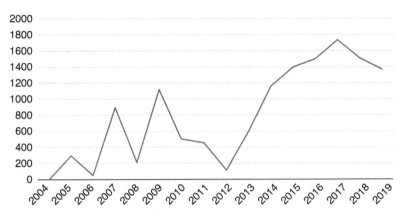

Figure 5 Number of 'Voluntary Returns' from Morocco organised by the IOM, 2005–19. Source: OIM Maroc 2019.

institutionalisation of the AVRR, its expansion and larger ownership by the Moroccan state. The budget support that the EU granted to Morocco for the implementation of the SNIA includes €1.2 million specifically for the AVRR. The programme, managed by the AECID, includes €200,000 for training Moroccan authorities about the management of the AVRR programme and €1 million for upgrading two training centres managed by Mutual Aid in Agadir and Khemisset, cities in the South and Centre of Morocco respectively. These centres should function both as structures providing professional training sessions, and as accommodation centres for migrants waiting to be voluntarily returned to their origin countries (European Commission 2016).

Contrary to mainstream understandings of the IOM's influence in Morocco, country's authorities have been central to the survival of Voluntary Return in the country. Over the years, the Moroccan government has provided the political and financial incentives necessary

"scandalous" that Morocco had to be alone in funding the AVRR for migrants on their territory, as Europe was equally concerned by the fate of these people. The IOM used the argument of the political responsibility of European states to support its own fundraising strategy: McKinley, in fact, complained that the IOM had launched multiple fundraising appeals to European countries, without managing to attract the desired budget (*Le Matin* 2006).

for the IOM to set up and institutionalise the AVRR, first as a punctual addition to the country's border security strategy, then as a component of the SNIA. In both phases, the IOM's Voluntary Return programme appears as an instrument to complement and externalise the country's deportation strategy. This allows the authorities to both share the financial burden of border security with donors and to gain the esteem of the international community on migration management.

Migrants' Suffering as the IOM Politics

Migrants' pressing demand for Voluntary Return is one of the main arguments put forward both by Moroccan authorities and by the IOM to justify the importance of the programme. As mentioned earlier, representative from the MDMCMREAM highlighted that "Voluntary Return has a lot of success among irregular migrants".[13] an IOM member of staff highlighted that the number of migrants applying for voluntary return has always outnumbered the agency's financial capacity. At the time of interview with the Voluntary Return team (July 2019), 2,500 people were registered on a "waiting list" for the programme, in contrast with a total of 400 people voluntarily repatriated since the beginning of the year.[14]

Migrants' pressing demand for Voluntary Return becomes particularly visible at moments of funding shortage, and consequent interruptions of the programme. In 2012 and 2016, migrants organised protests in front of the IOM office in Rabat to pressure the agency to resume registrations (Maâ 2019, 2020b). On both occasions, the stalemate ceased through the proactive intervention of the IOM. The agency, in fact, solicited donors to contribute the funding necessary to resume the programme.[15] Richard recalled that:

In 2012 there was almost no money left [for Voluntary Return], there were protests in front of our door, even this year [2016] ... as soon as there is no more money, we can feel it, and this is also how we raise the issue with the donors, we tell them "come and see in front of our door, when you have 200 migrants that are rebelling ...". We had it this year, and in 2012 as well.[16]

[13] Interview with officer of the MDMCMREAM, Rabat, June 2019.
[14] Interview with two IOM officers, Rabat, July 2019. [15] Ibid.
[16] Interview with Richard, IOM officer, Rabat, August 2016.

Migrants' visible and persistent physical presence in front of IOM doors is mobilised by the agency as a compelling evidence of the vulnerability of AVRR beneficiaries. IOM staff tends to depict Voluntary Return beneficiaries as "desperate" and claim Voluntary Return as a last-resort solution:

These are people for whom there is no other hope, they are ready to do anything, they really tell us "it is a question of life or death" [...] people do not have any other option, so they start camping in front of our office, they hold demonstrations.[17]

The same agency tends to use the 'vulnerability' label to draw a line between 'good' migrants (categorised as passive, desperate actors, who are deemed eligible for Voluntary Return) and 'bad' migrants (depicted instead as more active agents able to instrumentalise the Voluntary Return programme and its eligibility criteria to fit their own mobility strategy) (Maâ 2019). During the interview, IOM officer Richard emphasised the need to thoroughly assess migrants' vulnerability to avoid people from using the programme as a "travel agency", which means, to have people registering for the programme multiple times during subsequent journeys to and from Morocco.[18]

The IOM particularly leveraged the vulnerability argument in 2012, as the funding shortage coincided with a period of increased violence at the border. In a public fundraising appeal, the IOM invited donors to contribute €620,000 towards the Voluntary Return programme. This sum was needed to ensure migrants access to one of the only short-term "humanitarian" solutions available in a context of emergency (de Haas 2012; see also Bartels 2017). This unusual publicity for the Voluntary Return programme made the IOM the target of criticism. A few days after the launch of the appeal, Dutch academic Hein de Haas, in fact, published an entry on his blog titled "IOM's dubious mission in Morocco". In the blogpost, de Haas highlighted that the wording of the appeal suggested that "the IOM tries to make money out of the violations of migrants' rights by the Moroccan authorities", as "[...] these human rights abuses are now being instrumentalized [by the IOM] to justify a costly repatriation scheme" (de Haas 2012). Ten days after the publication of this blogpost, the then IOM Morocco

---

[17] Interview with two IOM officers, Rabat, July 2019.
[18] Interview with Richard, IOM officer, Rabat, August 2016.

mission chief Anke Strauss posted a comment under de Haas' blog post. In the comment, she clarified that the Voluntary Return programme "has to be seen as a complementary measure to the policy and advocacy response described above, which is implemented to provide a humanitarian response to the migrants' immediate needs in the short run". To further validate the IOM's position, Strauss concluded that "this IOM's response is seen by the UN Country Team and civil society partners as being the best solution to the challenge of many migrants wanting to return home" (de Haas 2012). Despite the criticism, the IOM managed to resume the Voluntary Return operations through the intervention of Switzerland, that accepted to fund the programme "as a 'durable solution' to save migrants from the increasing repression they suffered in Morocco" (Bartels 2017, 324).[19]

In the discourse and practice of the IOM, migrants are not subjects on whom the Voluntary Return programme is imposed. Rather, they are actors through which the Voluntary Return programme is produced and reproduced. Migrants' critical mass (both numerical, as names on the AVRR waiting list, and physical, as protestors in front of the agency's doors) and vulnerability transform are bargaining elements that the IOM uses to plead further aid from donors (Bartels 2017). Migrants' 'worthiness' within the AVRR economy, however, is directly linked to their vulnerability potential. In fact, migrants' capacity to sidestep and appropriate the rules of Voluntary Return to their own advantage is not welcomed by the IOM, whose officers consider these signs of noisy, unruly, and unwelcome agency.

Voluntary Return as the Outsourcing of Diplomatic Assistance

Embassies of countries of origin are key actors in the functioning of the Voluntary Return programme. Many migrants who request the IOM's assistance for voluntary return do not have papers. The collaboration of West and Central African embassies and consular authorities is thus

---

[19] In the following years, the protests and situations of tension during moments of funding shortage pushed the IOM to review its strategy and opt for a more discrete fundraising approach to Voluntary Return, based on funding cycles. The "cyclical funding" strategy structures resources for Voluntary Return "in cycles lasting just over 24 months [that] enables the IOM mission office to plan the available funds and arrange support from different donors for the different aspects of the programme" (International Organisation for Migration 2017, 42).

necessary to allow candidates to obtain the necessary travel documents. A diplomat from Guinea Conakry explained:

We have an identification role because those [the migrants] who come do not have documents. In Guinea there are more than 300 dialects and we identify them through a language test. After the identification, the IOM sends us a document and we produce a travel document, that they call a laissez-passer, but actually it is a travel document.[20]

A Senegalese diplomat explained that the identification role embassies are required to perform in the case of Voluntary Return is actually the same as that which is put in place in the case of forced returns. "When there are detainees, there is an agent of the [Senegalese] consulate who goes to the Ministry of Interior . . . and the other embassies do the same thing".[21]

During interviews, diplomats working in embassies and consulates of countries of origin did not portray their collaboration with the IOM as a burden on their everyday duties. Rather, they depicted the AVRR programme as a way to financially outsource the diplomatic assistance to their citizens in distress. The same Senegalese diplomat commented:

[. . .] we collaborate [with the IOM] without problems because this is convenient for us as well: [. . .] we do not have the means to assist them [stranded Senegalese migrants], while the IOM can participate to covering the medical expenses, sometimes even the accommodation during the period while they wait [to go back to their country] . . . *Honestly, if there was not the IOM, I do not know what the consulates of African countries would do*, especially when you have 5, 6, or 7 people every day arriving. The flight tickets for Senegal are very expensive . . . and the IOM can pay for that. [emphasis added]

This interviewee describes collaboration with the IOM as "convenient" because it allows the Senegalese embassy to externalise a number of different costs: flight tickets, accommodation, and medical expenses for Senegalese citizens that want to go back home. The financial advantage represented by the collaboration with the IOM seems to be particularly high because Morocco represents a context where mobilising

[20]   Interview with officer of the Embassy of Guinea Conakry, Rabat, June 2019.
[21]   Interview with officer of the Senegalese consulate, Casablanca, June 2019. Maâ, however, has highlighted elsewhere that the procedure of Voluntary Return is often obstructed by the unhelpful and dismissive behaviour of embassies of countries of origin (Maâ 2020a).

alternative channels of relief is particularly pricy. An Ivorian diplomat explained that:

We do not have the budget to assist them [stranded migrants] so these people, when they arrive, we send them to the IOM. Normally, if they are in need, we try to call their family, but sometimes even the family does not have the means [...] The tickets for African countries are expensive. There is just the RAM [Royal Air Maroc] [operating here], if there was Air Ivoire we would be able to negotiate ... but there is just the RAM, Air Ivoire does not operate here.[22]

The diplomats surveyed seemed to agree in considering the AVRR as a financially convenient option to outsource assistance to their fellow citizens in distress, in a context of resource scarcity. This discoursive commitment in providing assistance to members of their diaspora, however, somehow clashed with the fact that interviewees seemed to share a negative view of the kind of people that had to be assisted through Voluntary Return. The diplomat from Senegal, for example, told me that the number of Senegalese migrants who were voluntarily returned was not very significant before 2018. At the time of the interview (summer 2019), however, the consulate was seeing many more people pleading to return home voluntarily. He specified that voluntary returnees are "people who arrived here because they wanted to cross to Europe, but they did not manage to cross and now they come back towards the cities. They are tired, they are ill and everything ... and we refer them to the IOM". Later in the interview, he stated that "this population [people that apply for Voluntary Return] is very difficult". He then started listing "they do not have a job, they do not have resources, they sometimes have a lot of illnesses like tuberculosis, if they come to the consulate it is just to ask us for help". The representative from the Ivorian embassy concurred and drew a more precise line between "the people who apply for Voluntary Return" and "the students". "Because with them [people that are referred to the IOM's AVRR] it is not like with the students" he explained. "The students, all is well, but these people [those who apply for Voluntary Return] are those who tried to leave but did not manage. Because in Africa, you see, we are scared of going back home because we did not manage". Both interviewees depicted a similar image of AVRR applicants as

[22] Interview with an officer of the Embassy of Ivory Coast, Rabat, June 2019.

"problematic", essentially because they are seen (and devalued) as poor and resourceless after an unsuccessful migration project.

Beside negatively judging AVRR applicants for having financial and health troubles, interviewees also expressed disapproval because these migrants tend not to make themselves legible to the state apparatus. The diplomat from Guinea Conakry qualified candidates to Voluntary Return as "people who do not register with the embassy because they want to go directly to the North [of Morocco]". The Ivorian diplomat instead highlighted that the illegible presence of these migrants hinders the ability of consular authorities to facilitate repatriation assistance. As he put it:

These people do not register themselves [with consular authorities], they come here only when there are problems [...] there is an office of Ivorians abroad, if we had a list of people that want to return, they could make funding available ... but we do not have [a list of candidates to return]. We even asked migrant-led organisations to give us a list, to do a census of people but they did not give us any [list].

The dismissive attitude that diplomats interviewed showed vis-à-vis voluntary returnees echoes broader findings foregrounded by the literature on mobility in North Africa. Research, in fact, argues that the relationship between West and Central African migrants and their consular authorities are often quite tense. In his work on illegality in Rabat, Bachelet highlights that African embassies and consulates often behave quite obliviously vis-à-vis the needs of their citizens in Morocco, especially of those that are more exposed to violent border control practices (Bachelet 2016). Similarly, research conducted with returnees in Senegal and Mali shows that people who have been voluntarily or forcibly returned see the authorities of their countries of origin as uninterested in providing them with the necessary assistance needed to reintegrate back home (Chappart 2015; Lecadet 2016b; Rodriguez 2019).

The IOM's Voluntary Return programme can count on the collaboration of embassies of migrants' countries of origin. These consider the AVRR as a way to outsource the cost of assisting their citizens in distress abroad. The economic convenience of externalising return to the IOM seems particularly high given the negative description that the interviewees gave of AVRR applicants as a 'problematic' group, who defies state legibility, claims assistance from a situation of distress, and is qualified as unworthy – or at least, not as worthy as 'the students'.

Who Is Conducting 'Voluntary' Returns?

The Voluntary Return programme is an area of operation where the IOM seems to devote particular attention to issues of transparency. At the time of writing (December 2019), the IOM had published two quarterly reports on its website (April–June and July–September) as well as an annual report on Voluntary Return for 2018. The latter document provided figures about the number of migrants repatriated, and trends about nationality, age and gender, attempts to cross the border to Europe prior to applying for Voluntary Return, the reasons for returning, the period of time spent in Morocco, their vulnerabilities, and information about the reintegration component of the programme (International Organisation for Migration 2018). These publications supplemented the annual report that the IOM published in early 2019. This level and frequency of implementation details is not easily available for other projects: generally, the IOM only published a project leaflet, as well as a summary of the year's activity in the annual report. After the announcement of the new migration policy, in particular since 2016, the MDMCMREAM has also been particularly proactive in publishing data and statistics about the implementation of the new migration policy. In particular, the Ministry has published three reports covering the periods 2013–16, 2017, and 2018 respectively (MCMREAM 2016; MDMCMREAM 2017, 2018) which report figures about the various programmes composing the SNIA, including the Voluntary Return programme.

A closer look at this unusual abundance of details reveals that the figures shared by the IOM and the Moroccan authorities on Voluntary Return do not coincide. As the graph and table below show (see Figure 6 and Table 2), government's statistics report a significantly higher number of voluntary returns conducted from Morocco since 2004, in comparison to the figures published by the IOM.

The 2017 annual report on the implementation of the SNIA does not provide precise figures on the implementation of the programme in 2016 and 2017. However, it does specify that "1,554 voluntary returns have been facilitated [by the Ministry of Interior] between the 1st of January and the 9th of August 2017, bringing the number of voluntary returns

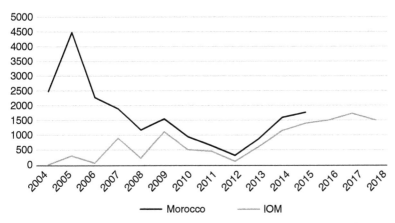

Figure 6 Number of 'Voluntary Returns' conducted by Moroccan authorities and the IOM in comparison. Source: MCMREAM 2016 and IOM 2018.

from Morocco up to 23,000 since 2014" (MDMCMREAM 2017, 98, translation by author). This last figure is quite surprising: the data shared by the IOM states that during the 2014–17 period, the number of people voluntarily returned by the agency was only 5,790 (OIM Maroc 2019). The government, in other words, declares that the number of people voluntarily returned from Morocco between 2014 and 2017 is four times higher than IOM's statistics suggest. Interestingly, the 2018 annual report on the implementation of the SNIA only quotes the statistics shared by the IOM in relation to voluntary returns, and reports that 11,175 individuals have been voluntarily returned from Morocco to their countries of origin since 2005 (MDMCMREAM 2018).

The date of inception of the programme also differs between the two sources. Whereas the IOM takes 2005 as the starting point for the agency's engagement in voluntary returns, Moroccan authorities state 2004 as the inception date for the AVRR. As the 2016 report on the implementation of the SNIA outlines, the programme was initially launched to manage the "return of irregular migrants originating from Nigeria". The episode "constituted a great experience that encouraged the IOM to get inspired from Morocco and to cooperate on this matter" (MCMREAM 2016, 85, translation by author).

Table 2 *Number of 'Voluntary Returns' conducted by Moroccan authorities and the IOM in comparison*

Year	Number of voluntary returned migrants	
	Morocco	IOM
2004	2,480	0
2005	4,485	295
2006	2,280	51
2007	1,890	892
2008	1,170	210
2009	1,550	1,119
2010	950	501
2011	640	453
2012	310	112
2013	874	597
2014	1,594	1,158
2015	1,772	1,399
2016	n/a	1,500
2017	n/a	1,733
2018	n/a	1,508

Source: MCMREAM 2016 and IOM 2018.

What are these discrepancies due to? The first and most straightforward explanation emerging from interviews is that the Moroccan government does not completely outsource Voluntary Return to the IOM. "The data from the Ministry of the Interior include the whole of the assistance to voluntary return" two IOM officers explained to me. "The returns organized by the IOM are just a percentage of this figure. There are some returns that are organized by the Ministry of Interior and the IOM is not involved"[23]. During an interview, a respondent of the MDMCMREAM was clearly uneasy talking about this point. "In the Memorandum of Understanding between the IOM and Morocco there are annual objectives" he explained to me. "However, the waiting lists [for voluntary return] are always very long, so in cases of urgency, Morocco can decide to go [to proceed with voluntary return] without the IOM"[24]. The respondent did not qualify what counted as an

[23] Interview with two officers from the IOM, Rabat, July 2019.
[24] Interview with an officer of the MDMCMREAM, Rabat, July 2019.

urgency for Moroccan authorities. The "emergency" and "humanitar- ian" argument is one that the authorities had already used to frame their sustained efforts at repatriation. In conversation with American diplomats in 2006, Khalid Zerouali, director of Migration and Border Surveillance in Morocco's Interior Ministry, stated that "the GOM [Government of Morocco] would continue to repatriate migrants pri- marily to send a message to the 'mafia' of traffickers that their activities will not be tolerated in Morocco". He then reassured his counterparts that "the repatriation procedures are always performed in accordance with international standards" (American Embassy of Rabat 2006c).

It seems clear that the Moroccan Ministry of Interior has been conducting returns qualified as 'voluntary' even without the IO. However, these returns are not clearly publicised by the authorities, nor by the IOM. In its 2016 report, the MDMCMREAM clearly points to the IOM as the body to which migrants must address themselves for voluntary return, and as the organisation which manages the entire voluntary repatriation process. The report includes a section specifying the "main activities of Moroccan authorities in the framework of assistance to voluntary return and durable reintegration". The list of activities suggests that Morocco plays only a support role in the AVRR programme run by the IOM, not that the authorities are directly involved as initiators and managers of voluntary returns (MCMREAM 2016, 87–88).

The voluntary nature of the returns conducted by the Moroccan authorities is a source of debate. In August 2018, Spain summarily sent back to Morocco 116 undocumented people who had irregularly crossed the border to Ceuta. In a report published in the summer 2018, the NGO GADEM argued that, once deported to Morocco, 43 of these people had been sent back to Cameroon and Guinea, their respective origin countries. These returns, however, seemed to have been classi- fied as "voluntary returns", rather than as a "deportations". Quoting a "reliable source", the NGO reports that "consular authorities present would have pressured the people into signing a document mentioning their will to return to their origin country." This procedure would facilitate and expedite voluntary returns, because "the existence of such a document would allow them to justify the voluntary return and proceed to expulsion without having to present them [the candi- dates to deportation] in front of a judge because they would have 'given their written consent'".

These circumstances suggest that the label of "voluntary return" is used in Morocco to clear and expedite the number of deportations conducted by the authorities, without ensuring the respect of the will of the returnee. As GADEM highlighted, "it is difficult to conceive of a real consent for people detained by security forces and for whom the consent has been extracted by consular authorities" (GADEM 2018a, 44, translation by author). The concern that the voluntary returns conducted by the Moroccan authorities might not really be "voluntary" was evoked by two respondents whom I jointly interviewed in June 2019. They explained to me that "Morocco has been doing voluntary returns for years, with or without the IOM . . .. Because with the IOM you need to follow certain standards, without the IOM they are [voluntary returns] *à la marocaine* [Moroccan-style]" they said, raising their hands towards their chest, as to indicate their scepticism vis-à-vis the conditions of implementation of such returns. At the end of the interview, both interviewees explicitly asked to be completely deidentified.[25]

The differences between the figures communicated by the IOM and Moroccan authorities in relation to Voluntary Returns, the unclear communication policy carried out by Rabat on the topic, and the anecdotes about the questionable "voluntariness" of returns, suggest that the IOM does not actually hold the monopoly over "voluntary" returns in Morocco. If this is the case, the label and publicity surrounding the IOM-run AVRR programme might be displacing attention away from state-run "voluntary" returns, which have therefore not undergone public scrutiny despite the existence of disturbing rumours surrounding them.

Conclusion

The Voluntary Return programme is emblematic of the complex power geometries characterising the workings of aid as an instrument of border control. AVRR is usually depicted as a quintessential European border externalisation tool. However, a closer analysis warrants the need to de-essentialise claims about the capacity of countries in the Global North to 'buy' the cooperation of their Southern neighbours through the promise of aid.

The implementation of the AVRR, in fact, relies on the active support of multiple actors, whose interests lie in completely different ends

---

[25] Interview with two deidentified individuals, Rabat, June 2019.

of the border control spectrum. The programme, however, is not explicitly imposed on African state partners by the IOM or European donors. Both Moroccan authorities and embassies of countries of origin cooperate with the IOM because they see the AVRR as a way to externalise the political and financial costs of dealing with a population deemed 'problematic' – for Morocco, 'irregular migrants'; for embassies of countries of origin, 'class B diaspora'. Morocco, over the years, has also sophisticated its way of strategising Voluntary Return for domestic interest. On the one hand, it has embraced AVRR as an alternative instrument to manage the number of irregular migrants in the country. On the other hand, the commitment to the running the AVRR has earned Moroccan authorities further esteem among the international community. Countries of 'origin' and 'transit' thus do not really seem to see the aid channelled by Northern donors through the AVRR programme as a sort of economic incentive for their cooperation into border control. Rather, they seem to conceptualise it merely as a way to level off the enormous social and economic costs that migration surveillance entails.

Migrants themselves, with their numerical and physical presence, also become a driving force in furthering and institutionalising the AVRR. Showcasing their 'interest' and 'vulnerability' by the IOM moves market and humanitarian arguments that have historically, although not consistently, contributed to the IOM's capacity to reproduce the AVRR. Voluntary Return thus works and expands its reach through migrants' participation to the programme, and by leveraging their demonstrations of dissent to advocate for more funding from donors.

7 | *The Left Hand of the Border*

In January 2016, Father Esteban Velazquez crossed the border between Morocco and Melilla. A Jesuit priest, Padre Esteban, as he was known to many, had been living and working for three years in Nador, where he had been coordinating a humanitarian project implemented by a Catholic organisation and funded by Switzerland. Along with a team of eight collaborators, Padre Esteban provided migrant people with emergency medical assistance, food parcels, clothes, and other small hygiene and shelter resources – forms of basic support that migrants relied on to survive the difficult living conditions in the forest camps. Padre Esteban complemented his humanitarian work by vocally criticising the violence unleashed by Moroccan and Spanish authorities against migrants in the borderlands. In an interview he granted to the Spanish newspaper *Publico*, he declared that his team "had seen everything", including "mandible fractures, smashed heads, lost eyes and also deaths" (*Público* 2016).

The Spanish press reported that Padre Esteban was under the constant impression that someone was watching him, following him, listening to his conversations. For three years, however, he managed to juggle his advocacy and humanitarian work, continuing to provide emergency care for migrant people brutalised at the border. But when he attempted to return to Nador in January 2016, Moroccan policemen stopped him at the border post in Beni Ensar. Claiming that his residency permit was no longer valid, they prevented him from re-entering the country. While Moroccan authorities did not publicly announce the reasons for this entry ban, the local Moroccan press reported that Padre Esteban was suspected of Christian proselytism. However, there is common agreement among aid workers and human rights activists that Padre Esteban was prevented from returning because of his outspoken advocacy. "Maybe he said something that bothered someone", an anonymous source suggested in an interview to the Spanish newspaper *Eldiario* (Eldiario.es 2016).

Since the early 2000s, humanitarian organisations have been providing emergency assistance to migrants stranded in the Moroccan borderlands, in particular in the area of Oujda and Nador, and, to a lesser extent, in the forests surrounding the Spanish enclave of Ceuta and in the city of Tangier. For twenty years, the violence unleashed by police forces and border infrastructure has forced migrant people into unbearable living conditions, which humanitarian organisations manage to relieve only marginally. But even this marginal relief is difficult to implement in the borderlands. The repression experienced by Padre Esteban is symptomatic of the inconvenient position occupied by humanitarians at the border. The closer to the fences, the more emergency work has to be conducted under the watchful eyes of Moroccan authorities. State surveillance monitors and obstructs humanitarian activities to prevent humanitarians from speaking out about violence against migrants. For three years, Padre Esteban infringed the unwritten rule regulating humanitarian presence in the borderlands: "if you stay, you shut up" (IRIDIA et al. 2017, 65).

This chapter investigates the uneasy place that aid-funded humanitarian projects inhabit in the governance of the frontier. In the areas surrounding the Spanish enclaves of Ceuta and Melilla, sovereign authorities deploy a violence against people racialised as 'sub-Saharan migrants' that has no equal in the rest of the country. Migrant life in the borderlands is thus subjected to power in its most explicit deductive form – a power that actively inflicts pain, coerces bodies, kills, *and* lets die. The ferocity of border containment changes the way NGOs and IOs operate. Rather than focusing on implementing integration projects, humanitarian organisations working at the border limit themselves to a form of limited assistance, that could be qualified as "minimal biopolitics" (Redfield 2013, 21). Minimal biopolitics does not aim at revolutionising the status quo by spurring people's life and potential. Rather, it aims at mitigating death in a punctual, temporary way, that does not at all challenge the structural degradation of migrant existence at the border (Williams 2015).

The elusiveness of border containment power plays out through the minimality of aid-funded assistance: aid reduces the chances of death without necessarily fostering the possibilities of migrants' life. Border containment power is not necropolitical or spectacular. It is minimal: it assists migrants at the margins, without moving them away from the margins (Williams 2015). In the Moroccan borderlands, much of that minimality depends on the fact that the very presence of humanitarians in the borderlands lies, somehow, suspended: aid sustains a *threatened* apparatus of minimal biopolitics, whose presence is constantly at risk of expulsion. In this chapter, however, I will show that humanitarians react differently to the threat of sovereign authorities. Some decide to speak out. Others, instead, decide to stay silent. Aid, I will show, tends to support a threatened and silent apparatus of minimal biopolitics that operates with discretion, and which privileges presence on the ground over denouncing state-sanctioned abuses against migrants.

Discussing the workings of aid-funded humanitarian projects is not possible without exploring the broader history of humanitarian borderwork in the Moroccan North-East. First, donors' appearance in the borderlands only dates back to the late 2000s. Until that point humanitarian provision in the area was mostly covered by MSF and by Moroccan grassroots organisations. Second, aid-funded NGOs and IOs capitalised on the work of MSF, which supported other organisations in visiting and establishing a presence in the borderlands. To the best of my knowledge, MSF did not receive direct funding from European state donors during the operation of its humanitarian projects in the borderlands, although it did collaborate and interact with aid-funded organisations. Throughout the chapter, I regularly alternate references to the work of MSF and data related to the work of aid-funded NGOs and IOs to highlight the continuities and interruptions characterising the shift between humanitarian work conducted by activist organisations and aid-funded actors.

The five sections of this chapter dissect this minimal biopolitical system by analysing its conditions of existence, rules of functioning, and points of fracture. The first section explores the conditions within which humanitarian work exists by tracking patterns of violence against migrants at the Spanish–Moroccan border. The second and third sections explore the rules which guide the functioning of border humanitarianism. Building on the work of Michel Agier, the second section uncovers the symbiosis between humanitarians and border violence. It explores how humanitarians alleviate a form of suffering that is produced, sustained, and regularly reproduced by the border itself. The third section continues this reflection by focusing on the coexistence of humanitarians and the state in the borderlands. The fourth and fifth sections investigate the points of rupture of minimal biopolitics. I do this by exploring the factors that undermine the precarious existence of the humanitarian system. The fourth section focuses on the challenging relation between humanitarianism and border crisis. Prolonged crisis constantly triggers the need for humanitarian action, while also exposing humanitarian incapacity to implement transformative change. The last section unravels the tension between humanitarian presence and duty to bear witness. It explores how pervasive policing and authoritarian repression oblige humanitarians to choose between operating transformative action and maintaining access to the field.

Violence as Migration Control

Humanitarians operate in a border environment characterised by pervasive violence. At the Spanish–Moroccan border (see Map 2), like in other critical crossing points in the world, the endangerment of life is a structural component of migration containment (see Slack et al. 2016 for an example of the US–Mexico border). The tightening of European borders has progressively transformed the borderlands into a space governed through practices which are in open violation of national and international law. In a report compiled in 2013, MSF argued that in 2012 alone its staff assisted 600 people who had been injured at the border between the Moroccan city of Nador and the Spanish enclave of Melilla. MSF patients had either been directly injured by Spanish and Moroccan border guards or were victims of "indirect violence, generally sustained as sub-Saharan migrants ran and fell trying to escape arrest during raids or fell or cut themselves on the barbed wire covering the multiple fences separating Nador and Melilla" (MSF 2013c, 15). The number of victims of border violence is however likely to be much higher. Data provided by humanitarian and human right groups, in fact, only shed light on the number of people *who sought assistance*, not on the number of people *actually injured* (MSF 2013b).

After the announcement of the new migration policy in 2013, police discontinued the generalised harassment of migrants and refugees in most areas of the country – at least until the summer of 2018. In the borderlands, however, time appears to have stood still. In particular, in the cities and forests surrounding the Spanish enclave of Melilla, police forces still carry out a policy of institutionalised deterrence of the migrant presence (AMDH Nador 2019). Mass arrests and practices of "infrastructural warfare" (Graham 2002) currently conducted by Moroccan authorities

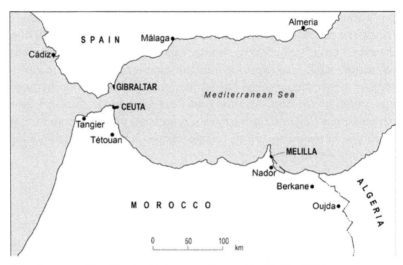

Map 2 Map of the North of Morocco. Created by Philip Stickler.

do not differ from the abuses characterising the period preceding the announcement of the new migration policy. Arbitrary arrests of migrants venturing into the city further restrict migrants' freedom of movement. This politics of institutional harassment, generally circumscribed to the area of Nador, sometimes extends to the city of Tangier (Lemaizi 2018). As an aid worker told me in an interview, "it is like if they [Moroccan authorities] were saying 'you can't stay here, go somewhere else because we know that if you come here, it's because you want to cross [to Spain]'".[1]

Drawing on its work with migrant communities, the NGO Caminando Fronteras estimated that between September 2015 and December 2016 at least "2,213 people were victims of forced displacement, 569 were victims of *devoluciones en caliente* (summary deportations), 739 were injured due to the violence exercised by [Spanish and Moroccan] security forces, and 6 people lost their life" at the Ceuta and Melilla borders (Caminando Fronteras 2017, 39, translation by author). The borderlands have therefore become a space of exception not only to the rule of law, but to the tolerance towards migrants that (at least between 2013 and 2018) seemed to have become the norm in the rest of the country.

[1] Interview, two NGO officers, Rabat, September 2016.

In the borderlands, migrants are stripped of all rights, their life becomes expendable, their abusers go unpunished (Agamben 1998). Such lethality is not only perpetrated through destruction, but through a purposeful abandonment of migrant people to dangerous environments, where racialised life is exposed to "an unconditional capacity to be killed" (Vaughan-Williams 2015, 65). The drive for migration control and the Euro–Moroccan cooperation on the matter has therefore normalised ultra-violence as a mode of power, which transforms the borderlands into no-go areas for black people on the move.

Humanitarianism and Border Violence

Humanitarianism works in symbiotic relation to border violence. Migration control creates the conditions that allow the emergence of humanitarian missions and defines the margins of everyday humanitarian action. The normalisation of migrants' precariousness at the frontier has led to the rise of a "humanitarian border", a complex system of discourses and practices that govern the frontier by "compensating for the social violence embodied in the regime of migration control" (Walters 2010, 139).

The rise of the humanitarian border in Morocco dates back to the early 2000s. MSF started its first migration project in Tangier in 2003, and worked with the population of migrants living in the medina of the city and in the forests surrounding the Spanish enclave of Ceuta (MSF 2005). In 2004, the NGO expanded its activities to the Moroccan region of the Oriental, in the areas of Oujda, Berkane, and Nador, and in 2007 also to the large coastal cities of Rabat and Casablanca (MSF 2010, 2013a). Over the years, multiple humanitarian actors have first worked alongside and then substituted MSF in the assistance of migrants stranded in the North-Eastern borderlands, including Moroccan NGOs, international and faith-based organisations, and the IOM. After MSF decided to leave the country in 2013, its project was taken over by an international medical NGO and by a Catholic organisation – the latter coordinated by aforementioned Padre Esteban in Nador between 2013 and 2016 (Servicio Jesuita a Migrantes España n.d.). The project was coordinated by the IOM and funded by Switzerland (OIM Maroc 2014). After 2015, the two charities continued the project without the involvement of the

IOM.[2] The IOM, however, continued operating in the area in partnership with other Moroccan NGOs (see OIM Morocco 2017). From
the late 2000s until 2019, Switzerland was by far the most engaged
donor in funding humanitarian assistance to migrants stranded at the
borderlands, with other actors (such as the EU, the Spanish
Decentralised Cooperation, Finland, USAID, and Denmark) having
had a much more dispersed and volatile presence.

Border violence creates the conditions which activate the need for
humanitarians' minimal biopolitics. Humanitarianism has historically
had a symbiotic relationship with the causes of suffering that emergency workers attempt to alleviate (Redfield 2013). Agier qualifies
humanitarianism as "the left hand of the empire": humanitarians, in
fact, operate in symbiosis with warfare to reinforce imperialist hegemony over other parts of the world (Agier 2003). As in most other
emergency settings, humanitarian organisations in the Moroccan borderlands operate as a left hand of the border. They engage in a sinister
symbiosis with the migration control apparatus by treating victims of
both slow and fast violence (see Nixon 2011; Povinelli 2011). In
reports compiled by MSF, the organisation argued that an extremely
high share of the migrants that it treated were victims of police assault
or had been injured trying to jump over the fences put in place to
protect European borders. The first report compiled by MSF in 2005
argues that "23.5% of the people treated in Tangier, Nador and Oujda,
medinas, outskirts (such as Mesnana) and forests (Bel Younech, near
Ceuta, and Gourougou, near Melilla), were direct or indirect victims of
violent acts". The report then specified that two-thirds of the victims of
violence that the MSF team was treating had been attacked by either
Spanish or Moroccan border guards:

Many of the sub-Saharan immigrants who come to our medical teams for
treatment for these injuries state that their assailants were institutional or
governmental officials from Morocco and Spain. Our patients say that they
have been victims of an excessive use of force in addition to humiliating and
cruel treatment whilst being detained or chased by certain members of the
Moroccan security forces (SF) and the Spanish security forces in Ceuta and
Melilla. [...] The distribution of violent acts committed against ISSs
[Irregular sub-Saharans] is somewhat uneven with the security forces of

both countries accounting for over 65% of cases, whilst criminal groups and human trafficking networks represent almost 30%. (MSF 2005, 7–8)

In a report published in 2010, the organisation highlighted that one-third of the women interviewed had been victims of sexual violence in Morocco, especially at the Algerian–Moroccan border (MSF 2010). Another publication released by the organisation in 2013 argued that "precarious life conditions" and "criminal and institutional violence" were the main causes of the medical cases that MSF staff were treating (MSF 2013c, 3). To date, not much has changed. As an aid worker put it poignantly during an interview in 2016:

He [an officer of the EU Delegation in Rabat] asked about the main problems that migrants have in Nador. I told him that already if they [the Spanish and Moroccan police] stopped beating them [the migrants], it would be already a lot. [...] but it is not just the police, it is the fence that kills them [...]. The fence is composed of three lines of barbed wire, which has been declared illegal by Europe, so what did they do? They put it on the Moroccan side of the border. This barbed wire cuts deeply into the skin, and it is produced in Malaga ....[3]

The symbiotic relation that humanitarians entertain with border violence also conditions the kind of support that emergency workers can provide to stranded migrants. Humanitarians, in fact, have to adapt project activities and working logistics to the undignified conditions and constant state of alert in which migrants have to live. Prevented from moving freely around Nador, migrants are forced to hide in the forests surrounding the city – wooded areas where living conditions are extremely precarious, especially in winter. All the activities planned and implemented by humanitarian organisations are conceived to allow migrants to better cope with these undignified conditions, to allow life to be "minimally managed under the persistent shadow of possible death" (Williams 2015, 18). The content of the humanitarian kits distributed by humanitarian organisations were meant to facilitate their survival in the forests surrounding Nador: tarpaulins to build shelters, hats and gloves to cope with cold winter weather (MSF 2013c), and jackets and blankets to migrants living in the forest camps.[4] The content of the kits was also modified to allow migrants to better cope with the

---

[3] Interview, humanitarian worker, Nador, November 2016.
[4] Interview, two NGO officers, Rabat, September 2016; Interview, humanitarian worker, Nador, November 2016; Interview, officer of a faith-based organisation,

violent policing methods adopted by Moroccan authorities. This emerges very clearly in this interview with a former humanitarian officer, who explained that his organisation decided to start distributing winter jackets rather than just blankets for pragmatic reasons:

At the beginning, we would just distribute blankets. But at every raid in the forest the police would burn down migrants' shelters, including the blankets. [...] So, we started distributing jackets as well. When they [the migrants] ran away from the police, at least they could run away with the jacket. [interview, former humanitarian officer, WhatsApp, October 2017]

Throughout the past fifteen years, migrants have consistently needed NGO assistance to physically visit healthcare facilities in border areas.[5] The harsh conditions and the constant state of anxiety endured by migrants in the forest provoke mental health problems that NGO psychologists barely manage to address. The psychological impact of border violence is so extreme that it can make migrants ineligible even for the most ambiguous form of care available to them in Morocco: voluntary return. As a humanitarian worker told me in 2017:

The more they [migrants] live in the forest, the more psychological problems they have, because they constantly live in a state of alert and at some point they completely crash .... We have the case of a woman that became completely schizophrenic, but we cannot give her accommodation for very long term, and she cannot stay in the forest ... I came to talk with the IOM to see if she could at least benefit from voluntary return, so to stay with her family rather than going to a psychiatric hospital here [in Morocco] ... but they said she will probably be declared unfit to travel, if she has this sort of severe psychological problems.[6]

The risk of arbitrary arrest and limited freedom of circulation experienced by migrants in Nador shapes how humanitarian organisations deliver assistance to migrants and refugees. To minimise the risk of arrests, humanitarian organisations do not expect migrants to go to their offices to claim assistance, but rather carry out the distribution of non-food items and medical checks directly in the forests (Tyszler 2019). In the case of a medical emergency, humanitarians reach

Tangier, August 2017; Interview, IOM officer, Rabat, September 2017; Interview, IOM officer, Rabat, September 2017.
[5] Interview, humanitarian worker, Nador, November 2016.
[6] Interview, humanitarian worker, Rabat, September 2017.

migrants in their refuges, conduct a triage, and attempt to treat the patient in place where possible. In the case of deliveries, intractable conditions, or the necessity to see a physician, the social workers would transport migrant people to the hospital and follow up on their admittance and treatment.[7]

In sum, border violence structures the conditions of existence and functioning of humanitarianism. Systematic abuse against migrants triggers the need for emergency relief, while also limiting humanitarian intervention to a form of minimal biopolitics that supports life in the interstices of border violence. The next section will unravel the symbiotic relation that humanitarians entertain with one particular source of border violence: the state.

Encountering the State(s) at the Border

The Moroccan state constitutes a significant actor in the creation of the conditions that lead to the emergence of the humanitarian border. Contrary to what one might expect, humanitarians engage with two different facets of the state at the border: a state that heals, as represented by the healthcare workers who cooperate with humanitarians to heal border violence; and a state that strikes, as portrayed by the police forces that endanger migrant lives and determine the conditions under which humanitarians can operate at the border. These two facets of the state lie on two opposite extremes of the biopolitical spectrum: the state is an entity that exposes migrants to lethal conditions, while at the same time rescuing them from death (Jusionyte 2017, 2018; Williams 2015, 2016).

The healthcare system forms part of a state that heals. Indeed, relief workers routinely engage with Moroccan public healthcare structures with which they have a collaborative relationship. Migrants have and still do struggle to access and be admitted to medical facilities without the help of an NGO, especially given the limited freedom of movement that they face in the city. However, hospitals generally accept migrants when they are accompanied by an NGO representative and, as MSF reported in 2013, over the years migrants have become more confident in autonomously seeking medical help (MSF 2013c). "This is because civil society has worked a lot there in the past decade" one NGO officer

---

[7] Interview, former humanitarian officer, WhatsApp, October 2017.

explained to me. "Now the medical staff is used to staying with the migrants."[8]

Humanitarians, aid workers and state physicians have all placed the protection of life at the heart of their mandate (Roborgh 2018). The treatment of foreign patients suffering from injuries caused by border control is therefore jointly conducted by humanitarians and local physicians. Humanitarians initiated and continue this collaboration for both strategic and practical purposes. According to MSF, supporting a parallel healthcare system would undermine the sustainability of medical assistance to migrants. It would also risk discriminating between foreign and Moroccan patients – as vulnerable foreigners would have more chances to access free medical assistance than poor Moroccans (MSF 2013c). Indeed, enhancing the capacity of public medical facilities was chosen and perpetuated after the end of the MSF mission as a more durable solution to tackle migrant vulnerability in the borderlands. Furthermore, directly providing medical treatment to migrants requires financial resources, logistical and medical skills that not all humanitarian organisations have.[9]

Moroccan medical facilities have not only been contributing to humanitarian work by showing an accommodating stance towards the work of humanitarians. At times, medics have openly challenged the repressive attitude of the state towards the presence of migrants in order to allow patients to access treatment. As a former humanitarian worker recalled:

One day I received a call from a Ghanaian guy who needed medical assistance. The guy had a broken leg and I told him that he needed to be transported to the hospital. The patient firmly refused. He feared that if he had gone to the hospital, the police would have arrested him and deported him at the border with Algeria. I went to the hospital of Nador and discussed the question with the medical staff. One of the physicians formulated an abstract hypothesis. "Well, the guy can come here, and we can get him in a cast. Then, if after we have done it, he goes out of the hospital without us realising it and by chance you pass with your car in front of the hospital in that very moment . . .."[10]

Beside encountering a state that heals, humanitarians at the border also have to navigate a complex coexistence with a state that strikes, to

---

[8] Interview, two NGO officers, Rabat, September 2016.
[9] Interview, officer of a faith-based organisation, Tangier, September 2017.
[10] Interview, former humanitarian officer, WhatsApp, October 2017.

borrow the words of Michel Agier (Agier 2003). Humanitarians and Moroccan police forces have very different stakes vis-à-vis migrant presence in the borderlands – the former providing emergency protection and the latter containing it through endangerment. The relations between these two actors, however, is more distinctively characterised by the sovereign capacity of the state to decide whether humanitarians can stay in the field and access their patients. In most liminal settings, humanitarians do not have the capacity to freely operate in the field. Their capacity to stay and access their beneficiaries is directly dependent on the tolerance of the various sovereign bodies regulating the area, entities that humanitarians often do not have many means to oppose (Magone et al. 2012). The Moroccan borderlands are no exception to this rule. As in many other humanitarian sites, the presence of humanitarians in a space so violently regulated by Moroccan police forces builds on a fragile equilibrium composed of explicit and implicit rules, margins of permissibility, and boundaries to be respected. This zone of indistinctiveness obliges humanitarians to resort to tactics which ensure their discretion. A former humanitarian officer recalled that his team had to enter the forest surrounding Nador around 7.30 a.m. and leave around 10 a.m. to conduct distributions of non-food items and medical visits. Arriving early was essential to avoid the Moroccan police, which would station in front of the entrance to the forest every morning from 8.30 until the evening. "Nobody told us we could visit migrants in the forest, but they saw us going out [of the forest] every day and didn't say anything" my respondent argued. "They tolerated our work. There was a sort of non-aggression pact."[11]

Despite the policy of institutionalised harassment against migrants, the authorities appear to tolerate the assistance provided by humanitarians to vulnerable foreigners. State authorities do not, however, necessarily provide a formal acknowledgement of humanitarians' right to work in the borderlands. In 2011, local authorities suddenly prevented MSF from working in Nador (MSF 2013b). For an entire year, the organisation engaged in negotiations with local authorities to be allowed to resume their activities. After a year of constant negotiations, MSF acknowledged the uselessness of this approach. As a former officer of MSF Morocco said, at some point the team "realised that nobody would ever take the responsibility to sign a document

---

[11] Interview, former humanitarian officer, WhatsApp, October 2017.

saying that we were allowed to go into the forests. So, we just decided to inform the authorities by letter and go, without waiting for their permission".[12] The absence of written permission becomes a tool through which humanitarian activities are kept in a space of uncertainty – not authorised, not prevented, but always preventable. As aforementioned Padre Esteban declared in an interview to the Servicio Jesuita a Migrantes before being banned from Morocco:

> The second thing that I would ask for is a written authorisation for the work that we conduct. There are verbal permissions that constitute a legal limbo, especially when the policeman on duty asks for a paper that we do not have, no? Sometimes, for effectiveness, it is better to keep on being in this limbo that does not imply the clash of two opposite opinions. I do not know, but the best thing would be to have written permission for work that has nothing to hide. (Servicio Jesuita a Migrantes España n.d., 31, translation by author)

In the case of IOs, the state more directly monitors their operations by limiting their capacity to open offices in the borderlands[13] (see Collyer 2012). The UNHCR, for example, has never been able to have a formal presence in the borderlands due to its legal mandate of international protection. So far, the agency has only managed to establish a partnership and referral mechanism with the Moroccan Organisation for Human Rights in Oujda. The latter was chosen as an operational partner for its historical proximity to the government as an attempt to reduce tensions with Moroccan authorities.[14] At the time of my field-work, the IOM focal point in Oujda represented the only formal presence of IOs in the area. However, this form of institutional presence is very low-key: as Richard, the IOM officer I mentioned in previous chapters, stressed during an interview, "this is not an office, it is a focal point."[15]

Moroccan authorities control humanitarian activities not only by denying written permissions, but also by surveilling organisations operating at the border (IRIDIA et al. 2017). During an interview, a former officer of MSF Morocco told me that during their mobile

---

[12] Interview, former officer of MSF Morocco, Skype, February 2017.

[13] Interview, officer of the Swiss Development Cooperation, Skype, September 2017; Interview, former officer of the IOM Morocco, Skype, October 2017; Interview, former officer of the UNHCR Morocco, Skype, October 2017.

[14] Interview, former officer of the IOM Morocco, Skype, October 2017; Interview, former officer of the UNHCR Morocco, Skype, October 2017.

[15] Interview with Richard, IOM officer, Rabat, August 2016.

medical clinics in the woods of Nador in 2011/2012, they could see and hear Moroccan military helicopters flying over the forests to watch over their work. A 2017 report by Iridia, Novact,[16] and Fotomovimiento on the Southern European border dedicates a section to the "Repression of the defence of human rights" on the Moroccan side of the fence. The authors of the report stress that many of their interviewees had asked for their identity to be kept anonymous "for fear of retaliation" (IRIDIA et al. 2017, 66, translation by author). As one of the respondents interviewed in the report put it:

In Morocco there is constantly a lot of police and a lot of people watching you: the gorilla,[17] the one living opposite you, the one at the bar, the one that is drinking a coffee. Everything is very ambiguous, nobody tells you what you can or what you can't do. You get signs or warnings, and you must learn to interpret them if you want to keep on working. Otherwise, you leave. And if you stay, you shut up. (IRIDIA et al. 2017, 65, translation by author)

These tactics of surveillance do not only target foreign-funded organisations, but also local organisations funded by Moroccan authorities. In the winter of 2017, the Moroccan NGO Manos Solidarias organised a medical caravan in the forest of Bel Younech, close to the Spanish enclave of Ceuta. Funded by the MDMCMREAM, the caravan was the third event of this kind organised by the NGO and aimed to provide humanitarian assistance to migrant people living in precarious conditions in the forests in Northern Morocco. Once the distribution was underway in Bel Younech, however, Moroccan police forces showed up and barred the NGO from continuing to provide assistance to migrants. This was particularly bizarre: the NGO officers, in fact, had submitted authorisation requests for the medical caravan to the local authorities of the nearby cities of Tétouan and Fnideq. Both requests, however, had gone incommunicado (Bentaleb 2017). What happened to Manos Solidarias, it must be said, contains a paradox: contrary to most humanitarian activities conducted in the borderlands, the medical caravan barred by Moroccan police forces had been funded by the Moroccan Ministry of Foreign Affairs. The state that was

---

[16] In June 2016 NOVACT closed its Moroccan branch after a year of very tense relations with Moroccan authorities. In 2015 Morocco expelled a NOVACT representative and prevented entry to another in 2016 (Gonzales 2016).
[17] In the original Spanish text.

preventing humanitarians from helping migrants was the same state that had funded that same assistance activity.

   Placed at the two ends of a biopolitical spectrum, the security and the medical branches of the state apparatus have very different relationships with humanitarians. State healthcare structures and humanitarians combine their efforts to form a broader left hand of the border. State security, conversely, not only creates the conditions requiring the intervention of humanitarians, it also polices the very presence of emergency workers in the borderlands, putting migrants' life at risk not only through direct violence, but also through the obstruction of emergency rescue.

Never-Ending Crisis and Humanitarian Purpose

Minimal biopolitics is a system of power built on an extremely fragile balance of forces and circumstances. Humanitarianism is punctuated by potential fracture points which constantly challenge the meaning, appropriateness, and duration of emergency action. 'Crisis' is one such potential point of fracture. Humanitarianism, in fact, has a deep and challenging relationship with the 'exceptional'. Although suffering can be found in multiple and variegated sites (Fassin 2011a; Ticktin 2006, 2011) the life upon which most humanitarian organisations focus "is not an ordinary one, in the sense of being burdened by everyday complaints", but is "the life located in an exceptional state of risk" (Redfield 2013, 33). However, in contexts characterised by severe conditions of precariousness, inequality, and injustice, the boundary between 'crisis' and 'normalcy' becomes blurred. The violence and precariousness produced by the border generate a critical albeit local need for emergency relief, which would be otherwise unthinkable (Pallister-Wilkins 2016).

   The relation between border humanitarianism and the exception is particularly evident in Morocco, which is an unusual setting for humanitarians. The Kingdom does not present any of the characteristics that normally justify the deployment of humanitarian relief (war, natural disaster, etc.). And yet, there are humanitarians. While recalling the beginning of IOM's work in the borderlands in 2012, a former employee of the IOM Morocco said: "Morocco is not really the country where you can do humanitarian work. However, the cases of victims of border violence that we were receiving [for Voluntary

Return] were too alarming, and we decided to dig into it."[18] The exceptional character of border violence transforms the borderlands into the only areas where humanitarian projects assisting migrants in Morocco are to be found. Trying to implement such a programme away from the border deprives humanitarians of the circumstances justifying their intervention: crisis. In 2007, MSF tried to replicate the humanitarian project implemented at the border in Rabat and Casablanca (MSF España 2007). Shortly after its inception, NGO staff realised that their emergency project was unnecessary in urban settings. Migrants in Rabat and Casablanca were not exposed to such high levels of violence and precariousness as in Oujda or Nador, which made a humanitarian approach useless and discriminatory towards the Moroccan population. Confronted with the redundancy of humanitarianism, MSF decided to shift the project to a development-like initiative aimed at ensuring migrants' access to healthcare by strengthening the capacity of Moroccan public authorities.[19]

And yet, the existence of a border is not sufficient to justify humanitarian intervention. Borders need to be characterised by an acute state of tension. As I mentioned earlier, in 2003 MSF set up a project in Tangier to assist the substantial migrant population living in precarious conditions in the historical centre and in the outskirts of the city. At that time, the city constituted one of the main points of departure of migrant boats heading to Spain. In the following years, the reinforcement of migration control in the Strait of Gibraltar reoriented migration routes towards the Canary Islands (Vives 2017a, 2017b). This determined a decrease in the number of attempts at crossing (Migreurop 2006) and of the precarious migrant population living in Tangier. Within this framework, MSF estimated that its work was no longer needed and decided to end the project in 2006. The reduction of border pressure had made humanitarian efforts redundant.[20]

The ordinary violence that characterises certain sections of the border generates a never-ending need for humanitarian relief. Prolonged

[18] Interview, former officer of the IOM Morocco, Skype, October 2017.
[19] Interview, former humanitarian officer, WhatsApp, October 2017. The decision to stay despite the absence of a clear-cut emergency can push humanitarian organisations to stretch their mandate towards development-like activities (Redfield 2013), such as promoting the resilience of beneficiaries (Feldman 2015) or elevating testimony as the main activity justifying their presence (Fassin 2008).
[20] Interview with former humanitarian officer, WhatsApp, October 2017.

emergencies, however, also challenge the very meaning of humanitarian operations (Barnett and Weiss 2008; Feldman 2015; Redfield 2013). Over the past fifteen years, humanitarians based in Moroccan borderlands have had to question more than once the meaning and validity of their interventions as the causes of suffering lay beyond their response capacity. The last report published by MSF poignantly exposed the difficulty for the organisation to operate transformative change in the field:

Although the medical and psychological needs of victims of human trafficking networks are extremely acute, the absence of other organisations providing assistance and, crucially, protection services, limits the impact of MSF's assistance.

"It's extremely frustrating, we provide medical and psychological assistance to victims of trafficking, but *we know that as soon as they leave the consultation room they face the same, horrific levels of violence and abuse that brought them to us in the first place*". MSF Medical Coordinator (MSF 2013c, 23)

The report issued by MSF conveys a certain humanitarian fatigue for minimal biopolitics. The medical coordinator interviewed as part of the report expressed frustration at recognising that the emergency intervention was only keeping abuse at bay. Frustration with minimal biopolitics can lead humanitarians to leave. After much discussion, in 2012 the perceived absence of purpose pushed MSF to announce the withdrawal of the Moroccan mission. In an interview with *Jeune Afrique*, the then head of the MSF mission in Morocco stated that the NGO had recognised that its engagement was "unsuitable for the situation in the field":

[The fact that we are closing the mission in Morocco] can seem contradictory. But we remarked that the work that is needed here is not the one of a medical NGO. We are not an organisation for the defence of human rights, even if we can denounce violations. (Jeune Afrique 2013)

The protracted temporality of border emergency does not only produce ethical challenges for NGOs but is also incompatible with donor funding policies. In 2015, the AECID rejected a proposal for an eighteen-month project on "Improved healthcare attention to the sub-Saharan population in Nador" presented by a Spanish faith-based organisation. According to the AECID evaluation form, the main official reason for the rejection appeared to be the lack of sustainability of the project. The evaluation committee questioned the fact that the project would substitute the action of the state. The proponent organisation, the report continued, had not clearly indicated how activities would be handed over to the Moroccan authorities after the end of the funding, nor how the provision of healthcare to migrants would be maintained afterwards (Cooperación Española 2015). A similar reason motivated a change in funding policy pursued by Swiss Development Cooperation in 2017. In September of that year, the donor announced its decision to stop funding humanitarian projects in Morocco.[21] As an officer of the Swiss Development Cooperation told me in an interview, until then Switzerland had funded projects in migration and protection in Morocco through the humanitarian aid line. However, the geographical priorities in the distribution of Swiss humanitarian aid had changed. As Morocco had adopted a new migration policy centred on migrant integration, Switzerland felt that it was no longer appropriate to work on migration issues with a humanitarian approach. "Morocco now has a migration policy, and the state considers itself responsible of its resources" my respondent told me. "By continuing to work in the same way we are feeding a system which supports a logic of substitution."[22] Whereas MSF voiced its frustration with minimal biopolitics in a more political way, donors tend to distance themselves from it through bureaucratic vocabulary, highlighting the "inappropriateness" and "incompatibility" of emergency action with the broader policies carried out in the country.

Frustration with minimal biopolitics is not a feeling shared by all actors operating in the borderlands. The ordinary character of a border crisis certainly pushes certain humanitarian actors out of the field. However, it also creates opportunities for groups of new, heterogeneous actors willing to engage in relief assistance. In 2010, MSF supported a Moroccan NGO funded by the Swiss Development Cooperation to set up a shelter for migrant women and their children in Oujda.[23] Between 2011 and 2012, when police violence in the borderlands escalated following the outbreak of the Libyan war, the

---

[21] Informal conversation, NGO officer, Rabat, September 2017.
[22] Interview, Officer of the Swiss Development Cooperation, phone, September 2017.
[23] Interview, former officer of MSF Morocco, Skype, February 2017; Interview, officer of the Swiss Development Cooperation, WhatsApp, September 2017.

IOM and the UNHCR sought the support of MSF to visit the border-lands and assess the needs and the possibility of establishing a stronger institutional presence in the area.[24] In 2012, after deciding to close the mission in the country, MSF started preparing the handover of its activities: it actively looked for other organisations that could continue delivering emergency assistance to migrants stranded in the area, and connected them to potential donors.[25] Although chronic crisis had pushed MSF to withdraw from the mission, the reality on the ground pushed staff to find a solution to ensure continuity so as not to leave migrants without assistance (Tyszler 2019). As I mentioned earlier in the chapter, by the time MSF left, the project had been taken over by an IOM-led initiative funded by the Swiss Development Cooperation. Many of the staff previously employed by MSF continued on the new project, including the person who then became the IOM focal point in Oujda in 2014. Donors thus stepped in at the moment when MSF was leaving. In this way, aid allowed for the continuation of humanitarian activities in a context where a radical organisation did not feel like its functional symbiosis with border violence made sense anymore.

Crisis challenges the purpose of border humanitarianism. The exception activates and localises the need for humanitarian action. The prolonged extent of the crisis, however, makes humanitarian efforts redundant for those actors that do not recognise themselves in a minimal biopolitical mandate. In Morocco, the prolonged extent of the crisis marks a fracture between those actors that leave and those that decide to stay. Crisis thus transforms the border environment. The departure of MSF and the infiltration of aid in the borderlands marked the beginning of a process of depoliticisation of humanitarianism. This became particularly apparent in the evolution of a key humanitarian activity: testimony.

Unspeakable Violence and Humanitarian Testimony

Like crisis, testimony also pushes humanitarians' minimal biopolitics to the edge of fracture. Testimony is central to humanitarian practice (Fassin 2008). Bearing witness, however, has a particularly complex

---

[24] Interview, officer of the Swiss Development Cooperation, Skype, September 2017.
[25] Interview, officer of a faith-based organisation, Tangier, September 2017.

relationship with maintaining access to the field (Terry 2000), which makes it one of the most divisive topics among and within humanitarian organisations.[26] Humanitarians see what the Moroccan state – and, in more indirect ways, European authorities – do to migrants at the border.[27] An aid worker operating in Nador recalled:

There has been the case of another 14-year-old kid, he stayed seven days in a coma, he arrived to Melilla and then he was sent back by the Spanish police . . . either he banged his head and then the Spanish police sent him back while he was unconscious, or it was the Spanish police or the fence, which is the same because they are devices paid for by the EU and it kills people. The Moroccan police beat this 14-year-old kid that was in a coma [. . .] . . . but these are cases that happen every day, it is systematic violence.[28]

The story of Padre Esteban that I started this chapter with is emblematic of the inconvenient position that humanitarians inhabit at the border. Esteban and his humanitarian team, in fact, "had seen everything" on migrants' bodies, including the most lethal expressions of border violence (*Público* 2016).

The presence of external actors in the borderlands is particularly problematic for Moroccan authorities. Border violence, in fact, contrasts with the way Morocco wants to present itself to the international community – as a modern, moderate country, respectful of human rights and engaged in the process of democratic transition. Since the early 1990s and more decidedly after 1999, Morocco has undertaken a reformist pattern, aiming to distance itself from the authoritarian imprint that had marked the reign of King Hassan II (Bono 2008). This process was sanctioned by the approval of two constitutional reforms in 1992 and 1996, the promotion of a regime of "alternation" in 1998 led by the by Socialist Union of Popular Forces' Abderrahman Youssoufi, and by the ratification of a number of human right treaties (Jiménez Álvarez et al. 2020). The political openings characterising the transition included the recognition of human rights abuses perpetrated by the regime in the previous decades (Catusse and Vairel 2003; Vairel 2004), a phase which is now publicly portrayed as over (Bono 2017).

---

[26] The affirmation of a moral need to speak out about the ordeals witnessed by humanitarian workers was the cornerstone of the rise of the MSF movement in the 1970s (Fassin 2008; Redfield 2006).

[27] For a lengthy discussion about the body as a site of state power, see (Fassin and d'Halluin 2005).

[28] Interview, humanitarian worker, Nador, November 2016.

Since its launch, the new migration policy itself has been inscribed into this transitional path, as a demonstration of the commitment of Morocco to maintain its international engagement on the respect of human rights (see Natter 2018). The formal alignment of Morocco to the international human rights regime, however, did not correspond to a disappearance of authoritarian techniques of ruling – like the suppression of dissident voices, the persistence of legislations constraining civil liberties, and the deployment of violence against marginalised groups (Amnesty International 2017; Human Rights Watch 2017a, 2017b; *Telquel* 2017). To borrow Can's reflections on Turkey, coercive and violent mechanisms of state power have not disappeared, but they "have become less sustainable for the image of the state at the national and international levels" (Can 2016, 352).

The announcement of the new migration policy and the establishment of a political climate more respectful of migrant rights has gone hand in hand with the denial of border violence. On 10 September 2013, King Mohammed VI gave his High Royal Orientations for the formulation of the new migration policy. The communiqué of the Moroccan Royal Cabinet, however, denied the existence of routinised violence against migrants in the country and specified that:

> If the operational management of irregular immigration results sometimes in certain excesses, which remain isolated, there is no systematic use of violence by police forces and even less of persecution. Morocco therefore categorically refuses all fallacious allegations that try to harm its reputation.
>
> (MAP 2013b, translation by author)

Testimony has a disruptive potential. By exposing the crude reality of violence against marginalised populations, testimony can challenge the status quo. In March 2013, MSF published the report "*Violences, Vulnérabilité et Migration: Bloqués aux Portes de l'Europe*" (Violence, Vulnerability and Migration: Blocked at Europe's Doors). In the document, MSF held Moroccan and Spanish authorities directly responsible for migrants' precarious healthcare conditions. MSF accused them not only of perpetrating violence against migrants, but also of fostering a climate of fear and terror which prevented migrants from seeking medical care (MSF 2013c). The report received a significant amount of media attention. It thus contributed to the construction of a climate of international shaming that drove Morocco to reform its migration policy (Jiménez Álvarez et al. 2020).

Speaking out, however, can hamper the relations between humanitarians and sovereign authorities. The state can punish organisations that trespass the boundaries of permissibility by forbidding them from accessing the field. The disruptive nature of testimony thus marks the boundaries of minimal biopolitics: the potential to operate transformative action entails the risk of losing the possibility to operate at all. Morocco's decision to ban Padre Esteban from returning to Nador seems to be intimately linked to the will of the authorities to keep critical voices away from the borderlands. As two NGO officers put it in an interview:

Lorena: Why was he [Padre Esteban] banned from entry again? Is it because he was speaking out [about border violence]?

Interviewee 1: I think it was for his relationship with the media, it was really ...

Interviewee 2: Well, he talked a lot [to journalists] but according to me it was necessary to talk ... it is true that he was very abrupt, very direct, so at a certain moment they [the Moroccan authorities] must have said "We are fed up with it". Maybe it [speaking out] could have been done differently, but it is not that it should have been avoided, everything that he said was well said, maybe the form was not ideal for Morocco ... .[29]

Each humanitarian organisation therefore has to balance access to the field and advocacy. The outcome varies depending on the nature of the organisation and its commitment to testimony. Speaking up or staying silent, in fact, are not foregone conclusions, but compromise solutions that organisations have to partake in. Here lies the main difference between the operations of MSF, the actions of Padre Esteban, and the workings of other aid-funded organisations that continued the work of MSF. Despite primarily adhering to a mandate of protecting life, MSF also has a strong duty to bear witness to the violence experienced by its beneficiaries (Redfield 2006, 2010, 2013). Over the years MSF had to elaborate a calculated advocacy strategy alternating "visibility" and "invisibility" in order to maintain access to the field. From 2003 to 2010, the organisation maintained a very low profile for its operations. As Moroccan authorities treated migration strictly as a security issue,

[29] Interview, two NGO officers, Rabat, September 2016.

MSF "had to be as invisible as the migrants were", as a member of the organisation recalled during an interview.[30] During this period of discretion, MSF staff directly witnessed some of the darkest pages of the history of migration control in the country.[31] Despite its strategy of "invisibility", the organisation still issued three critical reports – in 2005, 2008,[32] and 2010 respectively – denouncing the inhumane treatment of migrants at the border. In 2011, the organisation decided to abandon this approach, and to shift to full visibility.[33] This change occurred, unsurprisingly, around the same time as the decision to close the mission. Although MSF's decision decidedly played a role in communicating the ongoing abuses against migrants to the international community, the report was not unanimously welcomed by civil society organisations operating in Morocco (Tyszler 2019). Some of my respondents suggested that the ongoing strict surveillance of organisations working in the borderlands is linked to the fear that humanitarians and human rights organisations might expose Morocco again to international shaming.[34]

The replacement of MSF with other NGOs and IOs has produced a shift in the way humanitarian work is performed at the Spanish–Moroccan frontier. Whereas MSF had a clear duty to testify against human rights abuses, the actors who replaced the organisation occupy a very different position. The IOM, in particular, follows an openly acknowledged principle to avoid criticising state authorities in public (Olin et al. 2008, 22). The pamphlets and leaflets published by the Moroccan mission of the IOM never mention police violence against migrants. The publicly available material only mentions that migrants encounter "difficult life conditions" in Morocco (OIM 2017, 9, translation by author). It also specifies that "the passage [to Spain] is far from easy given the securitarian devices in place. In the hopes of reaching Spanish shores, migrants accumulate a certain number of vulnerabilities, which reinforce their precarity" (OIM 2016, 7, translation by

---

[30] Interview, former officer of MSF Morocco, Skype, February 2017.
[31] For example, in the aftermath of the Ceuta and Melilla events in 2005, MSF staff found hundreds of migrants who had been expelled in a desert area at the border with Algeria by Moroccan police forces. The staff of the organisation contacted journalists to alert the international community (Jiménez 2005).
[32] This report was handed to Spanish and Moroccan authorities and was not publicly released.
[33] Interview, former officer of MSF Morocco, Skype, February 2017.
[34] Interview, two NGO officers, Rabat, September 2016.

author). The causes underlying the production of migrants' "vulner-abilities" at the border are, however, never discussed.

Donor-funded humanitarian organisations now mainly engage with healing the bodily dimension of border violence, with very little to no space left for the engagement in advocacy activities. Especially since Padre Esteban has been barred from re-entering Morocco, humanitarian NGOs operating at the border only issue communications related to violence against migrants through collective and cautious publications that have a limited outreach.[35] The only organisation operating at the border that regularly diffuses pictures and communiqués on violence against migrants in the area is the Nador branch of the Moroccan Association of Human Rights (AMDH, in the French acronym). AMDH Nador, however, has a much more limited outreach than INGOs or IOs. The organisation and its members are also more vulnerable to the actions of the Moroccan state than international actors (see Frontline Defenders 2020).

The weakening of critical humanitarian voices feeds a broader choir of international institutions celebrating Morocco's engagement in migration governance. As I mentioned in the introduction already, this celebratory discourse also elicits criticism about state-perpetrated abuses against migrants at the border. A report published by GIZ in 2016 is very symptomatic of such a trend. In 2016, the GIZ published a report called "A Tale of Three Cities", comparing migrant integration in Tangier, Istanbul, and Offenbach. The document identified the weakness of local institutions and xenophobic attitudes expressed by the local population as the main challenges to migration governance and integration in Tangier (Integration Strategy Group 2016). Shortly after the report was publicly released, the Moroccan NGO Al-Khaima circulated on social media a letter addressed to the GIZ and criticising the report. The letter stated that:

After having read your document, we understand that it is not appropriate to take the city of Tangier as an example concerning integration in the Mediterranean area. Tangier is a border city and because of that the city

---

[35] One of these rare collective advocacy actions was the press release about border violence issued by the PNPM in 2016, and that I quoted in the introduction. The idea of the press release was not positively received by the Swiss Development Cooperation, which funded both the PNPM and some of its member organisations. As Tyszler argues, the donor tried to discourage the PNPM from publishing a statement so harshly criticising the local authorities (Tyszler 2019).

records a lot of human rights violations and violence against migrants. (Association Al-Khaima 2016)

A human rights activist that I interviewed in Tangier defined this sort of discourse as a "pact of silence". As they poignantly put it during our conversation:

[...] there is a *pacte du silence* [a pact of silence]. Morocco with this new migration policy has accepted to be the guardian of European borders . . . and donors try to correct here all the mistakes that they have done on integration in Europe. And Morocco wants to show everyone that they are a bastion in the respect of human rights in the region and that everything goes well, because this gives them more power in Africa . . .. *Et ça arrange tout le monde* [and this suits everyone].[36]

The departure of radical actors and the infiltration of aid has marked a depoliticisation of humanitarian border work. The forced departure of figures juggling advocacy and access to the field (like Padre Esteban), the establishment of organisations not prioritising testimony (like the IOM), and the influence of donors avoiding public controversy with Moroccan authorities (like Switzerland) meant that humanitarianism lost its subversive character. Within an aid environment supporting a sanitised portrayal of Morocco as a country of integration, humanitarianism contained itself to the role of provision of a minimal biopolitics – healing migrants' bodily injuries, keeping death at bay, but not attempting to structurally reverse the causes of border suffering.

Conclusion

Since the mid-2000s, humanitarian organisations have become a steady presence in the governance of Moroccan borderlands. Humanitarian projects develop in the interstices of border violence. They treat the direct and indirect victims of the border. They adapt their working patterns to the rhythm of the violent intrusion of the state in migrant existence. Within this symbiosis, humanitarians establish a double relation with the state: a conflictual relation with security forces which attempt to control and contain emergency outreach; and a collaborative interaction with state healthcare structures, which share the humanitarian mandate to protect life. By providing a form

---

[36] Interview, human rights activist, Tangier, December 2016.

of minimal biopolitics, humanitarian care has become instrumental to the reproduction of a border regime that structurally marginalises migrants' lives. In the borderlands, migrants are strictly confined to the margins, and humanitarian action can take care of these expendable lives just as long as relief is provided within the margins. Humanitarian care therefore does not work to reverse the conditions that have triggered the need for relief in the first place. It mainly operates to make this process of marginalisation less deadly.

The state of never-ending crisis unfolding at the border challenges the mandate of humanitarian organisations. Confronted with their incapacity to operate transformative action, activist organisations like MSF can decide to leave the field. However, the perpetual border crisis creates niches of opportunity for new organisations to assist migrants in distress. The presence of European donors is instrumental to the reproduction of the humanitarian border. It allows organisations like the IOM to expand their presence in the field when other, more activist actors decide that they have to leave. The arrival of donor-funded organisations, less prone to risk losing access to the field in favour of speaking out, has however led to a fundamental depoliticisation of humanitarianism. As more radical humanitarian formations have been substituted by actors with a weaker mandate to testimony, the border has become more and more silent. Aid thus sustains a threatened and silent apparatus of emergency relief, which maintains migrants' lives in the margins, without disrupting the conditions which enables life degradation in the first place.

Conclusion

In the second half of 2018, the increase in the number of irregular border crossings in the Western Mediterranean pushed Spain and the EU to revamp their cooperation with Morocco over the control of the Euro–African border (see Chapter 1). Spain lobbied the EU to grant Morocco more financial support for border control cooperation. The EU proactively reacted to these pressures, and allocated Morocco €74 million for two different border security projects. These projects, funded through the EUTF and implemented by the ICMPD and the FIIAPP respectively, specifically aimed at providing Moroccan authorities with technical equipment to more effectively control their land and sea borders (Statewatch 2019). This substantial increase in funding for border security was further topped up in December 2019, when the EU granted Morocco €101.7 million for a programme supporting the fight against human smuggling and the management of irregular migration (European Commission 2019). While the news about the escalation of violence against migrants in Northern Morocco flooded the international press, Morocco became the second largest receiver of migration-related aid in the EU neighbourhood (European Commission 2018b).

In December 2019, the Spanish press began publishing details about the technical equipment delivered to Moroccan authorities as part of these two EU-funded projects. In one such article at the time, the author listed the equipment which had been purchased: "384 vehicles", "200 off-road vehicles", "5 semi-rigid boats", "120 multi-purpose police vehicles", "26 minibuses or vans for the transport of irregular emigrants" (*Canarias7* 2019). The description of this last piece of equipment made the fast violence of aid-funded border containment appear in a perfectly clear light. During my last interviews in summer 2019, I had talked to a number of people that had been forced on "minibus[es] or vans for the transport of irregular migrants" and then forcefully displaced to the South of Morocco, hundreds of kilometres away from

194

their houses. Patrick, the Cameroonian man I mentioned in Chapter 6, was forcefully displaced from Tangier to Agadir, and then had to sleep for three months at the bus station because he had nowhere to go. Daouda, the Cameroonian man that I mentioned in Chapter 4, had been displaced multiple times from the North to the South and Centre of Morocco. When I met him, he had sought refuge with three other Cameroonian men in a small city of the Moroccan interior, a place where finding a job was extremely difficult. At least, he told me, the risks of being arbitrarily harassed and arrested by the Moroccan police were considerably lower. In summer 2019, the Moroccan press reported the story of Timothy Hucks, an Afro-American US citizen that had been arrested and displaced from Rabat to Beni Mellal in March of that year, together with another group of men, all black. In the months following the arrest, he tried to police his own movements, and avoid contact with the authorities. In a Twitter thread published in summer 2019, he stated:

I tried not to leave my house. I always carried my passport. If the police were walking, I chose the other side of the sidewalk. If they were circling their wagons, I waited until they left to keep walking. I acted like I was fine. I don't think I realized I wasn't. (Hucks 2019)

The Moroccan newspaper *Yabiladi* argued that Timothy Hucks had been arrested because he had been "mistaken for a sub-Saharan migrant in Morocco" (*Yabiladi.com* 2019). But the reality is that he had not been "mistaken" for a 'sub-Saharan migrant'. Like Patrick and Daouda, he had been profiled as an "irregular sub-Saharan migrant" because of his skin colour. By granting Morocco money to buy security equipment, the EU was directly fostering police violence against black people politically constructed as dangerous and expendable by border control policies.

When aid is used for hard border security, it is easy to see its migration containment potential. The technical language surrounding the description of the border equipment hardly masks the fast violence characterising its use. The purpose is clearly identifiable. The consequences are predictable and sinister. But as the different chapters of this book have argued, the border containment potential of aid is not always so explicit – there does not always seem to be something which can be clearly identified as control, and someone who can be unequivocally labelled as captive. In this book, I have taken the Moroccan migration industry as a vantage point to analyse the rise of aid as an instrument of slow border control. When aid for migration-related purposes is channelled through non-traditional security actors, it enables the rise of a political architecture of potential, ordinary, and elusive containment, which expands the reach of the border on migrant communities by infiltrating everyday sectors of social life. Contrary to what Jill Williams calls "hard power" instruments of migration control (Williams 2019, 3), aid does not further the border project by physically immobilising migrants away from Europe. Rather, it creates a dispersed network of marginalisation that produces 'sub-Saharan migrants' into a category of outsiders – identified as a problem to be managed, subordinated to forms of exclusionary care, and relegated to minimal lives.

Slow border control does not work in ways that are neat, coercive, or eye-catching. Aid-funded projects assisting migrant people often do not incorporate containment by design. Control, rather, constitutes a lingering possibility – any of the actors involved in aid implementation could potentially become an agent of border control by participating in mechanisms of domination. To enact this form of slow control, aid relies on a number of indirect techniques that attract (rather than coerce) non-traditional security actors into the control of mobility.

In the various chapters of this book, I have highlighted how aid diffuses mechanisms of containment away from border crossing points, and more pervasively in other, mundane sectors of societal regulation – like public discourse, social assistance, and labour integration. What characterises these power mechanisms is that containment never manifests itself as a fully fledged intention. Rather, it looks like a side effect that somehow seems to pass unobserved. An account of immigration in Morocco as a 'new', 'black', 'transit', 'irregular' experience included in a project factsheet compiled by the EU does not expressively have the intent to physically prevent border crossings. The formal purpose of the document, one could say, is another one: to lay out the background, objectives, and expected results of an aid-funded project. But the inclusion of such a description of immigration in Morocco in the background section of the factsheet *does* have a controlling effect. It contributes to transforming the idea of Morocco as a recent 'Immigration Nation' into the hegemonic image of the country. It makes the case for 'sub-Saharan migrants' to be considered as a 'problem' to be managed. Aid-funded projects do not need to be explicitly connected to containment to be experienced *as* the border

by those in their orbit. As I highlighted for the field of labour integration, border control is so pervasively built into the political environment surrounding aid-funded projects that displaced people police
their own behaviour as if labour integration projects were border
control sites.

The diffusion of migration containment away from physical borders
and into non-traditional security sectors triggers a hybridisation of care
and control. At the beginning of this book, I stated that trying to read
the ambiguities of aid work along logics of 'benevolence' and 'malevolence', alignment with or resistance to border control policies, risks
missing the complexity and productivity of the aid industry as an
instrument of migration containment. By blurring the boundaries
between care and control, aid expands the reach of the border regime
by facilitating the co-optation of non-security actors into borderwork.
Because control is fleetingly built into practices of assistance, it can look
a lot like care – so ordinary that the containment potential of aid
becomes elusive. Aid, in other words, transform border control into
a series of 'quasi-events' (Povinelli 2011): its negative effects cannot be
easily identified, and the contours of responsibility cannot be clearly
determined. In these circumstances, non-traditional security actors
struggle to see themselves, or the work they do, as borderwork. And
when they do, their concerns are quickly subdued: they enact sense-
making mechanisms which enable them to not see the work they do as
control, or to distance themselves from the complaints raised by
migrant people. Co-optation processes fracture relations within
Moroccan civil society, increasing the divide between organisations
that accept aid, those who distance themselves from it, and those who
are left on the doorstep of the aid market.

By infiltrating non-traditional security sectors, aid creates an
expanded network of containment involving donors, NGOs, IOs,
Moroccan authorities, embassies of countries of origin, and migrants
themselves. The presence of such a high number of intermediaries, and
the prevalence of indirect power techniques, unsettles our assumptions
about who governs the border. Aid, in fact, creates a political architecture where power is so diffused that *any* actor within the aid industry
could *potentially* become (or be perceived as) an agent of border
control – the community-based worker conducting a vulnerability
assessment, the Moroccan civil servant that negotiates an increasing
involvement of the IOM in Voluntary Return, or the asylum seeker

hesitating about participating or not in a labour integration project. This, of course, does not mean that structures of racialised inequality are erased, and that all actors participate equally to the construction of the border project. But deciphering the workings of aid through normative binaries opposing powerful and powerless actors takes border power as a given. Containment, as I have shown, is rather the dynamic result of contingencies, historical processes of inequality, and autonomous strategies of the actors involved in the transposition of aid policy on the ground. Acknowledging the distributed implementation of aid-funded projects challenges existing understanding of power relations between European and African actors. Morocco, in fact, does not at all correspond to the image of the passive aid-recipient state, co-opted into border control through the promise of aid, or the threat of cutting it. Much to the contrary, Morocco manages to attract, direct, or obstruct the implementation of aid-funded projects, depending on how these fit the Kingdom's own political agenda.

The dynamics of aid power examined in this book raise some important questions about the future of migration politics in Morocco. As I mentioned earlier on, the renewed anxiety of the EU over the Western Mediterranean border has placed hardcore migration security at the heart of EU development policies. This, in turn, has brought Moroccan state security back to the fore of the aid market, after a decade where talks of "vulnerability" and "integration" had dominated the expenditure of aid budgets in the field of migration in Morocco. This new architecture of securitised development will likely mark a new, dark turn for the Western Mediterranean border. At present, it seems very likely that these projects will produce a further tightening of the Gibraltar Strait route. They will probably also dangerously reinforce the operational capacity of the Moroccan security apparatus, with worrying consequences in terms of respect of migrant rights in the country. These projects might also become new battlegrounds of migration diplomacy. In the past, in fact, the EU has recorded significant difficulties in obtaining the cooperation of Moroccan authorities in the implementation of similar projects, namely on issues of monitoring and reporting of expenditure (Statewatch 2019; Wunderlich 2010). Interesting, in this regard, is the fact that the implementation of the two border security projects approved between 2018 and 2019 has not been delegated to Moroccan authorities directly, but rather to two IOs – ICMPD and FIIAPP. This seems to imply that the EU preferred to have someone mediating its relation with Moroccan authorities. It is to be seen whether these projects will become terrains of negotiation and contestation between Morocco and the EU, and how the mediation role that has seemingly being attributed to IOs will unfold in practice.

Civil society activists have not remained silent vis-à-vis the sinister twists of events unfolding in the Western Mediterranean. More interestingly, human rights organisations have started using strategic litigation to contest the use of development funding for border security, in Morocco and beyond. In 2019, the Guardian reported that an Ethiopian asylum-seeking boy was to sue the UK Department for International Development (DfID) for funding detention centres in Libya where he had experienced abusive treatment. The legal challenge aimed at pushing the UK government to stop funding such centres, and at granting compensation to the plaintiff for the ill-treatment received (*The Guardian* 2018). In 2020, the Spanish NGOs, Access Info Europe and Andalucía Acoge, submitted a formal claim to the Supreme Tribunal to contest Spain's decision to grant Morocco €30 million to support the Alaouite Kingdom in border control. The argument foregrounded by the two organisations is that such a decision amounts to the unproper use of the Spanish Contingency Fund, which should be only used in case of exceptional and unforeseeable emergencies (Andalucía Acoge 2020). If pursued, these two cases might set important precedents, and provide human rights activists with innovative examples on how to effectively contest the legitimacy of the use of aid for border control issues.

The outbreak and long-term consequences of the COVID-19 pandemic, furthermore, question how responses to the healthcare crisis are reshaping the workings of border control and of the aid industry in Morocco. The quarantine measures put in place to contain the spread of the virus have aggravated the exclusionary inclusion of migrants within Moroccan society. Stay-at-home orders and the shutdown of the economy at the beginning of the pandemic response have deprived the most vulnerable migrant people of their source of income. The need to track, trace, and isolate COVID-19 positive cases has further condensed the anxiety of the state over communities of poor foreigners – who, made vulnerable to exposure to the virus by racist structures of marginalisation, are conceptualised as dangerous to the body politic for their contagion potential. Moroccan security forces have been criticised for forcefully locking migrant people into 'quarantine sites' (that could be more accurately described as improvised detention centres) waiting for their COVID-19 tests to be processed (Gross-Wyrtzen 2020a). The pandemic has also constrained the capacity of aid-funded organisations and of solidarity networks to deliver assistance to migrant communities, obliging them to revisit their geographies and modes of operation (GADEM 2020; *Le Monde* 2020). But it has also given organisations like the IOM a window of opportunity to make their work more relevant vis-à-vis both donors and Moroccan authorities (IOM Morocco 2020)– apprehensive now, more than ever, to police the 'undeserving'.

The processes of border sophistication at work in Morocco illuminate the new architectures of migration control that aid is enabling in other countries of 'transit' and 'forced settlement' in Africa and in the broader Middle East. After the approval of the EUTF in 2015, the EU and its member states revamped and expanded their developmental strategy of border control in North, Western, Central, and Eastern Africa, with the ambition to create a region under surveillance from Rabat to Asmara, passing through Bamako, Niamey, and Cairo (Brachet 2016; Gabrielli 2016; Mouthaan 2019). In the Levant, the protracted temporality of the 'refugee crisis' has maintained the attention of donors focused on the countries that host the majority of Syrian refugees (Tsourapas 2019b). This has entailed an important mobilisation of both IOs and NGOs (Fine 2018; Wagner 2018), but also the affirmation of Southern donors, especially from the Gulf countries (Carpi 2020). Such an unprecedent mobilisation of aid as an instrument of border control opened new avenues of everyday and distributed containment in aid-recipient contexts, that merge and overlap with more traditional instruments of border security.

This book has opened a number of avenues of inquiry. The first one relates to the relation between the politics of remoteness and the production of border control. While discussing the work of frontline aid actors, I have argued that their proximity to the field affects their disposition vis-à-vis the migrant people they routinely deal with, and their way of understanding their position within the border regime. Exposure to the frontlines of aid work pushes street-level aid workers to enact sense-making mechanisms to distance themselves from their actual participation in border control. Proximity to the field therefore works as a self-making process, as it transforms the way people understand their roles as aid workers. But it is also a border-making process, as it shapes the way care for and control over migrant people are performed at the border. But how does distance from the field impact migration control? By distance from the field, I mean the physical, psychological, and political remoteness of aid organisations from the areas and communities they operate in. This remoteness is dictated both by the operational structure of the aid industry, organised in headquarters and field missions, with only a minimal percentage of (generally local and precariously employed) staff directly interacting with beneficiaries (Pascucci 2018); and with the complex geography of risk calculation that keeps aid workers at a distance from the areas where they 'operate' (Andersson 2019; see Duffield 2010).

The various chapters of this book have investigated what aid does to the border project, and to the migrant communities impacted by border control. One question that emerged, but remained unanswered is: what do migrant communities do to aid, and to the aid industry more broadly? Migrants are not passive subjects of aid and migration policies. They mobilise against it, through the organisation of fully fledged protests or through mundane acts of contestation. They aspire to be part of the industry, either by claiming their seat at the funding allocation table, or by seeking employment in aid-funded organisations (Magallanes-Gonzalez 2020; Rodriguez 2019). They utilise aid-funded projects as part of their own survival and social mobility strategy (Fiddian-Qasmiyeh 2014; Maâ 2019). The interaction of migrant people with the aid industry, however, is marked by the structural inequality that generate border control policies in the first place. Migrant civil society organisations integrate the aid market in a subordinate position (Chapter 3). Migrant aid workers are more precariously employed than their local or international colleagues (Andersson 2014). Their efforts to mobilise might be easily and violently bashed by police forces or dismissed by humanitarian organisations (Moulin and Nyers 2007; Pascucci 2014). But these encounters demonstrate the capacity of migrants to resist architectures of border containment, and beg further scholarly analysis.

The migration industry works at the intersection of multiple, long stories of domination and empire. As Leslie Gross-Wyrtzen and I highlighted in a recent article, migration scholarship has been marked by a presentist approach, hyper-attentive to the fast politics of the present but tendentially oblivious to "what is past but not over" (Stoler 2016, 25). However, the border project constitutes the latest transformation of a long-standing European enterprise aimed at containing and extracting value from countries in the South – first through colonialism, then through neoliberal policies, and simultaneously through the development project (Gross-Wyrtzen and Gazzotti 2020). As I have argued throughout this book, the aid sector is a site where the afterlives of domination materialise in multifold ways. One field where the traces of colonial past(s) resurge more evidently in the Moroccan aid industry is within architecture – for example, a former Spanish military fort converted into an aid-funded child protection centre (Jiménez Álvarez 2011) and Catholic churches that bear the mark of the Spanish and French protectorates providing assistance to migrants in distress (Robin 2014; Tyszler 2020). What does it mean when buildings created for a very different purpose, in support of or in direct connection to the colonial enterprise, are reconverted to structures of "assistance" and "care" for migrants? How do the materialities, memories, and spatialities of those infrastructures affect their present workings, and their role within the border regime?

This book has focused mostly on aid projects operating in nontraditional sectors of border control. But as I have highlighted at the beginning of this Conclusion, donors are also significantly investing in traditional border security projects. This presents a series of questions about the relation between border control, state-building and authoritarian ruling in countries on the receiving end of externalisation policies (Frowd 2018; Tsourapas 2019a). Details about the kind of equipment delivered to Morocco through aid-funded projects clearly suggests that aid strengthens the Moroccan security apparatus, especially of the Ministry of Interior, and its reach over the country's territory and population (see Wunderlich 2010). Researching this aspect of border externalisation, of course, is far from easy – not only because accessing sources inside or close to the security apparatus in hybrid or authoritarian contexts might be difficult or risky, but also because donors (such as the EU) can prove to be extremely reticent in sharing information about the implementation of aid-funded border security projects (Statewatch 2019). But research is also necessary at a time where, in Morocco as in Turkey, Libya, and elsewhere, international support for border security chronologically coincides with the escalation of authoritarian practices or of fully fledged civil conflicts.

Unveiling the mundane entanglements between aid and border control prompts a reflection about development and humanitarian practice in the field of migration. Aid workers inhabit a position of authority in the communities where they operate. The decisions that officers of donors, NGOs, and IOs take as part of their everyday jobs have powerful reverberations in the lives of the people qualified as "beneficiaries". This book, however, has also highlighted that aid workers do not always seem to be conscious of working at the intersection of multiple regimes of inequality, and of the power that emanates from it. The consequences of such power imbalances can reflect in both practices and in codified policies – as shown by the decision of Samuel's organisation to hire community-based workers as volunteers rather than to contract and pay them as employees. This warrants the need for aid-funded organisations to engage in a deep effort of conscientisation about their own positionality in the field, and to establish stronger structures of accountability to the communities they operate in. This does not only mean reflecting on their projects' political alignment, but also on the much more immediate effects that their protocols and operations have in aid-recipient sites. Such an endeavour is in line with the increasing pressures on the aid world to address its most exploitative practices – as demonstrated by the increasing calls to establish mechanisms of redress and reparation for victims of abuses perpetrated by aid workers (see REDRESS 2017) and the decision of some UN agencies to start paying interns (see Croxford 2018). Establishing protocols that make sure that all workers interacting directly with beneficiaries have been appropriately trained, reviewing hiring practices to make sure there is no undue or discriminatory use of unpaid and low-paid contracts, and starting a broader conversation about how the complaints of beneficiaries are received and dealt with in different organisations will not redress the inequalities and racism pervading the development and humanitarian system overnight, but would constitute important steps to at least mitigate its most obvious expressions.

When I discuss my research with aid workers, policy consultants, or informed citizens, I am often asked about what alternative aid policies should be pursued to improve the situation of migrants and refugees on the ground in non-European countries. I am always uneasy answering this question. It seems to imply that, even in absence of a change in context, it is possible to make aid policies work 'better' for migrant integration and the respect of human rights in Morocco. But if this book has done the job it was supposed to do, the reader will now have understood that development work cannot work 'well' for migrant integration in contexts marked by pervasive border control. Integration cannot happen if the people that are to be 'integrated' in society are the same people that are racially constructed and profiled as expendable – their freedom of movement is curtailed, their existence is not free of the fear of encounter with the authorities, and they are subjected to everyday forms of discrimination. A project providing social assistance to destitute foreigners cannot undo the structural sources of violence that has produced that same destitution, especially when precarity is generated by those same governments that provide aid. What aid produces is a distorted understanding of integration, where migrant, refugee, and asylum-seeking people are rendered visible within society by virtue of their own 'dangerousness', but socially left at its doorstep – limited in their capacity to move, work, access services. If we are to take migrants' rights seriously, the only policy recommendation that can possibly work in such a context is to decrease the structural causes of violence that place migrants in precarious conditions in the first place. Defunding border control is the first, immediate way to do this. Increasing avenues for legal migration and decriminalising irregular migration, both in the North and in the South, are the second, more comprehensive and challenging set of changes that need to happen for integration to work, in Morocco as everywhere else.

References

Abbas, Madeline-Sophie. 2019. "'I Grew a Beard and My Dad Flipped out!' Co-Option of British Muslim Parents in Countering 'Extremism' within Their Families in Bradford and Leeds". *Journal of Ethnic and Migration Studies* 45 (9): 1458–76. https://doi.org/10.1080/1369183X.2018.1466694

Abena Banyomo, Jackson. 2019. *Celui Qui Échoue Devient Sorcier: Parcours d'un Migrant Camerounais Parti d'Afrique et Arrivé … En Afrique.* Edited by Catherine Therrien. Québec: Presses de l'Université Laval.

Afailal, Hafsa. 2016. "Las Migraciones Inesperadas: Marruecos y Turquía Entre Diversidad y Seguridad". PhD Thesis, Universitat Rovira i Virgili, unpublished.

Agamben, Giorgio. 1942–. 1998. *Homo Sacer: Sovereign Power and Bare Life.* Translated by Daniel Heller-Roazen. Stanford, CA: Stanford University Press.

Agier, Michel. 2003. "La main gauche de l'Empire". *Multitudes* 11 (1): 67–77.

2011. *Managing the Undesirables.* Malden, MA: Polity Press.

Agustín, Laura María. 2007. *Sex at the Margins: Migration, Labour Markets and the Rescue Industry.* London: Zed Books.

Ahmed, Sara. 2007. "The Language of Diversity". *Ethnic and Racial Studies* 30 (2): 235–56. https://doi.org/10.1080/01419870601143927

2012. *On Being Included Racism and Diversity in Institutional Life.* Durham, NC: Duke University Press.

2017. *Living a Feminist Life.* Durham, NC: Duke University Press.

In press. *Complaint!* Durham, NC: Duke University Press.

Ait Akdim, Youssef. 2016. "Si le Maroc veut être en Afrique, il faut que l'Afrique soit au Maroc". *Le Monde.fr,* 13 December. www.lemonde.fr/afrique/article/2016/12/13/si-le-maroc-veut-etre-en-afrique-il-faut-que-l-afrique-soit-au-maroc_5048364_3212.html

Alami, Rajaa Mejjati. 2000. "L'ajustement structurel et la dynamique de l'emploi informel au Maroc". *Critique économique* 2 (Summer): 81–97. http://revues.imist.ma/index.php?journal=CE&page=article⊕view&path%5B%5D=2629

Alioua, Mehdi. 2009. "Le 'passage au politique' des transmigrants subsahariens au Maroc. Imaginaire migratoire, réorganisation collective et mobilisation politique en situation de migration transnationale". In *Le Maghreb à l'épreuve des migrations subsahariennes*. Edited by Ali Bensaâd, 279–303. Hommes et sociétés. Paris: Editions Karthala. https://doi.org/ 10.3917/kart.bensa.2009.01.0279

2011a. "L'étape Marocaine des Transmigrants Subsahariens En Route Vers l'Europe: L'épreuve de La Construction Des Réseaux et de Leurs Territoires". PhD Thesis, Université Toulouse II Le Mirail.

2011b. "Transnational Migration: A Staged Migration. The Example of Sub-Saharan Transmigrants Stopping over in Morocco". In *Transit Migrations in Europe: Contested Concepts and Diverse Reali*. Edited by Franck Düvell, Irina Molodikova, Hein De Haas, and Michael Collyer, 79–98. Amsterdam: Amsterdam University Press.

Alioua, Mehdi and Hicham Rachidi. 2017. "Le Maroc A-t-Il Toujours La Maîtrise de Sa Politique Migratoire?" 13 November. www.yabiladi.co m/articles/details/59310/maroc-a-t-il-toujours-maitrise-politique.html

Alioua, Mehdi, Jean-Noel Ferrié, and Helmut Reifeld, eds. 2017. *La Nouvelle Politique Migratoire Marocaine*. Rabat: Konrad Adenauer Stiftung.

AMAPPE. 2016. "Programme d'insertion Socio-Économique Des Réfugiés Urbains Au Maroc".

AMDH Nador. 2019. "Rapport Migration et Asile à Nador. De Graves Violations Au Service Des Politiques Migratoires Européennes".

American Consulate of Casablanca. 2006. "Despite Lack of Official Accord UNHCR Expands Rabat Office, Wikileaks Cable 06CASABLANCA1310_a". https://wikileaks.org/plusd/cables/06C ASABLANCA1310_a.html

American Embassy of Rabat. 2006a. "Asylum Seekers Overwhelm UNHCR in Rabat". https://wikileaks.org/plusd/cables/06RABAT2_a.html

2006b. "Official Moroccan Views on Refugee Resettlement, Confidence Building Measures. Wikileaks Cable: 06RABAT516_a". https://wiki leaks.org/plusd/cables/06RABAT516_a.html

2006c. "Official Moroccan Views on Refugee Resettlement, Confidence Building Measures". https://wikileaks.org/plusd/cables/06RABAT516_ a.html

Amnesty International. 2017. Maroc. Vague d'arrestations massives visant des manifestants dans le Rif. www.amnesty.org/fr/latest/news/2017/06/ morocco-rif-protesters-punished-with-wave-of-mass-arrests/

2018. "Maroc. Des Milliers de Réfugiés et de Migrants Subsahariens Sont Visés Par Une Répression Illégale Continue". www.amnesty.org/fr/lat est/news/2018/09/morocco-relentless-crackdown-on-thousands-of-su b-saharan-migrants-and-refugees-is-unlawful/

Andalucía, Acoge. 2020. "Entitated Sociales Impugnan Ante El Tribunal Supremo La Concesión de 30 Millones de Euros Del Fondo de Contingencia a Marruecos Para Control de La Migración". https://aco ge.org/entidades-sociales-impugnan-ante-el-tribunal-supremo-la-conce sion-de-30-millones-de-euros-del-fondo-de-contingencia-a-marruecos-para-el-control-de-la-migracion/

Anderl, Felix, Nicole Deitelhoff, and Regina Hack. 2019. "Divide and Rule? The Politics of Self-Legitimation in the WTO". In *Rule and Resistance beyond the Nation State: Contestation, Escalation, Exit.* Edited by Felix Anderl, Christopher Daase, Nicole Deitelhoff, et al., 49–68. London: Rowman and Littlefield.

Andersson, Ruben. 2010. "Wild Man at Europe's Gates: The Crafting of Clandestines in Spain's Cayuco Crisis". *Etnofoor* 22 (2): 31–49.

2014. *Illegality, Inc.: Clandestine Migration and the Business of Bordering Europe.* 1st ed. Oakland, CA: University of California Press.

2019. *No Go World: How Fear Is Redrawing Our Maps and Infecting Our Politics.* Oakland, CA: University of California Press.

Arab, Chadia. 2009. *Les Aït Ayad: la circulation migratoire des Marocains entre la France, l'Espagne et l'Italie.* Rennes, France: Presses universitaires de Rennes.

2018a. *Dames de fraises, doigts de fée. Les invisibles de la migration saisonnière en Espagne.* Casablanca: En toutes lettres.

2018b. Nous sommes tou·te·s des #DamesDeFraises, *Mediapart.* https:// blogs.mediapart.fr/chadia-arab/blog/130618/nous-sommes-tou-te-s-de s-damesdefraises

Aradau, Claudia and Martina Tazzioli. 2019. "Biopolitics Multiple: Migration, Extraction, Subtraction". *Millennium* 48 (2): 198–220. https://doi.org/10 .1177/0305829819889139

Arci. 2018. "Le Tappe Del Processo Di Esternalizzazione Del Controllo Alle Frontiere in Africa, Dal Summit Della Valletta Ad Oggi". www.integra tionarci.it/wp-content/uploads/2016/06/esternalizzazione_docanalisiA RCI_IT.pdf

Artigas, Xavi and Xapo Ortega. 2016. *Tarajal. Desmontando La Impunidad En La Frontera Sur/Tarajal. A European Phantasmagoria.* https://vime o.com/165289252

Association Al-Khaima. 2016. "A l'attention de La Direction de La GIZ". Letter from the NGO to GIZ. 9 November.

Azkona, Nerea and Jon Sagastagoitita. 2011. "Políticas de Control Migratorio y de Cooperación al Desarrollo Entre España y África Occidental Durante La Ejecución Del Primer Plan África". Bilbao and Madrid: Alboan and Entreculturas. www.entreculturas.org/files/documentos/estudios_e_in formes/InformeControlMigratorioyAOD_2011.pdf?download

Bachelet, Sébastien. 2016. "Irregular Sub-Saharan Migrants in Morocco: Illegality, Immobility, Uncertainty and 'Adventure' in Rabat". PhD Thesis, University of Edinburgh.

2018. "'Fighting against Clandestine Migration': Sub-Saharan Migrants' Political Agency and Uncertainty in Morocco". *PoLAR: Political and Legal Anthropology Review* 41 (2): 201–15. https://doi.org/10.1111/plar.12265

Bakewell, Oliver. 2008. "'Keeping Them in Their Place': The Ambivalent Relationship between Development and Migration in Africa". *Third World Quarterly* 29 (7): 1341–58.

Barnett, Michael and Thomas G. Weiss, eds. 2008. *Humanitarianism in Question: Politics, Power, Ethics.* Ithaca, NY: Cornell University Press.

Bartels, Inken. 2017. "'We Must Do It Gently.' The Contested Implementation of the IOM's Migration Management in Morocco". *Migration Studies* 5 (3): 315–36. https://doi.org/10.1093/migration/mnx054

Bastani, Niyousha and Lorena Gazzotti. In press. "'Still a Bit Uncomfortable, to Be an Arm of the State': Making Sense and Subjects of Counter-Extremism in the UK and Morocco". *Environment and Planning C: Politics and Space.*

Bateman, Milford and Ha-Joon Chang. 2012. "Microfinance and the Illusion of Development: From Hubris to Nemesis in Thirty Years". *World Economic Review* 1 (26 January). SSRN: https://ssrn.com/abstract=2385482

Becker, Cynthia. 2002. "'We Are Real Slaves, Real Ismkhan': Memories of the Trans-Saharan Slave Trade in the Tafilalet of South-Eastern Morocco". *The Journal of North African Studies* 7 (4): 97–121. https://doi.org/10.1080/13629380208718485

Belguendouz, Abdelkrim. 2003. *Le Maroc Non-Africain Gendarme de l'Europe?: Alert Au Projet de Loi 02–03 Relative à l'entrée et Au Séjour Des Étrangers Au Maroc, à l'émigration et l'immigration Irrégulières!* Salé: Imprimerie Beni Snassen.

2005. "Expansion et sous-traitance des logiques d'enfermement de l'Union européenne: l'exemple du Maroc". *Cultures & Conflits* 57 (March): 155–219. https://doi.org/10.4000/conflits.1754

Benargane, Yassine. 2018. "Migration: Le Maroc s'explique Devant Le Corps Diplomatique Africain". 31 August. www.yabiladi.com/articles/details/68508/migration-maroc-s-explique-devant-corps.html

Benjelloun, Sara. 2017a. "Mise En Oeuvre et Enjeux Diplomatiques de La Nouvelle Politique Migratoire". In *La Nouvelle Politique Migratoire Marocaine.* Edited by Mehdi Alioua and Jean-Noel Ferrié, 77–122. Rabat: Konrad Adenauer Stiftung.

2017b. "Nouvelle Politique Migratoire et Opérations de Régularisation". In *La Nouvelle Politique Migratoire Marocaine*. Edited by Mehdi Alioua and Jean-Noel Ferrié, 35–76. Rabat: Konrad Adenauer Stiftung.

2017c. "Nouvelle Phase d'intégration Des Migrants Irréguliers: Opérationnalisation et Enjeux Diplomatiques". www.Farzyat.Org. 3 January. http://farzyat.org/nouvelle-phase-dintegration-des-migrant s-irreguliers-operationnalisation-et-enjeux-diplomatiques

Bensaâd, Ali. 2009. "Le Sahara et la transition migratoire entre Sahel, Maghreb et Europe". *Outre-Terre* 23: 273–87. https://doi.org/10.391 7/oute.023.0273

Bentaleb, Hassan. 2017. "Les Autorités de Tétouan Interdisent sans Crier Gare. Le 'non' Injustifié à l'organisation d'une Caravane Médicale Au Profit Des Migrants Passe Mal". *Libé.Ma*, 6 February. www.libe.ma/L es-autorites-de-Tetouan-interdisent-sans-crier-gare_a83290.html

Berger, Peter L. and Thomas Luckmann. 1979. *The Social Construction of Reality: A Treatise in the Sociology of Knowledge*. Harmondsworth: Penguin.

Berrada, Abdelkader. 1986. "La Politique des Bas Salaires Au Maroc: Ébauche d'analyse". *BESM*, 157: 11–65.

Berrada, Abdelkader and Mohamed Saïd Saadi. 2013. "Le Grand Capital Privé Marocain". In *Le Maroc Actuel: Une Modernisation Au Miroir de La Tradition?* Edited by Jean-Claude Santucci, 325–91. Connaissance Du Monde Arabe.Aix-en-Provence: Institut de recherches et d'études sur le monde arabe et musulman. http://books.openedition.org/iremam/2434

Berriane, Johara. 2015. "Sub-Saharan Students in Morocco: Determinants, Everyday Life, and Future Plans of a High-Skilled Migrant Group". *The Journal of North African Studies* 20 (4): 573–89. https://doi.org/10.10 80/13629387.2015.1065042

Berriane, Mohamed, Mohammed Aderghal, Mhamed Idrissi Janati, and Johara Berriane. 2013. "Immigration to Fes: The Meaning of the New Dynamics of the Euro-African Migratory System". *Journal of Intercultural Studies* 34 (5): 486–502. https://doi.org/10.1080/ 07256868.2013.827825

Bialasiewicz, Luiza, Paolo Giaccaria, Alun Jones, and Claudio Minca. 2013. "Re-Scaling 'EU'Rope: EU Macro-Regional Fantasies in the Mediterranean". *European Urban and Regional Studies* 20 (1): 59–76. https://doi.org/10.1177/0969776412463372

Biehl, Joao. 2005. *Vita: Life in a Zone of Social Abandonment*. Berkeley, CA: University of California Press.

Bogaert, Koenraad. 2011. "Urban Politics in Morocco. Uneven Development, Neoliberal Government and the Restructuring of State Power". PhD Thesis, Ghent University.

Bono, Irene. 2007. "Outsourcing Nella Fabbrica Della Democrazia: Appunti Sulla Partecipazione in Marocco". *Meridiana* 58: 139–62.

——— 2008. "Cantiere Del Regno. Associazioni, Sviluppo e Stili Di Governo in Marocco". PhD Thesis, University of Turin.

——— 2010. "L'activisme associatif comme marché du travail. Normalisation sociale et politique par les 'Activités génératrices de revenus' à El Hajeb". *Politique africaine* 120 (4): 25–44. https://doi.org/10.3917/polaf.120.0025

——— 2014. "Indigenti Responsabili e Giovani Occupabili. Il Governo Neoliberale Di Chi ≪merita≫ Assistenza in Marocco". *Meridiana* 79: 127–50.

——— 2017. "Approcher, détourner, écarter le regard: L'observation du politique au prisme de ses représentations hégémoniques". In *Terrains marocains: Sur les traces de chercheurs d'ici et d'ailleurs*. Edited by K. Mouna, C. Therrien, and L. Bouasria, 53–66. Rabat, Casablanca: Centre Jacques-Berque. https://doi.org/10.4000/books.cjb.1287

Boswell, Christina. 2003. "The 'External Dimension' of EU Immigration and Asylum Policy". *International Affairs (Royal Institute of International Affairs 1944-)* 79 (3): 619–38.

——— 2011. "Migration Control and Narratives of Steering". *The British Journal of Politics & International Relations* 13 (1): 12–25. https://doi.org/10.1111/j.1467-856X.2010.00436.x

Boudarssa, Chadia. 2017. "Entre Travail et Engagement, Les Acteurs Expatriés et Nationaux de Solidarité Internationale Au Maroc: Volontaires, Salariés, Bénévoles et Stagiaires. Le Cosmopolitisme à l'épreuve?" PhD thesis, Université Paris Diderot, unpublished.

Bouilly, Emmanuelle. 2010. "La Lutte Contre l'émigration Irrégulière Au Sénégal: Carrière d'une Cause, Trajectoires d'acteurs et Jeu de Pratiques Dans Un Espace de Mobilisation Internationalisé". *Canadian Journal of African Studies/Revue Canadienne Des Études Africaines* 44 (2): 229–55. https://doi.org/10.1080/00083968.2010.9707550

Bourdieu, Pierre. 1994. "Rethinking the State: Genesis and Structure of the Bureaucratic Field". *Sociological Theory* 12 (1): 1–18.

Brachet, Julien. 2016. "Policing the Desert: The IOM in Libya Beyond War and Peace". *Antipode* 48 (2): 272–92. https://doi.org/10.1111/anti.12176

Bredeloup, Sylvie and Olivier Pliez. 2005. "Migrations Entre Les Deux Rives Du Sahara". *AUTREPART-BONDY PARIS* 36: 3.

Brigg, Morgan. 2002. "Post-Development, Foucault and the Colonisation Metaphor". *Third World Quarterly* 23 (3): 421–36. https://doi.org/10.1080/01436590220138367

Burridge, Andrew, Nick Gill, Austin Kocher, and Lauren Martin. 2017. "Polymorphic Borders". *Territory, Politics, Governance* 5 (3): 239–51. https://doi.org/10.1080/21622671.2017.1297253

Busher, Joel, Tufyal Choudhury, Paul Thomas, and Gareth Harris. 2017. "What the Prevent Duty Means for Schools and Colleges in England: An Analysis of Educationalists' Experiences". Centre for Trust, Peace and Social Relations, Coventry University. https://pureportal.coventry.ac.u k/en/publications/what-the-prevent-duty-means-for-schools-and-col leges-in-england-a

Butler, Judith. 1993. "Endangered/Endangering: Schematic Racism and White Paranoia". In *Reading Rodney King/Reading Urban Uprising*. Edited by Robert Gooding-Williams, 15–22. New York and London: Routledge.

Caillault, Clotilde. 2012. "The Implementation of Coherent Migration Management Through IOM Programs in Morocco". In *The New Politics of International Mobility. Migration Management and Its Discontents*, 133–56. Osnabrück, IMIS.

Cairoli, M. 1998. "Factory as Home and Family: Female Workers in the Moroccan Garment Industry". *Human Organization* 57 (2): 181–89. https://doi.org/10.17730/humo.57.2.082j824l32711736

Caminando Fronteras. 2017. "Tras La Frontera". https://abriendofronteras .net/wp-content/uploads/2017/06/ccf-itlf-arte-final-cuerpo.pdf

Can, Başak. 2016. "Human Rights, Humanitarianism, and State Violence: Medical Documentation of Torture in Turkey". *Medical Anthropology Quarterly* 30 (3): 342–58. https://doi.org/10.1111/maq.12259

Canarias7. 2019. "Más de 1.300 Vehículos Pagados Por La UE Vigilarán Las Costas de Marruecos". www.canarias7.es/politica/mas-de-1-300-vehicu los-pagados-por-la-ue-vigilaran-las-costas-de-marruecos-BD8445056

Capelli, Irene. 2016. "Cibler Les Mères Célibataires. La Production Bureaucratique et Morale d'un Impensable Social". In *Le Gouvernement Du Social Au Maroc*. Edited by Béatrice Hibou and Irene Bono, 199–232. Paris: Karthala.

Capello, Carlo. 2008. *Le Prigioni Invisibili: Etnografia Multisituata Della Migrazione Marocchina*. Milano: FrancoAngeli. https://books.google.c o.ma/books?id=2EMkAQAAIAAJ

Carpi, Estella. 2020. "Different Shades of 'Neutrality': Arab Gulf NGO Responses to Syrian Refugees in Northern Lebanon". In *Refuge in a Moving World. Tracing Refugee and Migrant Journeys across Disciplines*. Edited by Elena Fiddian-Qasmiyeh, 415–28. London: UCL Press. https://discovery.ucl.ac.uk/id/eprint/10105213/1/Refuge-in-a-Movin g-World.pdf

Casas-Cortes, Maribel, Sebastian Cobarrubias, and John Pickles. 2014. "'Good Neighbours Make Good Fences': Seahorse Operations, Border

Externalization and Extra-Territoriality". *European Urban and Regional Studies* 23 (3): 231–51. http://eur.sagepub.com/content/early/2014/08/12/0969776414541136.abstract

Cassarino, Jean-Pierre. 2018. "Morocco's Bilateral Agreements Linked to Readmission". Jeanpierrecassarino.Com. www.jeanpierrecassarino.com/datasets/ra/maroc/

Cassidy, Kathryn. 2018. "Everyday Bordering, Healthcare and the Politics of Belonging in Contemporary Britain". In *Borderless Worlds for Whom?: Ethics, Moralities and Mobilities*. Edited by Anssi Paasi, Eeva-Kaisa Prokkola, Jarkko Saarinen, and Kaj Zimmerbauer, 78–92. London: Routledge.

Castles, S., H. de Haas, and M. Miller. 2014. *The Age of Migration: International Population Movements in the Modern World*. Basingstoke: Palgrave MacMillan.

Catusse, Myriam. 2005. "Les réinventions du social dans le Maroc 'ajusté'". *Revue des mondes musulmans et de la Méditerranée* 105–106 (January): 175–98. https://doi.org/10.4000/remmm.2726

2010. "Maroc: Un Fragile État Social Dans La Réforme Néo-Libérale". In *L'État Face Aux Débordements Du Social Au Maghreb. Formation, Travail et Protection Sociale*. Edited by Myriam Catusse, Blandine Destremau, and Éric Verdier, 187–228. Paris: Karthala.

Catusse, Myriam and Frédéric Vairel. 2003. "'Ni tout à fait le même, ni tout à fait un autre'. Métamorphoses et continuité du régime marocain". *Maghreb-Machrek, printemps* 175: 73–91.

2010. "Question sociale et développement: les territoires de l'action publique et de la contestation au Maroc". *Politique africaine* 120: 5–23. https://doi.org/10.3917/polaf.120.0005

Centre for Strategy and Evaluation Services. n.d. "Final Report – Evaluation of Preparatory Actions B7-667 – Cooperation with Third Countries in the Area of Migration. Appendix D – Case Studies". www.asktheeu.org/en/request/8994/response/30266/attach/2/Final%20Report%20PDF.pdf?cookie_passthrough=1

Chappart, Pascaline. 2015a. "Retours Volontaires, Retours Forcés Hors d'Europe. Une Socio-Anthropologie de l'éloignement Des Étrangers. Le Cas de La France". PhD Thesis, Universite de Poitiers, unpublished.

Charef, Mohammed and Patrick Gonin. 2005. *Emigrés-immigrés dans le développement local*. Agadir: Sud Contact.

Chattou, Zoubir. 1998. *Migrations Marocaines En Europe. Le Paradoxe Des Itineraires*. Paris: L'Harmattan.

Chaudier, Julie. 2014. "Première: Un Quart Du Financement de l'aide Au Retour Volontaire des Migrants Assuré Par Le Maroc". *Yabiladi,*

7 March. www.yabiladi.com/articles/details/23892/premiere-quart-fin ancement-l-aide-retour.html

Cherti, Myriam and Michael Collyer. 2015. "Immigration and Pensée d'Etat: Moroccan Migration Policy Changes as Transformation of 'Geopolitical Culture'". *The Journal of North African Studies* 20 (4): 590–604. https://doi.org/10.1080/13629387.2015.1065043

Cherti, Myriam and Peter Grant. 2013. "The Myth of Transit. Sub-Saharan Migration in Morocco". Institute for Public Policy Research. www.ippr .org/files/images/media/files/publication/2013/07/myth-of-transit-moro cco-ENG_June2013_11051.pdf

Choukri, Mohammed. 1980. *Le Pain Nu*. Paris: La Découverte.

Claisse, Alain. 2013. "Le Makhzen Aujourd'hui". *In Le Maroc Actuel: Une Modernisation Au Miroir de La Tradition?* Edited by Jean-Claude Santucci, 285–310. Connaissance Du Monde Arabe. Aix-en-Provence: Institut de recherches et d'études sur le monde arabe et musulman. http://books.openedition.org/iremam/2431

CMSM and GADEM. 2012. "Recrudescence de La Répression Envers Les Migrants Au Maroc Une Violence Qu'on Croyait Révolu".

CNDH. 2013. "Conclusions et Recommandations Du Rapport: 'Etrangers et Droits de l'Homme Au Maroc: Pour Une Politique d'asile et d'immigration Radicalement Nouvelle'". www.cndh.org.ma/fr/rap ports-thematiques/conclusions-et-recommandations-du-rapport-etran gers-et-droits-de-lhomme-au

CNSS. 2019. "Le Salaire Minimum de Bénéfice Des Allocations Familiales Augmente". www.cnss.ma/fr/content/le-salaire-minimum-de-bénéfice-des-allocations-familiales-augmente

Coddington, Kate. 2019. "The Slow Violence of Life without Cash: Borders, State Restrictions, and Exclusion in the U.K. and Australia". *Geographical Review* 109 (4): 527–43. https://doi.org/10 .1111/gere.12332

Coleman, Nils. 2009. *European Readmission Policy: Third Country Interests and Refugee Rights*. Leiden and Boston, MA: Martinus Jinhoff Publishers.

Collett, Elizabeth. 2007. "The 'Global Approach to Migration': Rhetoric or Reality?" European Policy Centre. www.files.ethz.ch/isn/45563/PB_N ov_07_Global_Migration.pdf

Collyer, Michael. 2007. "In-Between Places: Trans-Saharan Transit Migrants in Morocco and the Fragmented Journey to Europe". *Antipode* 39 (4): 668–90. https://doi.org/10.1111/j.1467-8330.2007.00546.x

2009. "Euro-African Relations in the Field of Migration, 2008". *Panorama: The Mediterranean Year*: 283. www.researchgate.net/publication/23758 8383_Euro-African_Relations_in_the_Field_of_Migration_2008

2010. "Stranded Migrants and the Fragmented Journey". *Journal of Refugee Studies* 23 (3): 273–93. https://doi.org/10.1093/jrs/feq026

2012. "Migrants as Strategic Actors in the European Union's Global Approach to Migration and Mobility". *Global Networks* 12 (4): 505–24. https://doi.org/10.1111/j.1471-0374.2012.00370.x

2016. "Geopolitics as a Migration Governance Strategy: European Union Bilateral Relations with Southern Mediterranean Countries". *Journal of Ethnic and Migration Studies* 42 (4): 606–24. https://doi.org/10.1080/1369183X.2015.1106111

Committee on the Rights of the Child. 2018. "Concluding Observations on the Combined Fifth and Sixth Periodic Reports of Spain – CRC/C/ESP/CO/5–6".

Concord. 2018. "AidWatch 2018. Aid and Migration. The Externalisation of Europe's Responsibilities". https://concordeurope.org/wp-content/uploads/2018/03/CONCORD_AidWatchPaper_Aid_Migration_2018_online.pdf?1bf6b0&1bf6b0

Confédération Suisse. 2015. "Migration". 12 November. www.eda.admin.ch/countries/morocco/fr/home/cooperation-internationale/themes/migration.html

Conseil Economique, Social et Environnemental. 2018. "La Protection Sociale Au Maroc. Revue, Bilan et Renforcement Des Systèmes de Sécurité et d'assistance Sociales". www.cese.ma/media/2020/10/Rapport-La-protection-sociale-au-Maroc.pdf

Cooperación Española. 2015. "AECID. Convocatoria de Proyectos de ONGD 2015. III- Fichas de Valoración de Los Proyectos Admitidos a La Convocatoria En Magreb, Oriente Medio, Fipinias y Africa Subsahariana".

Council of the European Union. 2005. "The Hague Programme: Strengthening Freedom, Security and Justice in the European Union (2005/C 53/01)".

Crisp, Jeff. 2003. "UNHCR, Refugee Livelihoods and Self-Reliance: A Brief History". 22 October. www.unhcr.org/research/eval/3f978a894/unhcr-refugee-livelihoods-self-reliance-brief-history.html

Cronin, Ciaran. 1996. "Bourdieu and Foucault on Power and Modernity". *Philosophy & Social Criticism* 22 (6): 55–85. https://doi.org/10.1177/019145379602200603

Croxford, Rianna. 2018. "UN Agency's U-Turn after Unpaid Internships Row". *BBC*. www.bbc.co.uk/news/world-45605768

Cuttitta, Paolo. 2016. "Ricerca e Soccorso Indipendenti Nel Canale di Sicilia". *Rivista Di Storia Delle Idee* 5 (1): 130–39.

2020. "Non-Governmental/Civil Society Organisations and the European Union-Externalisation of Migration Management in Tunisia and Egypt". *Population, Space and Place* 26 (7): e2329.

De Genova, Nicholas. 2013. "Spectacles of Migrant 'Illegality': The Scene of Exclusion, the Obscene of Inclusion". *Ethnic and Racial Studies* 36 (7): 1180–98. https://doi.org/10.1080/01419870.2013.783710

Del Grande, Gabriele. 2007. *Mamadou va a morire. La strage dei clandestini nel Mediterraneo.* 2nd ed. Due Santi di Marino, Roma: Infinito edizioni.

Delcourt, Laurent. 2009. "Retour de l'Etat. Pour Quelles Politiques Sociales?" *Alternatives Sud* 16 (7).

den Hertog, Leonard. 2016. "Money Talks: Mapping the Funding for EU External Migration Policy". CEPS Paper in Liberty & Security in Europe, No. 58. www.ceps.eu/publications/money-talks-mapping-fund ing-eu-external-migration-policy

——— 2017. "Study. EU and German External Migration Policies: The Case of Morocco". Heinrich Böll Stiftung. https://ma.boell.org/sites/default/file s/eu_and_german_external_migration_policies_-_ceps.pdf

Denyer Willis, Laurie and Clare Chandler. 2019. "Quick Fix for Care, Productivity, Hygiene and Inequality: Reframing the Entrenched Problem of Antibiotic Overuse". *BMJ Global Health* 4 (4): e001590. https://doi.org/10.1136/bmjgh-2019-001590

Díaz, Sato. 2018. "José Palazón: 'No Me Imagino Melilla Sin La Actividad Económica de La Inmigración.'" *Cuarto Poder*, 31 July. www.cuartopo der.es/derechos-sociales/2018/07/31/jose-palazon-melilla-actividad-eco nomica-imigracion/

Dini, Sabine. 2017. "Migration Management, Capacity Building and the Sovereignty of an African State: International Organization for Migration in Djibouti". *Journal of Ethnic and Migration Studies* 44 (10): 1691–705. https://doi.org/10.1080/1369183X.2017.1354058

Duffield, Mark. 2007. *Development, Security and Unending War: Governing the World of Peoples.* Cambridge: Polity Press.

——— 2010. "Risk-Management and the Fortified Aid Compound: Everyday Life in Post-Interventionary Society". *Journal of Intervention and Statebuilding* 4 (4): 453–74. https://doi.org/10.1080/17502971003700993

Düvell, Franck. 2006. "Crossing the Fringes of Europe: Transit Migration in the EU's Neighbourhood". Centre on Migration, Policy and Society, University of Oxford. www.compas.ox.ac.uk/wp-content/uploads/WP-2006-033-Düvell_Fringe_Migration.pdf

Edogué Ntang, Jean-Louis and Michel Peraldi. 2011. "Un Ancrage Discret. L'établissement Des Migrations Subsahariennes Dans La Capitale Marocaine". In *D'une Afrique à l'autre. Migrations Subsahariennes Au Maroc.* Edited by Michel Peraldi, 35–52. Paris: Karthala.

El Aissi, Noureddine. 2018. "Soutien Des Migrants: L'Entraide Nationale s'engage". *L'Economiste*, 25 January. www.leconomiste.com/article/1 023237-soutien-des-migrants-l-entraide-nationale-s-engage

El Hamel, Chouki. 2012. *Black Morocco: A History of Slavery, Race, and Islam. African Studies*. Cambridge: Cambridge University Press. https://doi.org/10.1017/CBO9781139198783

El País. 2017. "Un Tribunal Ordena Reabrir El Caso Por La Tragedia Del Tarajal". 12 January. http://politica.elpais.com/politica/2017/01/12/ac tualidad/1484245825_186391.html

El Qadim, Nora. 2014. "Postcolonial Challenges to Migration Control: French–Moroccan Cooperation Practices on Forced Returns". *Security Dialogue* 45(3): 242–61. https://doi.org/10.1177/0967010614533139
2015. *Le gouvernement asymétrique des migrations. Maroc/Union européenne*. Paris: Dalloz.

El Qadim, Nora, Beste İşleyen, Leonie Ansems de Vries, et al. 2020. "(Im) Moral Borders in Practice". *Geopolitics* (April): 1–31. https://doi.org/10.1080/14650045.2020.1747902

Eldiario.es. 2016. "Qué Hacía y Qué Denunciaba El Sacerdote Español al Que Marruecos Ha Expulsado". *Eldiario.Es*. 25 January. www.eldiari o.es/desalambre/denunciaba-sacerdote-Marruecos-impide-entrad a_0_477353147.html

Ellermann, Antje. 2009. *States against Migrants: Deportation in Germany and the United States*. Cambridge: Cambridge University Press.

Elyachar, Julia. 2005. *Markets of Dispossession: NGOs, Economic Development, and the State in Cairo*. Durham, NC: Duke University Press.

Emperador Badimon, Montserrat. 2010. "Insérer Ou Controler Les Chomeurs? La Bicéphalie de La Politique de l'emploi à l'épreuve Des Mobilisations de Diplomés Chomeurs Au Maroc". In *L'Etat Face Aux Débordements Du Social au Maghreb. Formation, Travail et Protection Sociale*. Edited by Myriam Catusse, Blandine Destremeau, and Eric Verdier, 251–65. Paris: Karthala.

Enabel. n.d. "Appui à La Mise En Œuvre de La Stratégie Nationale d'immigration et d'asile". https://open.enabel.be/fr/MAR/2221/p/appui–la-mise-en-oeuvre-de-la-stratgie-nationale-d-immigration-et-d-asile.html
2018. "Le Programme d'appui à La Gestion de La Thématique Migratoire Est Lancé!" 22 May. https://open.enabel.be/fr/MAR/2222/606/u/le-pro gramme-d-appui–la-gestion-de-la-thmatique-migratoire-est-lanc.html

Ennaji, Mohammed. 1999. *Serving the Master: Slavery and Society in Nineteenth-Century Morocco*. Basingstoke: Macmillan.

Escher, Anton and Sandra Petermann. 2013. "Marrakesh Medina: Neocolonial Paradise of Lifestyle Migrants?" In *Contested Spatialities, Lifestyle Migration and Residential Tourism*. Edited by Michael Janoschka and Heiko Haas, 29–46. Abingdon, Oxon: Routledge.

Escoffier, Claire. 2006. "Communautés d'itinérance et Savoir– Circuler Des Transmigrant-e-s Au Maghreb". PhD Thesis, Université Toulouse II, unpublished.

EU Delegation in Rabat. 2016. "Projets Financés Par l'Union Européenne Au Maroc – En Cours".

2017a. "Contrats de Subvention Octroyés En Décembre 2017. Source de Financement: BGUE-B2017-22.045100-C8-NEAR".

2017b. "Programme: Promouvoir l'intégration Des Migrants Au Maroc. Lignes Directrices à l'intention Des Demandeurs".

Europe Aid. 2006. "AENEAS Programme – Programme for Financial and Technical Assistance to Third Countries in the Area of Migration and Asylum. Overview of Projects Funded 2004–2006". https://download .taz.de/migcontrol/eu/EU_AENAS_%20projects%20funded%20to%2 0third%20countries%202004%20-%202006_eng.pdf

2008. "Grants Awarded under Call for Proposals 126364 – Thematic Programme of Cooperation with Third Countries in the Areas of Migration and Asylum". https://bit.ly/3bkx7tT

European Commission. n.d.a "Annexe IV à l'Accord Instituant Le Fonds Fiduciaire 'European Union Emergency Trust Fund for Stability and Addressing Root Causes of Irregular Migration and Displaced Persons in Africa', et Ses Règles Internes. Vivre Ensemble sans Discrimination: Une Approche Basée Sur Les Droits de l'Homme et La Dimension de Genre (T05-EUTF-NOA-MA-01)".

n.d.b "Appui Aux Actions des Autorités Marocaines Contre Les Réseaux Facilitant Les Flux Migratoires Irréguliers". https://ec.europa.eu/trust fundforafrica/region/appui-aux-actions-des-autorites-marocaines-con tre-les-reseaux-facilitant-les-flux-migratoires_en

n.d.c "Assistance Aux Personnes Migrantes En Situation de Vulnérabilité (T05-EUTF-NOA-MA-03)". https://ec.europa.eu/trustfundforafrica/sit es/euetfa/files/t05-eutf-noa-ma-03.pdf

n.d.d "Soutien à La Gestion Intégrée des Frontières et de La Migration Au Maroc". https://ec.europa.eu/trustfundforafrica/region/north-africa/moroc co/soutien-la-gestion-integree-des-frontieres-et-de-la-migration-au-maroc_en

2016. "C(2016) 8836 Final – Décision d'exécution de La Commission Du 15.12.2016 Relative Au Programme d'action Annuel 2016 – Partie 3 En Faveur Du Maroc à Financer Sur Le Budget Général de l'Union".

2017. "Lignes Directrices. Programme: PROMOUVOIR L'INTEGRATION DES MIGRANTS AU MAROC (PROGRAMME D'APPUI AU PARTENARIAT POUR LA MOBILITE UE-MAROC) Lignes Directrices à l'intention Des Demandeurs Ligne(s) Budgétaire(s): BGUE-B2013-

19.080101-C1-DEVCO SPRING Référence: EuropeAid/156714/DD/ ACT/".

2018a. "Empowerment Juridique Des Personnes Migrantes (T05-EUTF-NOA-MA-02)". https://ec.europa.eu/trustfundforafrica/sites/euetfa/file s/t05-eutf-noa-ma-02_19.pdf

2018b. "EU Cooperation on Migration with Morocco". https://ec.europa .eu/neighbourhood-enlargement/sites/near/files/eu-morocco-factsheet .pdf

2018c. "T05-EUTF-NOA-MA-03". https://ec.europa.eu/trustfundfora frica/sites/euetfa/files/t05-eutf-noa-ma-03.pdf

2019. "EU Emergency Trust Fund for Africa: New Actions of Almost €150 Million to Tackle Human Smuggling, Protect Vulnerable People and Stabilise Communities in North Africa". https://ec.europa.eu/commis sion/presscorner/detail/en/ip_19_6744

European Council. 2005. "Brussels European Council. Presidency Conclusions. 15/16 December 2005". www.statewatch.org/news/2005 /dec/eu-summit-concl-dec-05.pdf

European Court of Human Rights. 2017. "Judgment – Affaire N.D. et N.T. c. Espagne". https://hudoc.echr.coe.int/spa#{"itemid":["001-201353"]}

Fassin, Didier. 2008. "The Humanitarian Politics of Testimony: Subjectification through Trauma in the Israeli–Palestinian Conflict". *Cultural Anthropology* 23 (3): 531–58. https://doi.org/10.1111/j.1548 -1360.2008.00017.x

2011a. *Humanitarian Reason.* Berkeley, LA and London: University of California Press. www.ucpress.edu/book.php?isbn=9780520271173

2011b. "The Trace: Violence, Truth, and the Politics of the Body". *Social Research: An International Quarterly* 78 (2): 281–98.

Fassin, Didier and Estelle d'Halluin. 2005. "The Truth from the Body: Medical Certificates as Ultimate Evidence for Asylum Seekers". *American Anthropologist* 107 (4): 597–608.

Feldman, Ilana. 2015. "Looking for Humanitarian Purpose: Endurance and the Value of Lives in a Palestinian Refugee Camp". *Public Culture* 27 (3 (77)): 427–47. https://doi.org/10.1215/08992363-2896171

Feldman, Ilana and Miriam Ticktin. 2010. *In the Name of Humanity: The Government of Threat and Care.* Durham, NC: Duke University Press.

Ferguson, James. 1994. *The Anti-Politics Machine: Development, Depoliticization, and Bureaucratic Power in Lesotho.* New ed. Minneapolis, MN: University of Minnesota Press.

Fernández, Fátima. 2018. "South-South Agreements in the Framework of North-South Integration: The Case of Morocco in the Euro-Mediterranean Process". PhD Thesis, Universidade de Santiago de Compostela, unpublished.

Ferrer-Gallardo, Xavier. 2008. "The Spanish–Moroccan Border Complex: Processes of Geopolitical, Functional and Symbolic Rebordering". *Political Geography* 27 (3): 301–21. https://doi.org/ 10.1016/j.polgeo.2007.12.004

Ferrié, Jean-Noel and Mehdi Alioua. 2017. "Politiques Migratoires et Sérénité de l'action Publique". In *La Nouvelle Politique Migratoire Marocaine*. Edited by Mehdi Alioua, Jean-Noel Ferrié, and Helmut Reifeld, 19–34. Rabat: Konrad Adenauer Stiftung.

Fiddian-Qasmiyeh, Elena. 2014. *The Ideal Refugees: Gender, Islam, and the Sahrawi Politics of Survival.* 1st ed. Syracuse, NY: Syracuse University Press.

FIDH and GADEM. 2015. "Maroc – Entre Rafles et Régularisations Bilan d'une Politique Migratoire Indécise". www.fidh.org/IMG/pdf/rapport_maroc_migration_fr.pdf

Fine, Shoshana. 2018. "Liaisons, Labelling and Laws: International Organization for Migration Bordercratic Interventions in Turkey". *Journal of Ethnic and Migration Studies* 44 (10): 1743–55. https://doi.org/10.1080/1369183X.2017.1354073

FitzGerald, David. 2019. *Refuge beyond Reach: How Rich Democracies Repel Asylum Seekers.* New York: Oxford University Press.

Foucault, Michel. 1979a. *Discipline and Punish: The Birth of the Prison.* Harmondsworth Penguin Book.

1979b. *Discipline and Punish: The Birth of the Prison.* New York: Vintage Books.

1980. *Power/Knowledge: Selected Interviews and Other Writings, 1972–1977.* Harlow: Longman.

1990. *The History of Sexuality: An Introduction.* Harmondsworth Penguin.

2002. *Archaeology of Knowledge.* London and New York: Routledge.

2007. *Security, Territory, Population Lectures at the Collège de France, 1977–78.* Basingstoke and New York: Palgrave Macmillan.

FRONTEX. 2017. "Africa-Frontex Intelligence Community Joint Report 2016". https://globalinitiative.net/wp-content/uploads/2018/01/FRONTEX-Africa-Frontex-2016-Intelligence-Community-Joint-Report.pdf

Frontline Defenders. 2020. "Preventive Detention of Omar Naji & 2 Other HRDs Because of Social Media Posts, in the Context of COVID-19". www.frontlinedefenders.org/en/case/preventive-detention-omar-naji-2-other-hrds-because-social-media-posts-context-covid-19

Frowd, Philippe M. 2018. *Security at the Borders: Transnational Practices and Technologies in West Africa.* Cambridge: Cambridge University Press. https://doi.org/10.1017/9781108556095

FTDES and Migreurop. 2020. "Politiques Du Non-Accueil En Tunisie". http://ftdes.net/rapports/ftdes.migreu.pdf

Gabrielli, Lorenzo. 2016. "Multilevel Inter-Regional Governance of Mobility between Africa and Europe. Towards a Deeper and Broader Externalisation". GRITIM Working Paper Series – Universitat Pompeu Fabra, 30.

GADEM. 2013a. "Communication Adressée Aux Membres Du Comité Pour La Protection Des Droits de Tous Les Travailleurs Migrants et Des Membres de Leur Famille". www.gadem-asso.org/communication-adr essee-aux-membres-du-comite-pour-la-protection-des-droits-de-tous-le s-travailleurs-migrants-et-des-membres-de-leur-famille/

2013b. "Rapport Sur l'application Par Le Maroc de La Convention Internationale Sur La Protection Des Droits de Tous Les Travailleurs Migrants et Des Membres de Leur Famille. Résumé Exécutif". www.g adem-asso.org/rapport-sur-lapplication-par-le-maroc-de-la-conven tion-internationale-sur-la-protection-des-droits-de-tous-les-travail leurs-migrants-et-des-membres-de-leur-famille-resume-executif/

2018a. "Coûts et Blessures. Rapport Sur Les Opérations Des Forces de l'ordre Menées Dans Le Nord Du Maroc Entre Juillet et Septembre 2018 – Éléments Factuels et Analyse". www.lacimade.org/wp-content/ uploads/2018/10/20180927_GADEM_Couts_et_blessures.pdf

2018b. "Expulsions Gratuites. Note d'analyse Sur Les Mesures d'éloignement Mises En Œuvre Hors Tout Cadre Légal Entre Septembre et Octobre 2018".

2020. "Communiqué de Presse GADEM – Samedi 21 Mars 2020. Covid-19: Le Gouvernement Marocain En Action Mais Quelles Mesures Pour Les Personnes Étrangères Au Maroc?" www.gadem-asso.org/covid-19-le-gouvernement-marocain-en-action-mais-quelles-mesures-pour-les-p ersonnes-etrangeres-au-maroc/

GADEM, Migreurop, La Cimade, and APDHA. 2015. "Ceuta et Melilla, Centres de Tri à Ciel Ouvert Aux Portes de l'Afrique". www.migreurop .org/article2666.html?lang=fr

Gammeltoft-Hansen, Thomas and Ninna Nyberg, Sørensen, eds. 2013. *"The Migration Industry and the Commercialization of International Migration"*. New York: Routledge Global Institutions Series, xviii.

García Andrade, Paula and Iván Martìn. 2015. "EU Cooperation with Third Countries in the Field of Migration". Study for the LIBE Committee, European Parliament. www.europarl.europa.eu/RegData/etudes/STU D/2015/536469/IPOL_STU%282015%29536469_EN.pdf

Garelli, Glenda and Martina Tazzioli. 2016. "Warfare on the Logistics of Migrant Movements: EU and NATO Military Operations in the Mediterranean". *OpenDemocracy* 15 June. www.opendemocracy.net/ mediterranean-journeys-in-hope/glenda-garelli-martina-tazzioli/war fare-on-logistics-of-migrant-movem

Gazzotti, Lorena. 2018. "From Irregular Migration to Radicalisation? Fragile Borders, Securitised Development and the Government of Moroccan Youth". *Journal of Ethnic and Migration Studies* 45 (15): 2888–909. https://doi.org/10.1080/1369183X.2018.1493914

2019. "Governing the 'Immigration Nation'. Development, Humanitarianism and Migration Politics in Morocco". PhD Dissertation, University of Cambridge.

2021. "(Un)making Illegality: Border Control, Racialized Bodies and Differential Regimes of Illegality in Morocco". *The Sociological Review* 69 (2): 277–95. https://doi.org/10.1177/0038026120982273

Gazzotti, Lorena and Maria Hagan. 2020. "Dispersal and Dispossession as Bordering: Exploring Governance through Mobility in Post-2013 Morocco". *Journal of North African Studies*. https://doi.org/10.1080/13629387.2020.1800209

Geddes, Andrew. 2000. *Immigration and European Integration: Towards Fortress Europe?* Manchester: Manchester University Press.

2008. *Immigration and European Integration: Beyond Fortress Europe.* 2nd rev. ed. Manchester: Manchester University Press.

Geha, Carmen and Joumana Talhouk. 2018. "From Recipients of Aid to Shapers of Policies: Conceptualizing Government–United Nations Relations during the Syrian Refugee Crisis in Lebanon". *Journal of Refugee Studies* 32 (4): 645–63. https://doi.org/10.1093/jrs/fey052

Geiger, Martin and Antoine Pécoud, eds. 2010. *The Politics of International Migration Management.* London: Palgrave Macmillan. http://link.springer.com/10.1057/9780230294882

Gentile, Michael. 2013. "Meeting the 'Organs': The Tacit Dilemma of Field Research in Authoritarian States". *Area* 45 (4): 426–32. www.jstor.org/stable/24029921

GIZ. n.d. "Projects in Morocco". www.giz.de/projektdaten/index.action?request_locale=en_EN#?region=3&countries=MA

Gonzales, Elena. 2016. "Marruecos Desmantela a Golpe de Expulsiones Una ONG Financiada Por La Cooperación Española". *El Diario*, 29 June.

Graham, Stephen. 2002. "'Clean Territory': Urbicide in the West Bank". *OpenDemocracy*, 7 August. www.opendemocracy.net/en/article_241jsp/

Gross-Wyrtzen, Leslie. 2020a. "Policing the Virus: Race, Risk, and the Politics of Containment in Morocco and the United States. Roundtable on Borders and the State in Light of COVID-19". *Security in Context.* www.securityincontext.com/publications/borders-roundtable-policing-the-virus

2020b. "Contained and Abandoned in the 'Humane' Border: Black Migrants' Immobility and Survival in Moroccan Urban Space".

Environment and Planning D: Society and Space 38 (5): 887–904. htt ps://doi.org/10.1177/0263775820922243

Gross-Wyrtzen, Leslie and Lorena Gazzotti. 2020. "Telling Histories of the Present: Postcolonial Perspectives on Morocco's 'Radically New' Migration Policy". *Journal of North African Studies.* https://doi.org/1 0.1080/13629387.2020.1800204

Groupe Thématique Migrations. 2007. "Cadre Stratégique". www.unhcr.o rg/4a93fc769.pdf

Guerini, Nausicaa. 2012. "Teatri Di Transito. Inter-Azioni e Ibridazioni Tra Associazioni e Migranti Subsahariani in Marocco". PhD Thesis, Università Di Bergamo, unpublished.

Haas, Hein de. 2003. "Migration and Development in Southern Morocco. The Disparate Socio-Economic Impacts of Out-Migration on the Todgha Oasis Valley". PhD thesis, Katholieke Universiteit Nijmegen.

2005. "Morocco's Migration Transition: Trends, Determinants and Future Scenarios". MDR Working Paper, No. 3.

2007. "Morocco's Migration Experience: A Transitional Perspective". *International Migration* 45 (4): 39–70.

2008. "The Myth of Invasion: The Inconvenient Realities of African Migration to Europe". *Third World Quarterly* 29 (7): 1305–22. http s://doi.org/10.1080/01436590802386435

2012. "IOM's Dubious Mission in Morocco". 4 October. http://heinde haas.blogspot.com/2012/10/ioms-dubious-mission-in-morocco.html

Hampshire, James. 2016. "Speaking with One Voice? The European Union's Global Approach to Migration and Mobility and the Limits of International Migration Cooperation". *Journal of Ethnic and Migration Studies* 42 (4): 571–86. https://doi.org/10.1080/ 1369183X.2015.1103036

Harrell-Bond, Barbara. 2002. "Can Humanitarian Work with Refugees Be Humane?" *Human Rights Quarterly* 24 (1): 51–85.

Haut Commissariat au Plan. 2009. "Les Résidents Étrangers Au Maroc. Profil Démographique et Socio-Économique". Royaume du Maroc. www.google.com/url?sa=t&rct=j&q=&esrc=s&source=web&cd=& ved=2ahUKEwiystLd_L_wAhUiyIUKHT1GA-MQFjAAegQIAhA D&url=https%3A%2F%2Fwww.hcp.ma%2Ffile%2F112337% 2F&usg=AOvVaw12j5H43tHjwpxSVZABtrbM

2015. "Populations Concernées Par Le Recensement Général de La Population et de l'Habitat". www.hcp.ma/file/165489/

2017a. "Chomage". www.hcp.ma/Chomage_r70.html

2017b. "Les Résidents Étrangers Au Maroc". www.google.com/url?s a=t&rct=j&q=&esrc=s&source=web&cd=&cad=rja&uact=8&ve d=2ahUKEwif7pXh_b_wAhWvxIUKHcnaA98QFjAAegQIBBAD&

url=https%3A%2F%2Fwww.hcp.ma%2Ffile%2F112337%2F&usg=AOvVaw12j5H43tHjwpxSVZABtrbM

2017c. "NOTE D'INFORMATION DU HAUT-COMMISSARIAT AU PLAN A L'OCCASION DE LA JOURNEE INTERNATIONALE DES MIGRANTS 18 DECEMBRE 2017". www.hcp.ma/Note-d-informa tion-du-Haut-Commissariat-au-Plan-a-l-occasion-de-la-journee-inter nationale-des-migrants-18-decembre-2017_a2067.html

Heath-Kelly, Charlotte and Erzsébet Strausz. 2019. "The Banality of Counterterrorism 'after, after 9/11'? Perspectives on the Prevent Duty from the UK Health Care Sector". *Critical Studies on Terrorism* 12 (1): 89–109. https://doi.org/10.1080/17539153.2018.1494123

Hellio, Emmanuelle. 2014. "Importer des femmes pour exporter des fraises?: Flexibilité du travail, canalisation des flux migratoires et échappatoires dans une monoculture intensive globalisée: le cas des saisonnières marocaines en Andalousie". PhD thesis, University of Nice, unpublished.

Hellio, Emmanuelle and Moreno Nieto Juana. 2018. "Les fruits de la frontière". *Plein droit* 1 (1): 31–34. www.cairn.info/revue-plein-droit-2018-1-page-31.htm

Hertog, Leonhard den. 2016. "Funding the Eu-Morocco 'Mobility Partnership': Of Implementation and Competences". *European Journal of Migration and Law* 18 (3): 275–301. https://doi.org/10.116 3/15718166-12342103

Hess, Sabine. 2010. "'We Are Facilitating States!' An Ethnographic Analysis of the ICMPD". In *The Politics of International Migration Management*. Edited by Martin Geiger and Antoine Pécoud, 96–118. Migration, Minorities and Citizenship. London: Palgrave Macmillan. https://doi.org/10.1057/9780230294882_5

Hibou, Béatrice. 1999. "La 'décharge', nouvel interventionnisme". *Politique africaine* 1: 6–15.

2004. *Privatising the State*. London: Hurst and Company.

2012. *La Bureaucratisation Du Monde à l'ère Néolibérale*. Paris: Paris: La Découverte.

Hibou, Béatrice and Mohamed Tozy. 2015. "Gouvernement Personnel et Gouvernment Institutionnalisé de La Charité. L'INDH Au Maroc". In *L'Etat d'injustice Au Maghreb. Maroc et Tunisie*. Edited by Irene Bono, Béatrice Hibou, Hamza Meddeb, and Mohamed Tozy, 379–428. Paris: Karthala.

Hucks, Timothy. 2019. "I Left My House for Two Minutes. And Two Minutes Was All It Took". https://twitter.com/Ame0baRepublic/sta tus/1167456566045548545?ref_src=twsrc%5Etfw%7Ctwcamp%5Et weetembed%7Ctwterm%5E1167456566045548545%7Ctwgr%5E&

ref_url=https%3A%2F%2Fen.yabiladi.com%2Farticles%2Fdetails%
2F82708%2Fordeal-african-american-mistaken-sub-saharan-migrant
.html

Human Rights Watch. 2014. "Maroc: Abus à l'encontre de Migrants
Subsahariens". Human Rights Watch. 10 February. www.hrw.org/fr/n
ews/2014/02/10/maroc-abus-lencontre-de-migrants-subsahariens

2017a. Morocco: Protest Leader Alleges Police Beat Him. www.hrw.org/
news/2017/06/22/morocco-protest-leader-alleges-police-beat-him

2017b. Maroc: Le roi ignore des preuves de violences policières. www.hr
w.org/fr/news/2017/09/05/maroc-le-roi-ignore-des-preuves-de-vio
lences-policieres

Hyndman, Jennifer. 2019. "Unsettling Feminist Geopolitics: Forging
Feminist Political Geographies of Violence and Displacement".
Gender, Place & Culture 26 (1): 3–29. https://doi.org/10.1080/
0966369X.2018.1561427

ICMPD. n.d. "Participants. Rabat Process". www.icmpd.org/our-work/mi
gration-dialogues/rabat-process/participants/

INAS and UNICEF. 2010. "'Mineurs Invisibles'. Les Mineurs Migrants et Le
Défi de Leur Protection Au Maroc".

Infantino, Federica. 2011. "Les Mondes Des Étudiants Sub-Sahariens Au
Maroc". In *D'une Afrique à l'Autre. Migrations Sub-Sahariennes Au
Maroc*. Edited by Michel Peraldi, 99–120. Paris: Karthala.

2016. *Outsourcing Border Control. Politics and Practice of Contracted
Visa Policy in Morocco*. New York: Palgrave Macmillan. www.pal
grave.com/de/book/9781137469830

Institute for Studies on International Politics (ISPI). 2010. "Regional Assisted
Voluntary Return and Reintegration (AVRR) Programme for Stranded
Migrants in Lybia and Morocco. External Evaluation". https://returnan
dreintegration.iom.int/system/files/resources/document/iom_regiona
l_assisted_voluntary_return_and_reintegration_for_stranded_migrant
s_in_libya_and_morocco_2010.pdf?type=node&id=153&lang=en

Integration Strategy Group. 2016. "A Tale of Three Cities: New Migration
and Integration Realities in Istanbul, O Enbach and Tangier". www.giz
.de/static/de/images/contentimages_320x305px/Bither_Kueppers_Zieb
arth_IntegrationThreeCities_Oct16_0.pdf

International Organisation for Migration. 2005. "Migration. Pakistan
Quake. A Race against Winter". https://publications.iom.int/system/fil
es/pdf/migration_dec_2005_en.pdf

2010. "Programme de Retour Volontaire Assisté de Migrants En
Situation Irrégulière Au Maroc et de Réinsertion Dans Leur Pays
d'origine (AVRR). OIM – Avril 2010". www.unhcr.org/50aa58de9
.pdf

2016. "Assistance à La Réintegration Au Maroc". http://morocco.iom.int/
sites/default/files/AVRR%20vers%20le%20Maroc.pdf

2017. "Voluntary Return and Reintegration: Community-Based
Approaches".

2018. "Assistance Au Retour Volontaire et à La Réintegration Depuis Le
Maroc. Rapport Annuel 2018". https://morocco.iom.int/sites/default/fi
les/Rapport%20Aide%20au%20Retour%20Volontaire%20et%20à
%20la%20Réintégration%20depuis%20le%20Maroc%20Année%2
02018%20.pdf

2019a. "2018 – Return and Reintegration Key Highlights". https://relief
web.int/sites/reliefweb.int/files/resources/2018_return_and_reintegra
tion_key_highlights.pdf

2019b. "Bilan OIM Maroc. Edition 2019". https://morocco.iom.int/sites/
default/files/BILAN%20edition%202019.pdf

IOM. 2018. "Formation Professionnelle et Opportunités de Subsistance
Pour Les Migrants Régularisés Au Maroc. Rapport d'évaluation Post
Projet". https://evaluation.iom.int/sites/evaluation/files/docs/resources/
IDF%2520Formation%2520Migrants%2520r%25C3%25A9gularis
%25C3%25A9s%2520Maroc%25202018.pdf

IOM Morocco. 2020. "IOM MOROCCO RESPONSE TO COVID-19.
Report N°7 COVID-19 From 01 April to 30 September 2020". http
s://morocco.iom.int/sites/default/files/Report%20n°7%20COVID19%
20IOM%20Morocco.pdf

IRIDIA, NOVACT, and Fotomovimiento. 2017. "La Frontera Sur. Accesos
Terrestres". http://ddhhfronterasur2017.org/assets/frontera-sur.pdf

Istituto Meme. 2008. "ALBAMAR: Sostegno Integrato a Favore Dei
Migranti Che Ritornano in Albania e Marocco". www.istituto-meme
.it/pdf/tesi/baldassarre-2008.pdf

Jeffrey, Alexander. 2013. *The Improvised State Sovereignty, Performance
and Agency in Dayton Bosnia. RGS-IBG Book Series.* Malden, MA:
Wiley & Sons.

Jeune Afrique. 2013. "Maroc: Sur Le Départ, MSF Lance Un Cri d'alarme Au
Sujet Des Violences Faites Aux Migrants". *JeuneAfrique.Com* (blog).
14 March. www.jeuneafrique.com/171800/societe/maroc-sur-le-d-part-
msf-lance-un-cri-d-alarme-au-sujet-des-violences-faites-aux-migrants/

2018. "Maroc: assouplissement des critères de régularisation des sans-
papiers". *JeuneAfrique.com* (blog). 29 March. www.jeuneafrique.co
m/546679/societe/maroc-assouplissement-des-criteres-de-regularisa
tion-des-sans-papiers/

Jiménez Álvarez, Mercedes. 2003. "Buscarse La Vida. Analisis
Transnacional de Los Procesos Migratorios de Los Menores
Marroquies No Acompanado En Andalucia". Fundacion Santa Maria.

2011. "Intrusos En La Fortaleza. Menores Marroquíes Migrantes En La Frontera Sur de Europa". PhD thesis, Universidad Autonoma de Madrid, unpublished.

Jiménez Álvarez, Mercedes, Keina R. Espiñeira, and Lorena Gazzotti. 2020. "Migration Policy and International Human Rights Frameworks in Morocco: Tensions and Contradictions". *Journal of North African Studies*. https://doi.org/10.1080/13629387.2020.1800208

Jiménez, Yasmina. 2005. "Médicos Sin Fronteras Localiza a Cientos de Inmigrantes Llevados al Desierto Por Marruecos". *El Mundo.Es*, 8 October. www.elmundo.es/elmundo/2005/10/07/solidaridad/11286 82072.html

Jones, Reece. 2016. *Violent Borders: Refugees and the Right to Move*. London and New York: Verso.

Jusionyte, Ieva. 2017. "The Wall and the Wash. Security, Infrastructure and Rescue on the US-Mexico Border". *Anthropology Today* 33 (3): 13–16.

2018. *Threshold: Emergency Responders on the US-Mexico Border*. Oakland, CA: University of California Press.

Kapur, Devesh. 2004. "Remittances: The New Development Mantra?" G-24 Discussion Paper Series, No. 24.

Karibi, Khadija. 2015. "Migrants Subsahariens à Rabat, Une Entrée Spatiale: L'épreuve Des Espaces Publics". In *Migrants Au Maroc: Cosmopolitisme, Présence d'étrangers et Transformations Sociales*. Edited by Nadia Khrouz and Nazarena Lanza, 134–39. Rabat: Centre Jacques Berque. https://books.openedition.org/cjb/910

Kettani, Meryem and Michel Peraldi. 2011. "Les Mondes Du Travail. Segmentations et Informalités". In *D'une Afrique à l'autre. Migrations Subsahariennes Au Maroc*. Edited by Michel Peraldi, 53–70. Paris: Karthala.

Khrouz, Nadia. 2015. "Quelle Politique d'immigration? La Problématique de l'accès Au Marché Du Travail". In *Le Maroc Au Présent: D'une Époque à l'autre, Une Société En Mutation*. Edited by Baudouin Dupret, 975–83. Casablanca: Centre Jacques Berque. http://books.openedition.org/cjb/99

2016a. "La Pratique Du Droit Des Étrangers Au Maroc. Essai de Praxéologie Juridique et Politique". PhD Thesis, Université Grenoble Alpes, unpublished.

2016b. "De La Respécification de La Notion de Transit". In *Migrants Au Maroc: Cosmopolitisme, Présence d'étrangers et Transformations Sociales*. Edited by Nazarena Lanza, 86–91. Description Du Maghreb. Maroc: Centre Jacques-Berque. http://books.openedition.org/cjb/893

Khrouz, Nadia and Nazarena Lanza, eds. 2016. *Migrants au Maroc: Cosmopolitisme, présence d'étrangers et transformations sociales*.

Description du Maghreb. Maroc: Centre Jacques-Berque. http://books
.openedition.org/cjb/865

Kingdom of Morocco and United Nations in Morocco. 2016. Programme
conjoint d'appui à la mise en œuvre de la Stratégie Nationale
d'Immigration et d'Asile.

Koch, Anne. 2014. "The Politics and Discourse of Migrant Return: The Role
of UNHCR and IOM in the Governance of Return". *Journal of Ethnic
and Migration Studies* 40 (6): 905–23.

Korvensyrjä, Aino. 2017. "The Valletta Process and the Westphalian
Imaginary of Migration Research". *Movements. Journal for Critical
Migration and Border Regime Studies* 3 (1): 191–204. http://move
ments-journal.org/issues/04.bewegungen/14.korvensyrjae–valletta-pro
cess-westphalian-imaginary-migration-research.html

La Cimade. 2017. "Coopération UE-Afrique Sur Les Migrations. Chronique
d'un Chantage". www.lacimade.org/wp-content/uploads/2017/12/Cim
ade_CooperationUEAfrique_8p.pdf

La Cimade and AFVIC. 2005. "Réfoulements et Expulsions Massives de
Migrants et Demandeurs d'asile. Récit d'une Mission de l'AFVIC et de
La Cimade".

    2006a. "ACTES DE LA FORMATION ASIL'MAROC. Formation
Organisée à Bouznika En 2005 Par l'AFVIC et La Cimade". http://arch
ives.rezo.net/archives/migreurop.mbox/YQVANTST4NZVH3DBTB3
ECS2IJIVKKDNX/attachment/Asilmaroc-ACTES%20juin%202006
%20(2)_.pdf

    2006b. "FORMATION ASIL'MAROC. Evaluation. Formation
Organisée à Bouznika En 2005 Par l'AFVIC et La Cimade". http://arch
ives.rezo.net/archives/migreurop.mbox/YQVANTST4NZVH3DBTB3
ECS2IJIVKKDNX/attachment/Asilmaroc-Rapport%20evaluation%2
0JUIN%202006_(2).pdf

Lachaud, Elsa. 2014. "Le Grand Agadir Comme Lieu de Résidence Pour Les
Migrants Européens au Maroc. Etude de Leurs Pratiques Socio-
Spatiales". MA Thesis, Aix-Marseille Université, unpublished.

Lahav, Gallya and Virginie Guiraudon. 2000. "Comparative Perspectives on
Border Control: Away from the Border and Outside the State". In *The
Wall around the West. State Borders and Immigration Controls in
North America and Europe*. Edited by P. Andreas and S. Snyder,
55–77. Lanham, MD: Rowman & Littlefield.

Landau, Loren B. 2019. "A Chronotope of Containment Development:
Europe's Migrant Crisis and Africa's Reterritorialisation". *Antipode*
51: 169–86. https://doi.org/10.1111/anti.12420

Lanza, Nazarena. 2014. "Pèleriner, faire du commerce et visiter les lieux
saints: Le tourisme religieux sénégalais au Maroc". *L'Année du*

Maghreb 11 (December): 157–71. https://doi.org/10.4000/
anneemaghreb.2289

Lavenex, Sandra. 2016. "Multilevelling EU External Governance: The
Role of International Organizations in the Diffusion of EU
Migration Policies". *Journal of Ethnic and Migration Studies* 42 (4):
554–70.

Lavenex, Sandra and Emek M. UçArer. 2004. "The External Dimension of
Europeanization". *Cooperation and Conflict* 39 (4): 417–43. https://d
oi.org/10.1177/0010836704047582

Lazar, Sian. 2004. "Education for Credit: Development as Citizenship
Project in Bolivia". *Critique of Anthropology* 24 (3): 301–19. https://d
oi.org/10.1177/0308275X04045423

Le Matin. 2006. "Le DG de l'OIM Juge «scandaleux» Que Le Maroc Assume
Seul l'opération d'aide Au Retour". 11 March. https://lematin.ma/jour
nal/2006/Immigration-Clandestine_Le-DG-de-l-OIM-juge-scandaleux-q
ue-le-Maroc-assume-seul-l-operation-d-aide-au-retour/61381.html

Le Monde. 2020. "Au Maroc, Les Migrants Subsahariens Fragilisés Par Les
Mesures Anti-Coronavirus". www.lemonde.fr/afrique/article/2020/05/
14/au-maroc-les-migrants-subsahariens-fragilises-par-les-mesures-anti-
coronavirus_6039631_3212.html

Lecadet, Clara. 2016a. *Le manifeste des expulsés: errance, survie et
politique au Mali*. Tours, France: Presses universitaires François-
Rabelais.

2016b. *Le Manifeste Des Expulsés: Errance, Survie et Politique Au Mali*.
Tours, France: Presses universitaires François-Rabelais.

Legal Flash. 2016. "Maroc: La Lutte Contre La Traite Des Êtres Humains
Encadrée Par Une Loi". 27 September. www.legalflash.ma/categories/
personnes/articles/16-09-394

Leite, Christopher C. and Can E. Mutlu. 2017. "The Social Life of Data: The
Production of Political Facts in EU Policy Governance". *Global
Governance: A Review of Multilateralism and International
Organizations* 23 (1): 71–82. https://doi.org/10.5555/1075-2846.23.1.71

Lemaizi, Salaheddine. 2018. "Traque Des Migrants Irreguliers. Opération
Coup de Poing". *LesEco.ma*, 16 August. www.leseco.ma/69155

Lemke, Thomas. 2016. *Foucault, Governmentality, and Critique*. Abingdon,
Oxon: Routledge.

LesEco.ma. 2017a. ANAM: les migrants recevront bientot leurs cartes
RAMED. www.leseco.ma/maroc/56028-anam-les-migrants-recevront-
bientot-leurs-cartes-ramed.html

2017b. Politique migratoire: la société civile aux avant-postes. www.lese
co.ma/maroc/56984-politique-migratoire-la-societe-civile-aux-avant-p
ostes.html

Limam, Mohamed and Raffaella Del Sarto. 2015. "Periphery under Pressure: Morocco, Tunisia and the European Union's Mobility Partnership on Migration". EUI Working Paper, RSCAS 2015/75.

Lipsky, Michael. 1980. *Street-Level Bureaucracy: Dilemmas of the Individual in Public Services*. New York: Russell Sage Foundation.

LO-FTF. 2018. "Morocco: Labour Market Profile". www.ulandssekretaria tet.dk/sites/default/files/uploads/public/PDF/LMP/LMP2018/lmp_mor occo_2018_final2.pdf

López García, Bernabé. 2008. "Españoles En Marruecos. Demografia de Una Historia Compartida". In *Españoles En Marruecos 1900–2007. Historia y Memoria Popular de Una Convivencia*. Edited by Oumama Aouad and Fatiha Benlabbah, 17–47. Rabat: Instituto de Estudios Hispano-Lusos.

——— 2013. "Aportación a La Historia Demográfica Del Magreb Del Siglo XX: Los Españoles En Marruecos". In *El Protectorado Español En Marruecos. La Historia Trascendida*. Edited by Manuel Aragon Reyes, Manuel Gahete Jurado, and Fatiha Benlabbah, 197–260. Bilbao: Iberdola.

——— 2014. "Le Grand Théâtre Cervantès: Un Mythe Centenaire". *Zamane*, 49 ed.

Lucas, Ángeles. 2017. "Una Marcha Recuerda En Ceuta a Los 15 Inmigrantes Fallecidos En Tarajal". EL PAÍS, 4 February. http://poli tica.elpais.com/politica/2017/02/04/actualidad/1486207197_991832 .html

Maâ, Anissa. 2019. "Signer La Déportation. Agencéité Migrante et Retours Volontaires Depuis Le Maroc". *Terrain. Anthropologie et Sciences Humaines*. http://journals.openedition.org/terrain/18653

——— 2020a. "Le Retour Incertain d'Aya et de Prince. Penser l'incertitude et l'intermédiation Des Retours Volontaires à Partir d'une Trajectoire Féminine En Instance de Départ Depuis Le Maroc". *Emulations – Revue de Sciences Sociales* 34: 51–75. https://doi.org/10.14428/ emulations.034.03

——— 2020b. "Manufacturing Collaboration in the Deportation Field: Intermediation and the Institutionalisation of the International Organisation for Migration's 'Voluntary Return' Programmes in Morocco". *Journal of North African Studies*. https://doi.org/10.1080/ 13629387.2020.1800210

Madariaga, M. R. de (María-Rosa). 2002. *Los Moros Que Trajo Franco–: La Intervención de Tropas Coloniales En La Guerra Civil Española*. 1st ed. Barcelona: Ediciones Martínez Roca.

Magallanes-Gonzalez, Cynthia. 2020. "Sub-Saharan Leaders in Morocco's Migration Industry: Activism, Integration, and Smuggling". *Journal of North African Studies*. https://doi.org/10.1080/13629387.2020.1800213

Magone, Claire, Michaël Neuman, and Fabrice Weissman. 2012. "Humanitarian Negotiations Revealed: The MSF Experience". www.msf-crash.org/en/publications/humanitarian-negotiations-revealed-msf-experience

Maleno Garzon, Helena. 2004. "Transacciones/Fadaiat". www.hackitec tura.net/osfavelados/fadaiat_tarifa/encuentro/aljaima.html

2018. "Estimado Pedro Sánchez, Hoy Tengo La Necesidad de Escribirte Públicamente". 16 August. www.eldiario.es/zonacritica/Estimado-Ped ro-Sanchez-escribirte-publicamente_6_804279590.html

2020. "Mujer de Frontera. Defender El Derecho a La Vida No Es Un Delito". Ediciones Península.

Malki, H. El and A. Doumou. 2013. "Les Dilemmes de l'ajustement". In *Le Maroc Actuel: Une Modernisation Au Miroir de La Tradition?* Edited by Jean-Claude Santucci, 313–23. Connaissance Du Monde Arabe. Aix-en-Provence: Institut de recherches et d'études sur le monde arabe et musulman. http://books.openedition.org/iremam/2433

MAP. 2013a. "Communiqué Des Départements de l'Intérieur, Des Affaires Etrangères et de La Coopération et de La Justice et Des Libertés Relatif à La Mise En Œuvre de La Nouvelle Politique d'immigration". www.ma pexpress.ma/wp-content/uploads/2013/09/Communiqué-conjoint-rela tif-à-la-mise-en-oeuvre-de-la-nouvelle-politique-migratoire.pdf

2013b. "SM Le Roi Préside à Casablanca Une Séance de Travail Consacrée à l'examen Des Divers Volets Relatifs à La Problématique de l'immigration Au Maroc (Cabinet Royal)". 10 September. www.mapnews.ma/fr/print/ 141246

Marín Sánchez, Isabel. 2006. "La Cooperación Espanola Para El Desarrollo Come Prevención de La Emigración Marroquí: Percepciones, Discursos y Realidades Entre Las Dos Orillas". PhD Thesis, Universidad de Granada, unpublished.

Martínez, José Ciro and Brent Eng. 2018. "Stifling Stateness: The Assad Regime's Campaign against Rebel Governance". *Security Dialogue* 49 (4): 235–53. https://doi.org/10.1177/0967010618768622

Mbembe, Achille. 2019. *Necropolitics*. Durham, NC: Duke University Press.

MCMREAM. 2015. Guide pratique pour faciliter votre intégration au Maroc. 1ère ed. http://docplayer.fr/8057025-Guide-pratique-pour-faci liter-votre-integration-au-maroc.html

2016. "Politique Nationale d'Immigration et d'Asile 2013–2016".

MCMREAM and CNDH. 2016. "3ème Édition Forum Annuel de l'Immigration. Politiques Migratoires: Quel Role Pour La Société Civile? Actes Du Forum". https://marocainsdumonde.gov.ma/ewha tisi/2018/02/acte-forum-immigration-2016.pdf

MDMCMREAM. 2017. "Politique Nationale d'Immigration et d'Asyle. Rapport 2017". https://marocainsdumonde.gov.ma/wp-content/uploa ds/2018/03/POLITIQUE-NATIONALE_Rapport-2017.pdf

2018. "Politique Nationale d'Immigration et d'Asile. Rapport 2018". htt ps://marocainsdumonde.gov.ma/wp-content/uploads/2019/01/Politiqu e-Nationale-dimmigration-et-dAsile-_-Rapport-2018.pdf

Médecins du Monde and Caritas. 2016. "Mineur-e-s Non Accompagné-e-s, En Recherche d'avenir". www.infomie.net/IMG/pdf/etude_mna_-_md mm_caritas_-_def.pdf

Menjívar, C. 2014. "Immigration Law Beyond Borders: Externalizing and Internalizing Border Controls in an Era of Securitization". *Annual Review of Law and Social Science* 10: 353–69.

Migreurop. 2006. "Guerre Aux Migrants. Le Livre Noir de Ceuta et Melilla". www.migreurop.org/IMG/pdf/livrenoir-ceuta.pdf

Migreurop and GADEM. 2015. "Gérer la frontière euro-africaine". Melilla, laboratoire de l'externalisa on des frontières de l'Union européenne en Afrique. www.migreurop.org/article2620.html?lang=fr

Minca, Claudio and Rachele Borghi. 2009. "Morocco: Restaging Colonialism for the Masses". In *Cultures of Mass Tourism: Doing the Mediterranean in the Age of Banal Mobilities*. Edited by Pau Obrador Pons, Mike Crang, and Penny Travlou, 21–53. Farnham: Ashgate Publishing.

Minca, Claudio and Nick Vaughan-Williams. 2012. "Carl Schmitt and the Concept of the Border". *Geopolitics* 17 (4): 756–72. https://doi.org/10 .1080/14650045.2012.660578

Ministère de l'Education Nationale, Royaume du Maroc. 2013. "Circulaire N° 13–487 Concernant l'intégration Des Élèves Étrangers Issus Des Pays Du Sahel et Subsahariens Dans Le Système Scolaire Marocain". www .ccme.org.ma/images/documents/fr/2013/11/Circulaire_13-487_Ministe re_de_Education_Nationale_inscription_eleves_etrangers_FR.pdf

Ministère du Tourisme, de l'Artisanat, du Transport Aérien et de l'Economie Sociale. n.d. "Evolution Par Nationalité des Arrivées Des Touristes Aux Postes Frontières". https://mtataes.gov.ma/fr/tourisme/chiffres-cles-tou risme/indicateurs-du-secteur-touristique/

Ministerio de Asuntos Exteriores y de Cooperaciòn, Gobierno de Espana. 2009. "Plan Director de La Cooperación Española 2009–2012". www .aecid.es/Galerias/publicaciones/descargas/plan_director_2009_2012.pdf

Mitchell, Timothy. 2002. *Rule of Experts: Egypt, Techno-Politics, Modernity*. Berkeley, CA: University of California Press.

Moulin, Carolina and Peter Nyers. 2007. "'We Live in a Country of UNHCR' – Refugee Protests and Global Political Society". *International Political Sociology* 1 (4): 356–72. https://doi.org/10.111 1/j.1749-5687.2007.00026.x

Mouna, Khalid, ed. 2016. "Espace Imaginé, Espace Vécu et Espace Négocié. Parcours Croisés Des Migrations Espagnoles et Subsahariennes à Tanger". AMERM. www.abhatoo.net.ma/maalama-textuelle/develop pement-economique-et-social/developpement-social/demographie/migr ation-interieure/espace-imagine-espace-vecu-et-espace-negocie-par cours-croise-s-des-migrations-espagnoles-et-subsahariennes-a-tanger

Mourji, Fouzi, Jean-Noel Ferrié, Saadia Radi, and Mehdi Alioua. 2016. *Les Migrants Sub-Sahariens Au Maroc. Enjeux d'une Migration de Résidence*. Rabat: Konrad Adenauer Stiftung.

Mouthaan, Melissa. 2019. "Correction to: Unpacking Domestic Preferences in the Policy-'Receiving' State: The EU's Migration Cooperation with Senegal and Ghana". *Comparative Migration Studies* 7 (1): 37. https:// doi.org/10.1186/s40878-019-0151-5

MSF. 2005. "Violence and Immigration. Report on Illegal Sub-Saharan Immigrants (ISSs) in Morocco". www.statewatch.org/media/docu ments/news/2005/oct/MSF-morocco-2005.pdf

2010. "Sexual Violence and Migration. The Hidden Reality of Sub-Saharan Women Trapped in Morocco En Route to Europe". www.lekari-bez-hr anic.cz/sites/czech/files/sexual_violence_and_migrants_201003253808 .pdf

2013a. "Medical Capitalization. Migration and Human Trafficking. Health Risks, Consequences and Service Delivery".

2013b. "Memoria Internacional 2012".

2013c. "Violences, Vulnérabilité et Migration: Bloqués Aux Portes de l'Europe". www.msf.fr/sites/default/files/informemarruecos2013_fr_0.pdf

MSF España. 2003. "Memoria 2002". www.msf.es/file/6901/download? token=cMqz_lqn

2007. "Memoria 2006".

Nations Unies. 2016. "Signature d'un programme conjoint d'appui à la Stratégie nationale d'immigration et d'asile". https://morocco.un.org/f r/19579-signature-dun-programme-conjoint-dappui-la-strategie-natio nale-dimmigration-et-dasile

Natter, Katharina. 2014. "The Formation of Morocco's Policy Towards Irregular Migration (2000–2007): Political Rationale and Policy Processes". *International Migration* 52 (5): 15–28. https://doi.org/10.11 11/imig.12114

2018. "Rethinking Immigration Policy Theory beyond 'Western Liberal Democracies'". *Comparative Migration Studies* 6 (March): 4. https://doi .org/10.1186/s40878-018-0071-9

2020. "Crafting a 'Liberal Monarchy': Regime Consolidation and Immigration Policy Reform in Morocco". *Journal of North African Studies* (July): 1–25. https://doi.org/10.1080/13629387.2020.1800206

Nixon, Rob. 2011. *Slow Violence and the Environmentalism of the Poor.* Cambridge, MA: Harvard University Press.

Norman, Kelsey P. 2016. "Between Europe and Africa: Morocco as a Country of Immigration". *The Journal of the Middle East and Africa* 7 (4): 421–39. https://doi.org/10.1080/21520844.2016.1237258

2019. "Inclusion, Exclusion or Indifference? Redefining Migrant and Refugee Host State Engagement Options in Mediterranean 'Transit' Countries". *Journal of Ethnic and Migration Studies* 45 (1): 42–60. https://doi.org/10.1080/1369183X.2018.1482201

OECD. n.d. "Net ODA". https://data.oecd.org/oda/net-oda.htm

Oeppen, Ceri. 2016. "'Leaving Afghanistan! Are You Sure?' European Efforts to Deter Potential Migrants through Information Campaigns". *Human Geography* 9 (2): 57–68.

OIM. 2016. "Assistance Directe Aux Migrants. Edition N°31 Janvier–Décembre 2016".

2017. "Protection et Résilience. Assistance Directe Aux Migrants".

OIM Maroc. n.d.a "FORAS – Renforcément Des Opportunités de Réintegration". https://morocco.iom.int/sites/default/files/FORAS-A4-2-FR-6.pdf

n.d.b "Qu'est-Ce Que Le Programme d'aide Au Retour Volontaire et à La Réintégration (AVRR)?" https://morocco.iom.int/sites/default/files/fiche%20AVRR.pdf

2014. "Lettre d'Information N° 24. Août–Octobre 2014. Maroc". www.iom.int/files/live/sites/iom/files/Country/docs/rabat-newsletter-FR-October-2014.pdf

2019. "Assistance Au Retour Volontaire et à La Reintegration Depuis Le Maroc. Rapport Annuel 2019". https://morocco.iom.int/sites/default/files/rapport%20AVRR%20à%20partir%20du%20Maroc%20annuel%202019.pdf

2020. "Termes de Références – Assistant/e Finance Du Projet FORAS II". www.tanmia.ma/wp-content/uploads/2020/03/TdR-AFI-FORAS-II-G5-v.pdf

OIM Morocco. 2017. "Opération de Distribution de Kits d'hygiène et Kits Alimentaires à Nador Dans Le Cadre Du Projet Santé". https://morocco.iom.int/news/op%C3%A9ration-de-distribution-de-kits-dhygi%C3%A8ne-et-kits-alimentaires-%C3%A0-nador-dans-le-cadre-du-projet

Olin, Anders, Lars Floring, and Björn Bengtsson. 2008. "Sida Evaluation. Study of the International Organization for Migration and Its Humanitarian Assistance". Swedish International Development Cooperation Agency. https://publikationer.sida.se/contentassets/fa22a604774249bd93a407a7148c9c0d/200840-study-of-the-international-organization-for-migration-and-its-humanitarian-assistance_1919.pdf

Omata, Naohiko. 2019. "'Over-Researched' and 'under-Researched' Refugees". *Forced Migration Review* 61: 15–18.

O'Neill, Kevin Lewis. 2015. *Secure the Soul: Christian Piety and Gang Prevention in Guatemala*. Oakland, CA: University of California Press.

Pack, Sasha D. 2019. *The Deepest Border: The Strait of Gibraltar and the Making of the Modern Hispano-African Borderland*. Stanford, CA: Stanford University Press.

Pallister-Wilkins, Polly. 2016. "Humanitarian Borderwork". In *Border Politics: Defining Spaces of Governance and Forms of Transgressions*. Edited by Cengiz Günay and Nina Witjes, 1st ed. 2017 ed., 84–103. New York: Springer.

Paoletti, Emanuela. 2011. *The Migration of Power and North-South Inequalities*. Basingstoke: Palgrave Macmillan. www.palgrave.com/us/book/9780230249264

Parker, Noel and Nick Vaughan-Williams. 2012. "Critical Border Studies: Broadening and Deepening the 'Lines in the Sand' Agenda". *Geopolitics* 17 (4): 727–33. https://doi.org/10.1080/14650045.2012.706111

Pascucci, Elisa. 2014. "Beyond Depoliticization and Resistance: Refugees, Humanitarianism, and Political Agency in Neoliberal Cairo". PhD Thesis, University of Sussex, unpublished.

2018. "The Local Labour Building the International Community: Precarious Work within Humanitarian Spaces". *Environment and Planning A: Economy and Space* 51 (3): 743–60. https://doi.org/10.1177/0308518X18803366

Pastore, Ferruccio. 2019. "From Source to Corridor: Changing Geopolitical Narratives about Migration and EU-Western Balkans Relations". *Journal of Balkan and Near Eastern Studies* 21 (1): 11–26. https://doi.org/10.1080/19448953.2018.1532683

Pécoud, Antoine. 2018. "What Do We Know about the International Organization for Migration?" *Journal of Ethnic and Migration Studies* 44 (10): 1621–38. https://doi.org/10.1080/1369183X.2017.1354028

Peraldi, Michel, ed. 2011. *D'une Afrique à l'autre, migrations subsahariennes au Maroc*. Paris: Karthala.

2018. *Marrakech, Ou, Le Souk Des Possibles: Du Moment Colonial à l'ère Néolibérale*. Souk Des Possibles. Paris: La Découverte.

Peraldi, Michel and Liza Terrazzoni. 2016. "Nouvelles migrations? Les Français dans les circulations migratoires européennes vers le Maroc". *Autrepart* 77: 69–86. https://doi.org/10.3917/autr.077.0069

Perrin, Delphine. 2008. "L'étranger rendu visible au Maghreb – La voie ouverte à la transposition des politiques juridiques migratoires européennes". *Revue Asylon(s)* 4 (May). www.reseau-terra.eu/article770.html

2016. "Regulating Migration and Asylum in the Maghreb: What Inspirations for an Accelerated Legal Development?" In *Migration in the Mediterranean – Mechanisms of International Cooperation.* Edited by Francesca Ippolito and Seline Trevisanut, 192–214. Cambridge, Cambridge University Press.

Pian, Anaïk. 2005. "Aventuriers et commerçants sénégalais à Casablanca: des parcours entrecroisés, Abstract". *Autrepart* 36: 167–82. https://doi .org/10.3917/autr.036.0167

2010. "La migration empêchée et la survie économique: services et échanges sexuels des Sénégalaises au Maroc, Blocked migration and economic survival: sexual services and exchanges of Senegalese women in Morocco, Resumen". *Cahiers du Genre* 49: 183–202. https://doi.org/ 10.3917/cdge.049.0183

Pickerill, Emily. 2011. "Informal and Entrepreneurial Strategies among Sub-Saharan Migrants in Morocco". *The Journal of North African Studies* 16 (3): 395–413. https://doi.org/10.1080/13629387.2010.484217

Picozza, Fiorenza. 2017. "Dubliners: Unthinking Displacement, Illegality and Refugeeness within Europe's Geographies of Asylum". In *The Borders of "Europe": Autonomy of Migration, Tactics of Bordering.* Edited by Nicholas De Genova, 233–54. Durham, NC: Duke University Press.

Piveteau, Alain, Khadija Askour, and Hanane Touzani. 2013. "Les Trajectoires d'industrialisation Au Maroc: Une Mise En Perspective Historique. Working Paper, Programme de Recherche Made in Morocco". Université Mohammed V-Agdal, Rabat.

Pliez, Olivier. 2006. "Nomades d'hier, nomades d'aujourd'hui. Les migrants africains réactivent-ils les territoires nomades au Sahara?" *Annales de géographie* 115 (652): 688–707. https://doi.org/10.3406/ geo.2006.21438

PNPM. 2016. "Violences Aux Frontières: Le Silence Assourdissant Des Responsables Politiques". www.cjhm.org/wp-content/uploads/2015/09/2 016.10.04-Communiqué-de-presse-Violences-aux-frontières-PNPM-1.pdf

2017a. "Contribution de La Société Civile Dans Le Cadre de l'Examen Périodique Universel Du Maroc – Mai 2017". https://uprdoc.ohchr.org/ uprweb/downloadfile.aspx?filename=3735&file=FrenchTranslation

2017b. "Etat Des Lieux de l'accès Aux Services Pour Les Personnes Migrantes Au Maroc: Bilan, Perspectives et Action de La Société Civile". www.pnpm .ma/wp-content/uploads/2017/12/Rapport-PNPM-11_2017_ACCES-AU X-SERVICES-POUR-MIGRANTS-AU-MAROC.pdf

Povinelli, Elizabeth A. 2011a. *Economies of Abandonment Social Belonging and Endurance in Late Liberalism.* Durham, NC: Duke University Press.

Principauté de Monaco. 2017. "Appui Au Développement de La Nouvelle Politique d'asile, à La Protection et à l'insertion Sociale Des Réfugiés Au Maroc". www.gouv.mc/Action-Gouvernementale/Monaco-a-l-Interna tional/L-Aide-Publique-au-Developpement-et-la-Cooperation-Internati onale/Projets-de-cooperation-internationale/Pays-mediterraneens/Mar oc/Appui-au-developpement-de-la-nouvelle-politique-d-asile-a-la-pro tection-et-a-l-insertion-sociale-des-refugies-au-Maroc

Publico. 2016. "Padre Esteban, el cura de los nadies al que Marruecos ha expulsado". www.publico.es/internacional/padre-esteban-cura-nadies-al.html

Qacimi, Mounia. 2015. "Les migrants et les réfugiés politiques bénéficieront désormais du Ramed". http://fr.le360.ma/politique/les-migrants-et-les-refugies-politiques-beneficieront-desormais-du-ramed-55525

Rachidi, Hicham. 2016. "Chronologie de l'action de La Société Civile Marocaine Pour Les Droits Des Migrants Depuis 2003". Intervention for the Third Annual Forum on Immigration, Rabat.

Radoine, Hassan. 2012. "French Territoriality and Urbanism: General Lyautey and Architect Prost in Morocco (1912–1925)". In *Colonial Architecture and Urbanism in Africa: Intertwined and Contested Histories*. Edited by Fassil Demissie. Intertwined and Contested Histories. Farnham, Surrey: Routledge.

Rahman, Aminur. 1999. *Women and Microcredit in Rural Bangladesh: Anthropological Study of the Rhetoric and Realities of Grameen Bank Lending*. Boulder, CO: Westview Press.

Redfield, Peter. 2006. "A Less Modest Witness: Collective Advocacy and Motivated Truth in a Medical Humanitarian Movement". *American Ethnologist* 33 (1): 3–26.

   2010. "The Impossible Problem of Neutrality". In *Forces of Compassion: Humanitarianism between Ethics and Politics*. Edited by Erica Bornstein and Peter Redfield, 53–70. Santa Fe, NM:SAR Press.

   2013. *Life in Crisis: The Ethical Journey of Doctors Without Borders*. Berkeley, CA: University of California Press.

REDRESS. 2017. "Sexual Exploitation and Abuse in Peacekeeping Operations. Improving Victims' Access to Reparation, Support and Assistance". https://redress.org/wp-content/uploads/2017/08/REDRES S-peacekeeping-report-English.pdf

Robin, Julie. 2014. "Entre Église catholique, bailleur européen et Gouvernement marocain, l'action de Caritas Maroc auprès des migrants subsahariens". *L'Année du Maghreb* 11 (December): 173–93. https://doi.org/10.4000/anneemaghreb.2302

Roborgh, Sophie E. 2018. "Beyond Medical Humanitarianism – Politics and Humanitarianism in the Figure of the Mīdānī Physician". *Social Science*

& Medicine (1982) 211 (August): 321–29. https://doi.org/10.1016/j.socscimed.2018.06.037

Rodier, Claire. 2012. *Xénophobie business*. Paris: La Découverte.

Rodriguez, Anne-Line. 2015. "Three Stories About Living Without Migration in Dakar: Coming to Terms with the Contradictions of the Moral Economy". *Africa* 85 (2): 333–55. https://doi.org/10.1017/S0001972015000042

——— 2019. "European Attempts to Govern African Youths by Raising Awareness of the Risks of Migration: Ethnography of an Encounter". *Journal of Ethnic and Migration Studies* 45 (5): 735–51. https://doi.org/10.1080/1369183X.2017.1415136

——— 2019. "RSC Research in Brief 13. Exploring Assumptions behind 'Voluntary' Returns from North Africa". www.rsc.ox.ac.uk/files/news/rsc-research-in-brief_returns-from-north-africa_web.pdf

Rothenberg, Janell. 2015. "The Social Life of Logistics on the Moroccan Mediterranean Coast". PhD Thesis, University of California Los Angeles, unpublished.

Sanchez, Gabriela. 2018. "Pedro Sánchez pasa de denunciar las devoluciones en caliente a defenderlas con los mismos argumentos que el PP". *Eldiario.es*. www.eldiario.es/desalambre/Gobierno-Sanchez-argumento-PP-devoluciones_0_803169816.html

Satzewich, Vic. 2015. *Points of Entry: How Canada's Immigration Officers Decide Who Gets In*. Vancouver: UBC Press.

Scheel, Stephan and Philipp Ratfisch. 2014. "Refugee Protection Meets Migration Management: UNHCR as a Global Police of Populations". *Journal of Ethnic and Migration Studies* 40 (6): 924–41. https://doi.org/10.1080/1369183X.2013.855074

Schuetze, Benjamin. 2019. *Promoting Democracy, Reinforcing Authoritarianism: US and European Policy in Jordan*. Cambridge: Cambridge University Press.

Servicio Jesuita a Migrantes España. n.d. "Por Un Estado de Derecho … También En La Frontera Sur". https://socialjesuitas.es/noticias/11-noticias-info/310-por-un-estado-de-derecho-tambien-en-la-frontera-sur

Slack, Jeremy. 2019. *Deported to Death: How Drug Violence Is Changing Migration on the US-Mexico Border*. Oakland, CA: University of California Press.

Slack, Jeremy, Daniel E. Martínez, Alison Elizabeth Lee, and Scott Whiteford. 2016. "The Geography of Border Militarization: Violence, Death and Health in Mexico and the United States". *Journal of Latin American Geography* 15 (1): 7–32. https://doi.org/10.1353/lag.2016.0009

Slaughter, Amy, Anubhav Dutt Tiwari, Caitlin Wake, et al. 2017. "Refugee Self-Reliance. Moving Beyond the Marketplace. Refugee Studies Centre Research in Brief 7". University of Oxford.

Soleterre Onlus. 2017. "Le botteghe del sole". 18 October. https://soleterre .org/cosa-facciamo/inclusione-sociale-e-lavorativa/le-botteghe-del-sole/

Soukouna, Sadio. 2011. "L'Échec d'une Coopération Franco Malienne Sur Les Migrations: Les Logiques Du Refus Malien de Signer". Mémoire de Master 2 Science Politique, Université Paris I Panthéon Sorbonne.

Statewatch. 2019. "Analysis: Aid, Border Security and EU-Morocco Cooperation on Migration Control". www.statewatch.org/analyses/n o-347-eu-morocco-aid-border-security.pdf

Stierl, Maurice. 2015. "The WatchTheMed Alarm Phone. A Disobedient Border-Intervention". *Journal for Critical Migration and Border Regime Studies* 1 (2). http://movements-journal.org/issues/02.kaempfe/ 13.stierl–watchthemed-alarmphone.html

Stoler, A. L. 2016. *Duress: Imperial Durabilities for Our Time.* Durham, NC: Duke University Press.

Strasser, Sabine and Eda Elif Tibet. 2020. "The Border Event in the Everyday: Hope and Constraints in the Lives of Young Unaccompanied Asylum Seekers in Turkey". *Journal of Ethnic and Migration Studies* 46 (2): 354– 71. https://doi.org/10.1080/1369183X.2019.1584699

Suárez-Navaz, Liliana and Mercedes Jiménez Álvarez. 2011. "Menores en el campo migratorio transnacional. Los niños del centro (Drari d'sentro)". *Papers. Revista de Sociologia* 96 (1): 11–33. https://doi.org/10.5565/re v/papers/v96n1.94

Sukarieh, Mayssoun and Stuart Tannock. 2019. "Subcontracting Academia: Alienation, Exploitation and Disillusionment in the UK Overseas Syrian Refugee Research Industry". *Antipode* 51 (2): 664–80. https://doi.org/ 10.1111/anti.12502

Swearingen, Will Davis. 2016. *Moroccan Mirages: Agrarian Dreams and Deceptions, 1912–1986.* Place of publication not identified: Princeton University Press.

Taylor, Chloë. 2017. *The Routledge Guidebook to Foucault's The History of Sexuality.* London: Routledge.

Tazzioli, Martina. 2014. *Spaces of Governmentality: Autonomous Migration and the Arab Uprisings.* London and New York: Rowman & Littlefield International.

    2018. "Containment through Mobility: Migrants' Spatial Disobediences and the Reshaping of Control through the Hotspot System". *Journal of Ethnic and Migration Studies* 44 (16): 2764–779. https://doi.org/10.10 80/1369183X.2017.1401514

2019. "Governing Migrant Mobility through Mobility: Containment and Dispersal at the Internal Frontiers of Europe". *Environment and Planning C: Politics and Space* 38 (3): 2399654419839065. https://do i.org/10.1177/2399654419839065

TelQuel. 2016. "L'ONU Plutôt Satisfaite de La Politique Migratoire Du Maroc." 16 September. https://telquel.ma/2016/09/16/lonu-plutot-satis faite-politique-migratoire-du-maroc_1514581

2017. "Hirak: des associations des droits de l'homme craignent des 'atteintes graves aux droits humains'". http://telquel.ma/2017/06/23/u n-rapport-associatif-sur-le-hirak-souleve-des-interrogations-sur-sa-neutralite_1551377

Terre des Hommes – Espagne. 2014. "Femmes Migrantes Au Maroc: Une Approche Médicosociale. Rapport de Capitalisation Sur Le Volet Médicosocial Du Projet 'Tamkine-Migrants' 2011–2014 d'appui à La Prise En Charge de Femmes Migrantes Enceintes et de Leurs Enfants". https://resourcecentre.savethechildren.net/sites/default/files/documents/ rapport_capitalisation-_sante_materno_infantile_migrants_maroc_tam kine_migrants_final_sept_2014_0.pdf

Terry, Fiona. 2000. "The Principle of Neutrality: Is It Relevant to MSF?" MSF.

The Guardian. 2018. "Asylum Seeker to Sue UK for Funding Libyan Detention Centres". 20 December. www.theguardian.com/uk-news/20 18/dec/20/asylum-seeker-to-sue-uk-for-funding-libyan-detention-centres

Therrien, Catherine. 2002. "La Mémoire Des Traces: Vie Quotidienne et Enjeux Identitaires de Femmes Qui Ont Vécu l'époque Internationale de Tanger". MA Dissertation, Université Laval, unpublished.

Therrien, Catherine and Chloé Pellegrini. 2015. "French Migrants in Morocco: From a Desire for Elsewhereness to an Ambivalent Reality". *The Journal of North African Studies* 20 (4): 605–21. https://doi.org/1 0.1080/13629387.2015.1065044

Ticktin, Miriam. 2006. "Where Ethics and Politics Meet". *American Ethnologist* 33 (1): 33–49.

2011. *Casualties of Care: Immigration and the Politics of Humanitarianism in France*. Berkeley, CA: University of California Press.

2014. "Transnational Humanitarianism". *Annual Review of Anthropology* 43 (1): 273–89.

Tsourapas, Gerasimos. 2019a. *The Politics of Migration in Modern Egypt: Strategies for Regime Survival in Autocracies*. Cambridge: Cambridge University Press.

2019b. "The Syrian Refugee Crisis and Foreign Policy Decision-Making in Jordan, Lebanon, and Turkey". *Journal of Global Security Studies* 4 (4): 464–81. https://doi.org/10.1093/jogss/ogz016

Turner, Lewis. 2017. "Who Will Resettle Single Syrian Men?" *Forced Migration Review* 54: 29–31.

    2018. "Challenging Refugee Men: Humanitarianism and Masculinities in Za'tari Refugee Camp". PhD Thesis, School of Oriental and African Studies, unpublished.

Tyszler, Elsa. 2019. "Derrière Les Barrières de Ceuta & Melilla. Rapports Sociaux de Sexe, de Race et Colonialité Du Contrôle Migratoire à La Frontière Maroco-Espagnole". PhD Thesis, Université Paris 8, unpublished.

    2020. "Humanitarianism and Black Female Bodies: Violence and Intimacy at the Moroccan-Spanish Border". *Journal of North African Studies*. https://doi.org/10.1080/13629387.2020.1800211

UN Office of the High Commissioner for Human Rights. 2015. "OHCHR Intervention before the European Court of Human Rights in the Case of N.D. and N.T v. Spain". www.refworld.org/type,AMICUS,ESP,57 a876f34,0.html

UNHCR. 2005a. "Country Operations Plan. Executive Committee Summary. Country: Morocco. Planning Year: 2006". www.unhcr.org/43327c712.pdf

    2005b. "Handbook for Self-Reliance". www.refworld.org/docid/4a54bb f40.html

    2011a. "Promoting Livelihoods and Self-Reliance. Operational Guidance on Refugee Protection and Solutions in Urban Areas". www.unhcr.org/publications/operations/4eeb19f49/promoting-livelihoods-self-reli ance-operational-guidance-refugee-protection.html

    2011b. "UNHCR Resettlement Handbook". www.unhcr.org/46f7c0ee2 .pdf

    2015. "Morocco – UNHCR Operational Update". 1 October–31 December. www.refworld.org/docid/58402b194.html

    2016. "Refworld | Morocco - UNHCR Operational Update". 1 July–1 October. www.refworld.org/docid/58402c4a4.html

UNHCR Morocco. 2020. "Factsheet September 2020". https://reporting.u nhcr.org/sites/default/files/UNHCR%20Morocco%20Fact%20Sheet %20-%20September%202020.pdf

UNICEF. 1994. "Support to Women's Productive and Income-Generating Activities. Evaluation and Research Working Paper Series, Number 1". https://www.gdrc.org/icm/wind/wind-unicef-wp.html

UNODC. 2016. "GloAct. Action Mondiale Pour Prévenir et Combattre La Traite des Personnes et Le Trafic Illicite Des Migrants (2015–2019)". https://morocco.iom.int/sites/default/files/GloACT_Project_Summary_ FR_2016.pdf

UNWomen. n.d. "Projet 'Améliorer l'accès Aux Services Judiciaires Des Femmes et Enfants Victimes de Traite Au Maroc'". http://maghreb.un

women.org/-/media/field%20office%20maghreb/documents/publica
tions/2015/fichesprojets/ficheprojet%20%20traite%20des%20femme
s%20et%20des%20enfants%20phase%20i.pdf?la=fr&vs=1658

Vacchiano, Francesco. 2013. "Fencing in the South: The Strait of Gibraltar
as a Paradigm of the New Border Regime in the Mediterranean".
Journal of Mediterranean Studies 22 (2): 337–64.

Vacchiano, Francesco and Mercedes Jiménez. 2012. "Between Agency and
Repression: Moroccan Children on the Edge". *Children's Geographies*
10 (4): 457–71. https://doi.org/10.1080/14733285.2012.726074

Vairel, Frédéric. 2004. "Morocco During the Black Years: Fairness and
Reconciliation?" *Politique africaine* 4 (4): 181–95. https://doi.org/10.3
917/polaf.096.0181

Valluy, Jérôme. 2006. "Contraintes et Dilemmes Des Actions de Solidarité
Avec Les Exilés Subsahariens En Transit Au Maroc Oriental Dans Le
Contexte Créé Par Les Politiques Européennes d'externalisation de
l'asile". http://barthes.enssib.fr/TERRA/IMG/doc/Valluy191206.doc

2007a. "Chronique de La Banalisation des Rafles et de l'usure des
Solidarités Avec Les Exilés Au Maroc". Programme ASILES (ACI-TTT
Ministère de la recherche). www.reseau-terra.eu/IMG/doc/VALLU
Y030207.doc

2007b. "Contribution à une sociologie politique du HCR: le cas des politiques
européennes et du HCR au Maroc". *Recueil Alexandries*. http://barthes
.enssib.fr/TERRA/article571.html

2007c. "Le HCR au Maroc: acteur de la politique européenne
d'externalisation de l'asile". *L'Année du Maghreb* III (November):
547–75. https://doi.org/10.4000/anneemaghreb.398

Vaughan-Williams, Nick. 2015. *Europe's Border Crisis: Biopolitical
Security and Beyond*. First ed. Oxford: Oxford University Press.

Vermeren, Pierre. 2016. *Histoire du Maroc depuis l'indépendance*. 5e éd.
Paris: La Découverte.

Vianello, Gaia. 2007. "Les Retours Féminins Au Maroc. Étude de Cas Sur
Les Femmes Migrantes de Retour Dans Les Régions Tadla-Azilal et
Chaouia-Ouardigha". Tesi Di Master, Università Ca' Foscari Venezia,
unpublished.

Vives, Luna. 2017a. "Unwanted Sea Migrants across the EU Border: The
Canary Islands". *Political Geography* 61: 181–92.

2017b. "The European Union–West African Sea Border: Anti-Immigration
Strategies and Territoriality". *European Urban and Regional Studies* 24
(2): 209–24. https://doi.org/10.1177/0969776416631790

Wagner, Ann-Christin. 2018. "Giving Aid Inside the Home". *Migration and
Society* 1 (1). www.berghahnjournals.com/view/journals/migration-an
d-society/1/1/arms010105.xml

Wagner, Lauren and Claudio Minca. 2014. "Rabat Retrospective: Colonial Heritage in a Moroccan Urban Laboratory". *Urban Studies* 51 (14): 3011–25. https://doi.org/10.1177/0042098014524611

Walters, William. 2010. "Foucault and Frontiers: Notes on the Birth of the Humanitarian Border". In *Governmentality: Current Issues and Future Challenges*. Edited by Ulrich Bröckling, Susanne Krasmann, and Thomas Lemke, 138–64. New York: Routledge.

Watkins, Josh. 2017a. "Australia's Irregular Migration Information Campaigns: Border Externalization, Spatial Imaginaries, and Extraterritorial Subjugation". *Territory, Politics, Governance* 5 (3): 282–303. https://doi.org/10.1080/21622671.2017.1284692

2017b. "Bordering Borderscapes: Australia's Use of Humanitarian Aid and Border Security Support to Immobilise Asylum Seekers". *Geopolitics* 22 (4): 958–83. https://doi.org/10.1080/14650045.2017.1312350

2020. "Irregular Migration, Borders, and the Moral Geographies of Migration Management". *Environment and Planning C: Politics and Space* 38 (6): 1108–27. https://doi.org/10.1177/2399654420915607

Webber, Frances. 2011. "How Voluntary Are Voluntary Returns?" *Race & Class* 52 (4): 98–107.

Wihtol de Wenden, Catherine. 2010. *La question migratoire au XXIe siècle: Migrants, réfugiés et relations internationales*. Paris: Presses de Sciences Po. https://doi.org/10.3917/scpo.wende.2010.01

Williams, Jill M. 2015. "From Humanitarian Exceptionalism to Contingent Care: Care and Enforcement at the Humanitarian Border". *Political Geography* 47 (Supplement C): 11–20. https://doi.org/10.1016/j.polgeo.2015.01.001

2016. "The Safety/Security Nexus and the Humanitarianisation of Border Enforcement". *The Geographical Journal* 182 (1): 27–37. https://doi.org/10.1111/geoj.12119

2019. "Affecting Migration: Public Information Campaigns and the Intimate Spatialities of Border Enforcement". *Environment and Planning C: Politics and Space* 38 (7–8): 1198–215. https://doi.org/10.1177/2399654419833384

Willis, Laurie D. 2018. "'It Smells Like a Thousand Angels Marching': The Salvific Sensorium in Rio de Janeiro's Western Subúrbios". *Cultural Anthropology* 33 (2): 324–48.

Wright, John. 2007. *The Trans-Saharan Slave Trade*. London and New York: Routledge.

Wunderlich, Daniel. 2010. "Differentiation and Policy Convergence against Long Odds: Lessons from Implementing EU Migration Policy in Morocco". *Mediterranean Politics* 15 (2): 249–72. https://doi.org/10.1080/13629395.2010.485052

2012. "Europeanization through the Grapevine: Communication Gaps and the Role of International Organizations in Implementation Networks of EU External Migration Policy". *Journal of European Integration* 34 (5): 485–503.

Yabiladi.com. 2019. "The Ordeal of an African-American Who Was Mistaken for a Sub-Saharan Migrant in Morocco". 30 August. https://en.yabiladi.com/articles/details/82708/ordeal-african-american-mistaken-sub-saharan-migrant.html

Zacka, Bernardo. 2017. *When the State Meets the Street: Public Service and Moral Agency.* Cambridge, MA: The Belknap Press of Harvard University Press.

Zaragoza-Christiani, Jonathan. 2016. "Empowerment through Migration Control Cooperation. The Spanish-Moroccan Case". PhD Thesis, European University Institute, unpublished.

Zardo, Federica and Chiara Loschi. 2020. "EU-Algeria (Non)Cooperation on Migration: A Tale of Two Fortresses". *Mediterranean Politics* (May): 1–22. https://doi.org/10.1080/13629395.2020.1758453

Zeghbib, Hocine and Catherine Therrien. 2016. "Les Migrants Français Au Maroc: De Quelques Aspects Juridiques et Administratifs". In *La Migration Des Français Au Maroc. Entre Proximité et Ambivalence.* Edited by Catherine Therrien, 199–276. Rabat: La croisée des chemins.

Index

For EU product safety concerns, contact us at Calle de José Abascal, 56–1°,
28003 Madrid, Spain or eugpsr@cambridge.org.

www.ingramcontent.com/pod-product-compliance
Ingram Content Group UK Ltd.
Pitfield, Milton Keynes, MK11 3LW, UK
UKHW020354140625
459647UK00020B/2472